MARKETS AND MORALS

Considering efficiency, equality, and morality, this book argues for qualified market expansion, particularly in legalizing kidney sales and prostitution. Legalizing prostitution will benefit both men and women, as argued in a chapter jointly written with Yan Wang. Blood donation without monetary compensation can still result in adequate blood supply if schools educate children that blood donation can actually benefit a donors' health. As a society becomes more advanced, with higher incomes and a better educated populace, more activities can be subject to market exchange, with gradual popular acceptance. Without serious misinformation and irrationality, inequality/fairness as such cannot be a valid reason for limiting the scope of the market. The book supports the use of markets to increase efficiency while also increasing the effort to promote equality, making all income groups better off, as was previously argued by the author in the *American Economic Review*.

Yew-Kwang Ng is Professor in Economics, Nanyang Technological University; Emeritus Professor, Monash University; Fellow of the Academy of the Social Sciences in Australia; and member of the Advisory Board, Global Priorities Institute, University of Oxford. He will be Special Visiting Professor at the School of Economics, Fudan University, from mid-2019. In 2007, he received the highest award (Distinguished Fellow) of the Economic Society of Australia. He delivered the inaugural Atkinson Memorial Lecture at the University of Oxford in 2018. He has 11.5 papers (joint papers counted fractionally) in the top five journals in economics, including one published when an undergraduate. He has also published more than 30 books and more than 250 refereed journal papers in economics, biology, cosmology, informetrics, mathematics, philosophy, psychology, and sociology, including the *American Economic Review, The Economic Journal, Journal of Political Economy,* and *The Review of Economic Studies.*

Markets and Morals

JUSTIFYING KIDNEY SALES AND LEGALIZING PROSTITUTION

YEW-KWANG NG

Nanyang Technological University, Singapore
School of Economics, Fudan University, Shanghai.

CAMBRIDGE
UNIVERSITY PRESS

CAMBRIDGE
UNIVERSITY PRESS

University Printing House, Cambridge CB2 8BS, United Kingdom

One Liberty Plaza, 20th Floor, New York, NY 10006, USA

477 Williamstown Road, Port Melbourne, VIC 3207, Australia

314–321, 3rd Floor, Plot 3, Splendor Forum, Jasola District Centre,
New Delhi – 110025, India

79 Anson Road, #06–04/06, Singapore 079906

Cambridge University Press is part of the University of Cambridge.

It furthers the University's mission by disseminating knowledge in the pursuit of
education, learning, and research at the highest international levels of excellence.

www.cambridge.org
Information on this title: www.cambridge.org/9781107194946
DOI: 10.1017/9781108163828

First published 2019

Printed and bound in Great Britain by Clays Ltd, Elcograf S.p.A.

A catalogue record for this publication is available from the British Library.

Library of Congress Cataloging-in-Publication Data
NAMES: Ng, Yew-Kwang, author.
TITLE: Markets and morals : justifying kidney sales and legalizing prostitution / Yew-
Kwang Ng, Nanyang Technological University, Singapore.
DESCRIPTION: Cambridge, United Kingdom ; New York, NY : Cambridge University
Press, 2019. | Includes bibliographical references.
IDENTIFIERS: LCCN 2018038855| ISBN 9781107194946 (hardback) | ISBN 9781316646571
(paperback)
SUBJECTS: LCSH: Economics – Moral and ethical aspects. | Capitalism – Moral and
ethical aspects.
CLASSIFICATION: LCC HB72 .N4896 2019 | DDC 174/.4–dc23
LC record available at https://lccn.loc.gov/2018038855

ISBN 978-1-107-19494-6 Hardback
ISBN 978-1-316-64657-1 Paperback

Contents

Preface   *page* vii

Acknowledgements   xi

1   Introduction   1
2   The Well-Known Case of Lateness Fees   6
3   Extending Economic Analysis   11
4   The Anti-Market Sentiment   14
5   The Inequality/Exploitation Case against
    Commodification Is Invalid   24
6   Repugnance? Similar to 'Honour' Killing   41
7   Crowding Out or Crowding In?   46
8   Market Expansion Is a Mark of Progress   53
9   The Case for Legalizing Kidney Sales   60
10 Making Presumed Consent the Default Option   68
11 Blood Donation   73
12 Prostitution   75
    Ms Yan Wang and Prof. Yew-Kwang Ng
13 Conscription   86
14 Profiteering   93
15 Water: A Typical Case of Under-Pricing   99
16 Fines, Imprisonment, or Whipping?   103
17 Some Specific Areas   109
    17.1   From Slavery to Surrogate Pregnancy   109
    17.2   From Vote Trading to Corruption   111
    17.3   From Friendship to Nobel Prizes   113
    17.4   Paying Others for Line Standing/Sitting   115
    17.5   Selling Permits for Hunting Rhinos   116

17.6   Educational Equality, University Admission, Hospital
       Priority, Jury Service   116
18   **Concluding Remarks**   119

Appendices:

Appendix A   *Welfare versus Preference*   126

Appendix B   *Happiness as the Only Ultimate Value: A Moral*
               Philosophical Perspective   130
               B.1 What Is Happiness?   130
               B.2 Happiness as the Only Intrinsic Value   135
               B.3 Answering Some Objections   141
               B.4 Rejecting Kant's Categorical Imperatives   145
               B.5 A Critique of Rawls   148
               B.6 Further Opposing Arguments Considered   152

Appendix C   *Extending Economic Analysis to Analyze Policy*
               Issues More Broadly   156

Appendix D   *Immigration Typically Makes Existing Residents*
               Better Off   170

Appendix E   *A Democratic Decision on COEs: Striking a*
               Balance between Elitism and Populism   175

References   178

Index   200

Preface

This book addresses a very important problem of general interest, the appropriate scope of using the market. After the collapse of the USSR and the transition of many countries from non-market to market economies, most people accept the use of the market in the traditional sphere of 'normal' goods and services. However, whether the use of market exchanges, especially those involving monetary payment, should be expanded to cover such areas as kidney sales and prostitution is much more controversial. This book tackles this fundamental problem, in both general and specific cases.

Since this book deals with the desirability of allowing or banning certain market exchanges, it needs to have some normative foundation. I am fully open on my stance in this matter. I am a 100% welfarist, believing that, ultimately speaking, only welfare or happiness is of intrinsic value and that public policies should be for the promotion of social welfare in the long run, although we should not rule out the consideration of animal welfare. The moral philosophical argument justifying this position is provided in Appendix B. However, even Kantians (those believing in some intrinsic deontic rules not justified by welfare considerations) may find the book useful, as something useful is still possible within the constraints of not violating those rules.

In my usage, welfare and happiness differ only in two trivial senses. First, we tend to use happiness to describe the current situation and welfare for the longer term. Given the time period that this book deals with, this difference disappears. Strictly speaking, we are using an a-temporal analysis, largely ignoring the complication of multi-periods, but referring to 'the future' where necessary. Second, welfare is more formal and happiness less so. Ignoring this formality, we use the two terms, and also 'subjective well-being', synonymously.

I use happiness in its subjective, affective, or feeling sense, and not the cognitive sense which, in my view, should be called life satisfaction. I prefer using happiness instead of life satisfaction since the latter is related to how one contributes to the happiness of others, and may thus constitute double counting. For any given period, say from the time you wake up until now, your net happiness is all (including the sensuous or bodily and the spiritual) your affective feelings (those feelings that matter to you, that make you feel either positively or negatively) over this period, counting the happy feelings positively and the unhappy feelings negatively, with intensities taken into account. Other non-affective or non-subjective definitions of happiness tend to confuse morality with fact, and/or is confused by the effects on the happiness in the future or on others. Please see Appendix B for details.

Given my welfarist position, many apparently unsolvable issues are all resolved at the level of costs and benefits in terms of welfare. For example, consider: 'the reasons that matter most to each side [of the pro and anti-market debate] come in with different weights: market advocates weigh autonomy and the negative liberty/anti-paternalism reasons as the heaviest, most important reasons, whereas nonmarket advocates weigh promoting an attitude of dignity and social civic community as heaviest, most important reasons' (Gillespie 2017, pp. 12–13). With different weights used, it seems impossible to reach any agreement. However, if we agree that the ultimate value is welfare, the correct weights for different elements should ultimately be based on their contributions to welfare in the long run, taking all relevant effects into account. One may still differ on the likely magnitudes, but the ultimate basic value could be the same.

From time immemorial and without record, through Mencius' compassion (惻隱之心) and 'being ashamed of evil deeds' (羞惡之心), Adam Smith's moral sentiments, to recent evolutionary theory of morality for cooperation (e.g., Frank 1987, Stanford 2018), morality as an important element of human nature has been much discussed. Our inborn moral sentiments help us to survive by having better interpersonal relationships, including cooperating better, for example, in market exchanges. They are further shaped by our experience, education, and other social influences. Our higher material achievements facilitated by markets also enhance our moral capability. Markets and morals are thus mutually reinforcing. However, they also have some negative or limiting effects on the each other. As ably put by Friedman and McNeill:

Markets need morals. . . . Though few realize it, markets have also made us more moral. They not only encourage cooperation, but since they've increased wealth, they've enabled boons like police and public health systems. As we brought morals and markets into alignment a few hundred years ago, warfare dropped off and so did crime. Markets bred the world of peace we live in today. ... But if the benefits run both ways, so do the hazards. ... Morals sabotage markets. ... Markets can also corrupt morals.

(2013, p. 6)

Could we use markets more without too much corrupting effects on morals? Could we keep the high benefits of morality while expanding the scope of markets? Hopefully, this book will contribute a little towards answering such questions. The important points made in this book include:

- The basic framework of economic analysis may be extended to include such effects as the possible crowding out of intrinsic motivation and morality in using the market. This may help answer the questions posed in this book and other questions involving factors beyond narrow economic effects more adequately (Chapter 3 and Appendix C).
- Such an extended analysis, although providing some useful insights, does not give a general answer as to the desirability of extending the scope of markets; we have to look at each specific case closely.
- Most people (the present author included) have anti-market sentiments, partly, if not largely, based on mistaken views (Chapter 4).
- One mistake is to regard the wider scope for markets as being unfair to the poor, allowing the rich to acquire, say, their kidneys when they are desperate for money.
- In the absence of serious misinformation and irrationality, inequality/ fairness as such cannot be a valid reason for limiting the scope of the market. We may use markets more to increase efficiency while also increasing the effort to promote equality, making all income groups better off (Chapter 5).
- As a society progresses in achieving higher degrees of division of labour, higher incomes, better education, more liberalism, and more understanding of economics, it will typically allow a wider scope for using markets (Chapter 8).
- In most cases, it is almost certain that kidney sales should be legalized, with adequate counselling. Instead of feeling repugnant against kidney trade, we should feel sympathy towards those desperate enough to buy and sell kidneys, and be glad that more lives are saved (Chapter 9).
- We may keep blood donation free of monetary compensation and yet have enough blood supply if we simply have a lesson in schools on the

point that blood donation is actually good also for the donors (Chapter 11).

- Partly because of our biological nature and partly because of the much higher costs of prohibition, the legalization of prostitution will most certainly promote welfare not only for men, but also for women (Chapter 12).
- A strong case is made for having presumed consent as the default option for using organs of the dead (Chapter 10).
- The case (made in Appendix B) for using welfare (happiness) as the ultimate objective, as it is the only thing of intrinsic value, is both the normative foundation for the position of this book and a contribution to moral philosophy in itself.

Other issues, including conscription, profiteering, slavery, fines versus imprisonment, inadequate pricing of some goods like car park space and water, among others, are also addressed briefly. While not pretending to have covered all relevant aspects of these complicated issues, at least some useful arguments, some quite novel, have been advanced. I understand that government has to take into account not just economic efficiency, but also the perception of fairness by the public, even if not based on valid grounds, making many of my proposals to improve both efficiency and equality possibly politically infeasible. However, as an academic and economist, I have the duty to explain the real issues involved, even if this proves to be very unpopular. For example, my case against some popular fallacies on immigration following the Population White Paper in Singapore in 2013 attracted 9–1 responses against me; a similar negative response was evoked for my case in favour of increasing water prices towards the full costs in 2017. Hopefully, over time, with better learning and education, the public opinion may gradually shift.

I hope to make the book readable by general readers. Thus, the main text is written to be largely understandable even without any training in economics. The more technical parts are put into appendices. Throughout the whole book, no equation is used, except a few in a small part of Appendix C. There are not even any graphs/diagrams used. Specific scholarly references and points are put in footnotes. However, references to publications (papers or books) may be made in the text by just citing the surnames of the relevant authors and the years of publication (e.g., Arrow 1972 which refers to the publication in 1972 written by Arrow). The full list of publications referred to appears at the end, listed alphabetically according to the surnames of the authors. Happy reading!

Acknowledgements

I am grateful to Nanyang Technological University for research funding [M4081118.100] and to Ms Jingying Bi, Mr Zhang Chen, Mr Leon Sim, Ms Yan Wang, Dr. Shuying Wang, Mr. Nicholas Yeo, and Ms Zhou Zhou for research assistantship and to Ms Yan Wang for co-authoring Chapter 12 on prostitution. Minor parts (Appendix B, in particular) of the book are based on some previously published papers but are revised or improved/extended, and the whole manuscript has largely been freshly written.

1

Introduction

If each individual or family could not rely on the market but had to produce all goods by themselves, their productivities would be very low. Most would probably perish. Even for those who could survive, they would not have much, if any, time for leisure, thinking, and invention. The use of market exchange has facilitated the division of labour, which in turn has helped to promote scientific and technological advances. These have resulted in huge increases in productivity and have increased the per-capita real income of the world by more than 10 times since 1800, to a population of more than 6 times, or an increase in total gross domestic product (GDP) of more than 60 times in real terms, not counting price increases. Although the increases have been uneven, even the poorest in Africa have more than tripled in real per-capita income (McCloskey 2006). 'Over the long run, markets drive the prices of most goods we want to consume way down. This means that all of us are in a real sense spending less time in getting those goods, more of us are getting them, and we are getting more of them. It is basic economics to say that our standard of living is higher now because the costs of pretty much everything in terms of time and labor are much lower now. For instance, between 1835 and 1850, the price of light in Britain in terms of average labor hours was cut in half. Between 1850 and 1890, it was further cut by about 97%. Quite literally, we can now buy more lights with 10 seconds of labor than a cave-person could have bought with 60 hours of labor'(Brennan & Jaworski 2016, p. 166). This is 21,600 times![1]

More recently, the transition of China in the past four decades from a centrally planned economy into a largely market economy has resulted in double-digit annual real growth rates over most years, leading to an increase in real per-capita income to more than 22 times over 38 years (World Bank 2017).

[1] On the history of lighting, see Nordhaus (1996).

Hundreds of millions of individuals escaped poverty. Although China has also benefited much from foreign investment and learning from overseas, the replacement of central planning by the market has played a crucial role. Many economists regard this replacement as the most important factor accounting for its rapid growth (e.g., Lardy 2014, Li 2017, p. 9, Naughton 2017). On the other hand, it may be tempting to blame the recent low morality in China on the extensive use of markets. However, as I argue elsewhere (Ng 2013a), the real culprits are Mao's movements (including the Great Leap Forward and the Cultural Revolution) and the one-child policy.

The economic success of China largely explains why it tops the world in its belief in the market system: 'A similar international divergence is observed for beliefs in the merits of "the free enterprise system and free market economy". The average degree of agreement that this is "the best system on which to base the future of the world" was 61 percent in the 2005 World Public Opinion Survey. Countries near the top include China at 74 percent, the United States at 71 percent, and Germany at 65 percent. Those at the bottom include Argentina at 42 percent, Russia at 43 percent, and France at 36 percent' (Bénabou & Tirole 2016, pp. 154–155).

The market-facilitated increase in productivity has also led to an enormous expansion in the scope of market usage. Not only has the amounts of goods involved increased many folds, the variety has also multiplied. We traded mainly in goods before, but now most parts of our GDP consist of services. Moreover, many esoteric types of services have emerged, such as those for line sitting (standing in queues) and for surrogate pregnancy. The emergence of such esoteric services has raised objections from certain scholars including the communitarians and/or anti-commodification (or commercialization) theorists. While these two terms need not mean exactly the same thing, I will use them largely interchangeably in this book for convenience. Also, while communitarianism as championed by Amitai Etzioni and others is rich in content, I will focus here on the aspect of anti-commodification as emphasized by Sandel (2012a, 2013, 2018).

According to Etzioni (2008, p. 170), 'The communitarian position I have come to share with a considerable global network [www.communitariannet work.org] of colleagues and public leaders assumes that there is a tension between the individual (and their rights) and the common good (and hence one's social responsibilities) and that a good society seeks a carefully crafted balance between the two, relying as much as possible on moral suasion and not on power.' With this description, I regard myself also a communitarian. Most economists recognize this tension at least through possible inequality issues and through external effects like pollution. More effects like the morality and intrinsic motivation aspects that the communitarians may emphasize are also allowed in my extended framework of analysis discussed in Chapter 3 and Appendix C. However, agreement on this central aspect of communitarianism needs not imply the same view regarding the expansion of the market.

Most of the critiques of market expansion are not against the use of markets in the traditional economic spheres of the production and exchange of 'normal' goods (including services). They are against many types of market expansion into social spheres where the use of markets, prices, exchange, and money should not prevail for some alleged reasons; they object to the expansion of the market economy into a market society. 'The difference is this: A market economy is a tool – a valuable and effective tool – for organizing productive activity. A market society is a way of life in which market values seep into every aspect of human endeavor. It's a place where social relations are made over in the image of the market.' (Sandel 2012a, pp. 10–11).

The concern of the communitarians on the excessive commodification or commercialization has some validity. Although the expansion of the market may generate some substantial benefits, the possible crowding out of intrinsic motivation and morality (as discussed in Chapter 7) may bring about negative effects. The excessive use of commercial advertisement may also combine with environmental disruption, relative competition, and excessive materialism/consumerism to result in welfare-reducing growth (Ng 2003).[2] However, an economist like me will be inclined to regard these negative effects as apart from the intrinsic effects of the market and its expansion. Rather, they are due to the external costs (costs imposed on others without compensation/payment) of such factors as pollution, competitive instead of informative advertisement, and invidious relative competition. These negative factors should be treated with the appropriate measures like taxes on pollution, income, and consumption, and not by limiting the expansion of the market.

The anti-commodification objection has been based on a variety of arguments. Brennan & Jaworski (2016) have provided a comprehensive, largely convincing, and, in most instances, compelling, critique of these various arguments.[3] Their main point is that the use of markets or monetary exchange itself is not the problem; what may be possessed or done may be bought and sold. Child pornography should not be bought and sold because child porn itself should not be created and possessed. It may be bad or not to have extra-

---

[2] Earlier concerns with some negative effects of economic growth and commercialization include Mishan (1967/1993), Hirsch (1976), and Scitovsky (1976/1992).

[3] For a critique of Brennan & Jaworski, see, e.g., Sparks (2017).

marital sex with a stranger, but whether monetary payment is involved or not is beside the point. When I was at the initial stage of reading their book, I found their position is somewhat extreme in being too pro-market. However, after reading this excellent book from the first word to the last, I am largely convinced by their arguments. However, being a welfarist, I still have to make some concessions to the anti-commodification theorists. For example, if many people deeply feel that the sale of human organs is highly repugnant, society may have to take this strong feeling into account, even if it is based on mistakes. However, in the long run, we will most probably be better off adopting policies not based on mistaken feelings. Through better knowledge and education, I hope that we may make improvements on this front, although the shift toward populist policy making as seen from the recent election results of Brexit and the Trump election do not give us much encouragement.[4]

Instead of tackling all aspects or arguments advanced by the anti-commodification theorists as done by Brennan and Jaworski, I shall concentrate on three more arguable and important points:

1. The use of markets or monetary payment allow the rich to exploit the poor.
2. Markets crowd out intrinsic motivation and morality.
3. Some markets are repugnant.

I will argue that, for most cases, including kidney sales and prostitution as focused on in this book, none of these arguments provide a convincing case in favour of the prohibition of voluntary exchange, especially in the absence of strong ignorance and/or irrationality. However, I will also argue in favour of keeping blood donation without monetary payment, based on a different reason. If some readers find that my conclusions are not justified as I have ignored some other possible objections to commodification other than the points discussed in this book (mainly, although not exclusively, the previously mentioned three points), they are advised to read Brennan & Jaworski (2016), which covers also many other points such as: markets are corrupt, give wrong signals, treat things as mere commodities, lead to low quality, and unjust allocation. They provide a very strong defence of markets against these and other objections; they also discuss some reasons giving rise to the incorrect anti-market attitudes and the 'pseudo-morality of disgust' against the use of

---

4   As Sandel (2018, p. 359) concludes, 'Disentangling the intolerant aspects of populist protest from its legitimate grievances is no easy matter. But it is important to try. Understanding these grievances and creating a politics that can respond to them is the most pressing political challenge of our time.'

markets in certain areas. As I believe that their arguments are largely persuasive and even compelling, I will not repeat them in this book.

Before discussing the various arguments mentioned earlier, we shall first discuss the widely reported case of the failure of charging lateness fees in reducing the late picking up of children in day care centres in the next chapter. In Chapter 3, we argue that that the traditional economic analysis may be extended to cover effects like repugnance and crowding out to provide a more comprehensive analysis of broader social changes like the expansion of markets. Although a general case either in favour or against the market expansion cannot be concluded, a more complete framework is provided to analyze the relevant issues more adequately. Readers more academically inclined and trained in economics may find reading Appendix C instead of Chapter 3 more rewarding.

2

The Well-Known Case of Lateness Fees

In 1998, some day care centres in Haifa, Israel introduced (after the suggestion of some researchers) a small fine of Israeli new shekel NIS 10 (about
US$2.70 then or about US$4 in 2017 prices) on parents who were late by
more than 10 minutes in picking up children. However, instead of discouraging lateness, more parents turned up late. In fact, the numbers of late pick-
ups are more than doubled.[1] The centres then scrapped the fine.
The incidence of lateness remained at the higher levels rather than falling
back to the original or pre-fine position. This well-reported incidence is
interpreted by the communitarians as a strong case that demonstrates the
limitation of the market. Not only did a fine fail to work, its introduction
apparently crowded out intrinsic motivation, moral behaviour, and values.[2]
As Gneezy & Rustichini (2000) and Rothman & Rothman (2006) put it,
'Once a commodity, always a commodity.' On the other hand, it is also
possible that, as a reviewer of the present book proposal suggested, a parent
might think, 'Oh, I thought I was really putting them out by picking up my
kids late. However, now that they've attached a low price to it, I see that I was
mistaken. In fact, I was barely harming them at all.'

Being eclectic, I concede to the existence of some crowding out (on which,
more discussion is in Chapter 6). However, is it clear-cut that no fines or
charges (a market way of doing things; see the last Chapter 18 on the differences between fees and fines) should be imposed for such cases like being late
for the picking up of children? The incidence may also be given a different
interpretation. The fact that more parents turned up late with the fine shows

---

[1] Gneezy & Rustichini (2000) and subsequent authors citing them only reported 'nearly
doubled', but the figures reported actually showed clearly more than doubling.
[2] On crowding out, see, e.g., Frey & Oberholzer-Gee 1997, Faravelli & Stanca 2014, Beretti et al.
2017.

6

that they had high demand for being able to be late on occasions. Paying a fine relieved them of the bad conscience of being late. This explains the higher incidence of lateness. Perhaps a fixed fine of $2.70 was too low; perhaps, at today's prices, a fine of US$8 per 10 minutes of being late may be more appropriate in reflecting the costs of the day care centre. The fine of NIS 10 is not substantial, compared to the childcare fee per month of NIS 1,400, fine for illegal parking of NIS 75, and for driving through a red light of NIS 1,000 plus additional penalties, and the average gross salary per month of NIS 5,595 in Israel at the time; see Gneezy & Rustichini (2000), pp. 4–5. Additionally, those with children in day care centres probably earned more than the average.

Thus, even if more parents are still late, this may actually be a better situation. The centres or schools get fully compensated for the extra costs in looking after the children longer. The parents have the additional option of paying for being late. When it does not cost them much to be punctual, they can choose to pick-up on time, avoiding paying the fine. When it is much costlier to be punctual, they may rationally choose to pay the price. These costs could include both monetary and non-monetary opportunity costs forgone by being punctual. They may just be the need to be hasty, the feeling of being pressured, having to drive faster, or giving up important business/appointments. These include the costs (including on others) of hasty driving and could be very substantial. Especially for those who view punctuality as important, the costs for being punctual could be very high, both on the person directly involved and on others. Thus, from an overall social point of view, it seems very sensible to allow the payment of a price equalling the costs imposed on the school for being late. Calling this a charge (instead of fine) of additional childcare may in fact relieve the bad conscience further and lead to more lateness and charge paying. But this is efficient, as a bad conscience is largely a dead weight loss. The bad feeling of being late does not benefit the school, but the monetary payment does.

We may view the extra childcare after hours as just a service available for purchase. The supply of this additional service relieves parents of either the costs of having to be punctual or the guilt feeling of being late, at a charge equalling the extra costs sustained by the school. Why not make such a service available?

My research assistant Ms Yan Wang and I did an informal investigation of the practice of pre-school childcare centres and kindergartens in Singapore regarding late pick-ups. We found that practices vary. Some do not levy fines for parents who are late to pick-up their children. 'One of the main reasons is because we only have one or two of such cases.' Others have written in their parents' handbook that 'late pick up by parents will be subjected to a surcharge of $5.00 per child, computed at per block of 5 minutes'. (One Singapore dollar equals about US$0.75.) One kindergarten has increasing steps from $5 per 5 minutes initially, increasing to $20 per 5 minutes after 1 hour. We also asked some parents regarding the practice and were told that late fees were very common and 'of course, the charging of late fees leads to less instances of lateness'. The different responses from the Israel case reported earlier may at least partly be explained by the higher fees charged in Singapore. The charging of late fees in Singapore also reflects the use of efficient pricing in many spheres in Singapore. For example, to restrict cars, one has to have a certificate of entitlement before owning a car. These certificates are auctioned instead of distributed by lotteries, as in Beijing. Moreover, Singapore uses the most efficient method of second-price auction, ensuring no misrepresentation of preferences and that the certificates go to those who value them most, as discussed in Appendix D.

Some commentators are not against charging lateness fees, but think that the levels should be much higher than the Haifa day care centre case in order to be effective in reducing lateness. In my view, there may be no need to reduce lateness. If we view it as the provision of an additional service instead of a penalty, the appropriate fees should just reflect the additional costs imposed on the day care centres concerned. Parents may then decide how often to use this additional service efficiently. Whether we have more or less lateness is then immaterial in terms of overall social efficiency. If or when parents have higher demand for more of such services, they pay more fees; with lower demand, they pay less. We may just treat extra care as just another economic service and allow the price mechanism to perform its efficient function of resource allocation more comprehensively. 'Resources' here include, of course, time and, in fact, with differentiation between less urgent and more urgent time. We should let people choose as they like, as long as they pay the costs of their choice's consequences. If I choose to buy a kilo of apples, I should pay for the costs of producing these apples. If I choose to be late or cannot avoid being late, I should similarly pay for the costs of such lateness. For the case of picking up children, these are mainly the additional costs imposed on the schools concerned for providing extra time to keep the children.

There may also be costs sustained by the children themselves. However, most parents should already have taken these possible costs on their own children into account. These are 'internal' costs. Just like the government does not have to charge/tax a factory for the costs of their raw materials and labour that the factory has to pay itself, the school does not have to include the costs imposed on the children in their lateness fees. The government should charge factories the 'external costs', like pollution and greenhouse gas discharges. The extra costs sustained by the school of looking after the children after the pick-up time is 'external' to the parents and should be charged. However, once the extra-care fee has been charged, the external effects have been internalized through the fees/ prices and the market may be left to function efficiently. What about some irresponsible parents? My knowledge from both theory and experience says that most parents care too much instead of too little for the good of their children. For the extremely rare cases of parental irresponsibility, they should be treated separately. Obviously, potential parental irresponsibility may be much more harmful at home than in being late in picking up children.

The communitarians may object that if one may just pay some money for being late, this will destroy people's sense of the virtue of punctuality and hence decrease punctuality all round, possibly resulting in great costs for the whole of society. Would this happen?

Consider the following two alternatives. The current situation, situation A, is our status quo, where a parent has to be punctual in both picking up the child and in some other activities, say an important meeting. The alternative is situation B, which is derived from A by allowing lateness in picking up children with the payment of a charge in accordance to the costs imposed on the school, and similar in all other aspects. It is likely that most people will find situation B better. When one can be punctual without incurring high costs, one may pick-up the child in time without having to pay the charge. When one is pressed for time or engaged in something important, one does not have to risk incurring accidents by rushing back fast or forgoing important activities. The question is: Will the increased incidents of being late in picking up children erode the punctuality in attending important meetings, creating greater costs there?

There are at least three different effects involved. The first is the efficiency gain as people buy the additional service, as discussed earlier. The second may be called the contagion effect of the lateness habit in picking up children, possibly increasing lateness elsewhere and even decreasing the adherence to social and moral principles in general. This contagion effect may be largely, if not completely, avoided by renaming the 'fine for being late' charge as an 'additional childcare fee'. This is especially so after some initial periods when people routinely take the fee as paying for some additional service.

A third effect may exist as observing punctuality (and possibly other principles) requires time, effort, and even mental and other resources.[3] Imagine that if

---

[3] This is in line with Arrow (1972) and Robertson (1954). On the other hand, the communitarians (e.g., Sandel 2013) also has a point in emphasizing that love, altruism, morality, etc. are not fixed in supply but grow in use.

you have to be punctual in sending children to school, getting to work, picking up children, attending meetings, etc., there are substantial requirements in having to plan carefully, to remind yourself of the time, to set alarm clocks, etc. If being punctual in picking up children becomes less important as the service of additional childcare is available, you will probably be relieved of these pressures at least to some extent. You are likely to be able to observe punctuality in other more important business like essential meetings better. This is so because the scarce 'resources' needed to meet punctuality may now be used over a smaller scope. You do not have to go mad having to be punctual in so many occasions each week.

The first effect is the well-known efficiency gain of rational exchanges as both sides to the transaction typically gain some consumer or producer surpluses. As we have abstracted away the traditional external effects like pollution and serious informational inadequacy, most economists believe that the market then functions efficiently and see no reason to limit the function of the market. This market efficiency of the invisible hand is formalized in the first theorem in welfare economics: under certain conditions, a market economy under perfect competition results in a most efficient allocation, both in resource, inputs or factors of production, and in final goods (taken to include services). Efficiency here is defined in the sense of Pareto optimality, where no one can be made better off without making another worse off. Perfect competition requires that all sellers and buyers have no influence on prices and take market prices as given; this requires that there are many sellers and buyers in each market. Apart from this, the main additional conditions for the theorem to hold are perfect relevant information, rational choice, and the absence of real external effects like pollution. Since issues like pollution and imperfect competition are not the concern of the communitarians here, the first theorem seems to suggest that this leaves information inadequacy, irrationality, and inequality in income distribution (which is beyond Pareto efficiency) to be possible sources of the differences between the communitarians and economists. However, these are not really the main sources. Most economists would accept government regulation such as food safety based on informational inadequacy and they will also accept the possible need for redistribution. While most economists would prefer more efficient means of redistribution and, being more aware of the costs involved, are likely wary of excessive redistribution, these are not the main sources of the differences either, as discussed in the following chapters.

3

Extending Economic Analysis

The communitarians would probably regard the main sources for the differences with economists as beyond the scope of the first welfare theorem, being in the realm of morality. While many, if not most, communitarians regard the narrow analysis of economics as ignoring morality, a reconciliation or significant reduction of the differences may be possible if an extended analysis is used that incorporates both economic factors and those beyond. Social welfare may be taken as a function of individual welfares or utilities (differences between them, including ignorance, a concern for the welfare of others, and irrationality, are ignored here, but discussed in Appendix A). Thus, for non-welfarist philosophers like the Kantians, some moral principles are beyond the scope of such an (even though extended) analysis. (Utilitarianism says that the maximization of the unweighted or equally weighted individual utilities is desirable. Welfarism says that social welfare is a function of, i.e., depends on, individual utilities; welfarism is utilitarianism generalized to a social welfare function beyond the unweighted summation of individual utilities.) However, for one thing, it may be argued that, provided we appropriately allow for effects on others and in the future, there is really no need to go beyond individual welfares. This argument is provided in Appendix B. For another thing, even for those accepting welfarism, communitarians and economists still have huge differences related to the appropriate market limits. Thus, an analysis within welfarism but going beyond the traditional economic factors may be useful, as discussed later.

As already mentioned, the concept of the invisible hand and the first theorem in welfare economics show the efficiency of the market mechanism. However, this is based on some important simplifications. In particular, external effects (effects affecting others without compensation) like pollution are ignored. Nevertheless, economists have a well-developed analysis of such external effects and how to deal with them. Basically, real external costs like

11

pollution should ideally be taxed at their marginal damages to others.[1] A practical problem arises due to the difficulties in estimating these damages, especially for environmental disruption including global warming which may affect the whole world for generations to come. For most of such cases where some abatement investment in alleviating the disruption has been undertaken, I have argued that these disrupting activities should be taxed at least at the marginal costs of abatement, which is much easier to estimate (Ng 2004a). Moreover, the amount of revenue so collected would be larger than the optimal amount of abatement investment. Thus, both practical problems of estimation and funding could be relatively easily overcome, if the political will to deal with the problem is available.

The point here is that the traditional first theorem in welfare economics and the theory of external effects could be extended relatively simply to analyze wider changes including the expansion of the market more adequately, taking into account effects beyond the traditional economic ones to include such factors like repugnance, crowding out of altruism, and/or effects on morality. This extension is done more formally in Appendix C. Here, the main points of that extension are reported. I expect that many, if not most economists are favourable to this extension. Most economists are not narrowly confined or focused on the monetary/financial aspects of the economy only. For example, a 2016 Nobel laureate in economics suggests in his Nobel lecture that we 'have to take into account the full portfolio of activities that the agent can engage in, the array of instruments, many nonfinancial' (Holmström 2017, Abstract).

As remarked earlier, if we accept welfarism, or if we confine our focus to the effects on welfare, the traditional economic analysis of having social welfare as a function of individual utilities/welfares may be used. The extension to include wider effects beyond the traditional economic ones may then be done by just including such factors like morality into the individual utility/welfare functions. Important principles like law and order, freedom, democracy, sovereignty, etc. are not ignored, but taken as important only in affecting the welfare levels of others including those in the future. Although this makes the actual estimation of the relevant costs and benefits difficult, this is a matter of practical difficulties, not of unaccountability in principle.

Even before the extension, the traditional economic analysis gives us the following propositions:

---

[1]   Real external effects are in contrast with pecuniary external effects which affect others only through market prices. Such pecuniary effects typically do not cause inefficiency. For example, your higher demand for a good may push up its market price, adversely affecting other consumers of that good. But these negative effects on other consumers are offset by the positive effects on the producers.

Proposition 1: A social equilibrium may be Pareto-inefficient even in the absence of any monopolistic power if there are uncorrected real external effects like untaxed pollution. (Perfect Pareto efficiency requires the impossibility of making someone better off without making anyone worse off.)

By analogy to this proposition, the extension gives us (see Appendix C for derivation):

Proposition 2: A social equilibrium may be Pareto-inefficient even in the absence of any monopolistic power and uncorrected real external effects like untaxed pollution, if uncorrected generalized external effects (including effects on morality) exist.

Proposition 3: In general, a conceptual/theoretical analysis without empirical evidence is insufficient to establish whether a certain expansion/limitation of the market (or some other policy or social change) is desirable or undesirable according to a Paretian social welfare function, even in the absence of ignorance, imperfect information, and irrationality and in the absence of traditional real external effects like pollution.

Proposition 4: In judging the likely signs and sizes of the different effects involved in the desirability of a policy or social change, in general, long-term effects as well as current effects should be taken into account.

Proposition 5: The objection (including feelings of repugnance) to the expansion of the market is likely to decrease over time as people become accustomed to the transaction of these goods, and as the society becomes more advanced in the degree of division of labour (and specialization), education (especially with more understanding of basic economics), and liberal thinking.

Although a definite general answer is not available, these propositions help us in estimating the relevant costs and benefits of a given measure, change, policy, etc. and, hence, its likely overall desirability, as done in the remaining chapters.

4

The Anti-Market Sentiment

Falk and Szech (2013) published a paper in *Science*, a top-ranked scholarly journal, claiming to show that 'markets erode moral values'. Their experiments are very simple. In treatment 1, a single individual decides whether to get 10 euros or save a mouse from being killed. In treatment 2, two persons bargain to share 20 euros, and, in treatment 3, more persons are involved. Significantly lower proportions of people under treatment 1 opted to receive the money than under the other treatments. Falk and Szech interpret the situations in treatments 2 and 3 involving bargaining as more market-like, and, thus, conclude that 'markets erode moral values'. This conclusion is clearly unwarranted from their experiments.

Breyer and Weimann (2015) have a more comprehensive criticism, focusing on the statistical aspects. Here, I want to focus on two simple common-sense considerations that make the claim of morality-erosion of markets of Falk and Szech based on their experiments completely invalid.

In treatment 1, the individual concerned is fully responsible for the mouse being killed if she accepts the 10 euros. In the other two treatments, she is only one of two or more individuals involved. Clearly, this is going to have a huge difference in the perception of responsibility. It is thus not surprising, even fully to be expected, that if there are no other significant effects, we will likely have higher proportions of decisions to accept the money instead of saving the mice under treatments 2 and 3. Thus, the experimental results of Falk and Szech cannot be accepted as evidence that shows the morality-erosion of markets at all. This responsibility-dilution effect itself is sufficient in negating their conclusion. The morality-erosion effects of markets may or may not exist, but these effects have not been demonstrated by their experiments.

We may in fact go further than this pure responsibility-dilution effect for the difference between treatment 1 and other treatments. In treatment 1, the individual knows that she can save the life of the mouse by refusing to take

14

the money. In other treatments, there are other individuals involved. Thus, even if the individual concerned prefers not to take the money (to save the mouse), she has other individuals to consider. She may thus think: 'Since these other individuals may gain some money by letting the mouse die, I should not just do as I please' (saving the mouse). This consideration may again reinforce the responsibility-dilution effect to increase the proportions of individuals who take the money under treatments 2 and 3.

Both this consideration of others and the several points discussed by Breyer and Weimann may be somewhat subtle and not easily seen. However, the responsibility-dilution effect is clear and conspicuous. In fact, Falk and Szech (2013, p. 708) themselves, commenting on treatment 2, note that 'it takes two people who agree on trading to complete a trade, implying that responsibility and feelings of guilt may be shared and thus diminished'. Despite this recognition, they draw their invalid conclusion. This is quite remarkable. Equally, if not more remarkable, is the fact that a paper that draws such an obviously invalid conclusion passed through the screening processes of referees and editors of one of a few top journals in the whole academic world. Apart from the fact that we are all human, there are likely to be some background factors that facilitate this outcome. A likely factor is the anti-market sentiment of the general public, including many scholars.

The anti-market sentiment has a long history: from 'an anticommercial theme originating in Aristotle' (McCloskey 2006, p. 2) to the recent concern by the Pope on allowing market exchanges in the permits/quota for the emission of greenhouse gases (Monast et al. 2017). It is fostered by a number of factors, including the following. First, although the use of markets has led to tremendous increases in wealth, it has also resulted in high degrees of inequality in the distribution of incomes and wealth. (Inequality within a country has increased for most countries since 1975, after more than a century of decline. However, at the level of the whole world, inequality has decreased a lot due to the faster growth of China and India in the past four decades or so.) From both nature and nurture, most of us have a preference for equality. We thus hate or at least dislike the inequality outcomes partly fostered by the market. Reinforcing this dislike is the fact that the manifestation of inequality, especially in the forms of extreme richness and poverty, are very conspicuous and often widely reported. On the other hand, the market's contributions to efficiency and growth are less conspicuous or are taken for granted, and are at least much less reported by the mass media. This perception bias is somewhat similar to that which causes the anti-immigration bias. For example, the filling of jobs that could have been taken by locals but by immigrants instead is conspicuous; the creation of more jobs by immigrants or by having a larger population is indirect and inconspicuous. For details, see the discussion of many such fallacies in Ng (2011), which is available in open access; the anti-immigration fallacy is also discussed in Appendix D.

Second, the incentives for monetary gains are large and may lead to both huge positive achievements that also benefit others and terrible negative activities including tax evasion, corruption, robberies, kidnappings, murders, wars, etc. Again, people tend to focus more on the conspicuous and widely reported negative effects and largely ignore the positive effects. This focus leads people to have a negative view on money and markets, and in fact all things material.

From media headlines, most people believe that markets foster crime. In fact, markets cut crime: 'Historians combing the archives of medieval European towns estimate an annual homicide rate of about 50 per 100,000 residents. . . . and by the time of the great market takeover it was below 10 per 100,000. By around 1880, the annual homicide rate in London was less than 2 per 100,000 and headed lower. . . . Markets also broaden social webs, strengthen bonds, and foster moral behavior. So the market takeover transforms the moral system' (Friedman & McNeill 2013, pp. 160–161).

The anti-market sentiment was reinforced in recent years by a number of factors. First, the global financial crisis around 2008, including the role played by the money grabbers in it, intensified the sentiment. Second, the increasing degrees of inequality in the distribution of incomes and wealth within each country in the last four decades or so has become more noticeable and more salient in recent years due to the slower growth after the global financial crisis.[1]

Scholars are also members of the general public. The anti-market sentiment thus also affects them, particularly so for those not well versed in the intricate functioning of the market mechanism. (Those anti-market scholars who believe that they are in fact so well versed should see whether they have taken into account the argument for 'treating a dollar as a dollar' or efficiency supremacy in specific issues discussed in the next chapter.) When an anti-market conclusion, such as the one that markets erode moral values, appears to be obtainable, they thus grab onto it without much careful reasoning. Their pens (or fingers for the keyboard) were dictated by their hearts, not their heads. This applies equally to authors, referees, and editors, even of top journals. We should thus be very cautious of such anti-market conclusions.

---

[1] See Piketty 2014, but see also McCloskey 2014, Krusell & Smith 2015, and Facchini & Couvreur 2015 for some qualifications on the analysis, and Ng 2015b for a logical flaw in its fundamental proposition.

Most people, myself included, do not mind if an invited dinner guest brings a bottle of wine or a box of chocolates as a gift. However, if she contributes an equivalent value of say $30 cash towards the cost of the dinner, most people will not like it and may even be offended. This instance of 'anti-money sentiment', although appearing rather similar to the 'anti-market sentiment' discussed earlier, may have more valid justification. When we invite someone for dinner, we typically enjoy their company and do not expect payment for the costs of preparing the dinner. Thus, we typically do not expect and may likely reject cash payment. However, a bottle of wine or a box of chocolates may be justified not as a payment, but as something to complement the dinner, or as an introduction to a particular brand which might be relevant to your host's future interests. Some guests may partly use the wine as a hidden *quid pro quo* for the dinner. But, because it is hidden and may have other significance, it is normally acceptable, while an outright cash payment is not. While this explanation is certainly valid, nevertheless, our resoluteness in rejecting the cash payment may also partly be accounted for by the anti-market, anti-money sentiment that most people, myself included, have.

Another similar example is: 'a wealthy college student who disliked doing communal chores in a group-living home could get away with paying a needy student to become his de facto servant, not by directly paying the student (which would be a taboo violation) but by paying the student's share of the electricity bill. "Getting away with it" means less reputational cost to the wealthy student who avoids the chores' (Tetlock et al. 2017, p. 97, reporting on McGraw & Tetlock 2005).

An economist tends to emphasize the point that money is just a medium of exchange that has helped enormously in facilitating and reducing the costs of exchange, and, hence, contributed to more division of labour and a much higher standard of living. Money itself, as an instrument, is not evil. It is the possible misuse of money and the associated market exchange that may be undesirable. Paying cash for an invited dinner is a possible misuse of money. However, this depends much on how the act is viewed by the relevant persons. In Chinese societies, there has been a long tradition of giving red packets containing cash at Chinese New Year, typically from parents to unmarried children and children of close relatives, and from married children to parents and aged relatives. Thus, if A wants to help B financially, A typically use the occasion of a Chinese New Year to give B a big red packet, which may be more likely accepted with less unease than cash assistance at other times.

Another consideration relevant to the anti-market sentiment, and, in particular, the anti-economic efficiency aspect, is due to the insufficient distinction between economic markets and financial markets. The former refers to the exchange of goods and services; the latter to the exchange of financial instruments only, including cash, deposits, loans, shares, and derivatives. Finance serves an important function in a modern economy, especially in channelling savings into investments. However, the financial sector also involves much speculation and manipulation. Although speculation may also be productive or useful (as discussed in Chapter 14), the existence of some unproductive elements and even fluctuation-creating ones cannot be denied, although this is usually associated with some imperfect information and irrationality (i.e., may not be the inherent results of markets as such). The issue of the acceptability of commodification or the expansion of markets usually involves economic markets of goods and services, although ones that are normally less traded or usually not using money. For example, blood donation, organ sales, prostitution, line sitting/standing, etc. involve some real goods (defined widely enough to include human organs) and/or services. The insufficient distinction between economic and financial markets makes people extend their hatred for financial markets to economic markets. Let me explain further.

A few days before presenting a keynote speech at a conference on environmental economics in August 2017, I mentioned this to a colleague in our Humanities School (which is housed in the same building as our Social Sciences School). She remarked, 'Environmental economics! That sounds like a contradiction [oxymoron]!' I asked why. She explained that economics is concerned with GDP and money making which are bad for the environment. I explained to her that she probably confused economics with finance or business studies. The latter focuses much on money making, especially at the level of firms, but economics is mainly concerned with efficiency and social welfare at the level of the whole economy, and takes much account of issues of equality and environmental disruption.

The excessive fluctuation in financial markets and the causes may partly be seen by the following examples at the height of the global financial crisis, as reported in Bloomberg on 28 October 2008 (when the Australian dollar was trading at higher than 65 US cents):

- 'RBC recommends selling the Australian dollar when it trades at less than 63.36 cents, targeting a decline to 55 U.S. cents. They should exit the bet if the currency strengthens to 67.9 U.S. cents, RBC said, citing technical analysis.'
- 'Goldman Sachs Inc. analysts said yesterday in a note that the Australian dollar's decline to 63.3 U.S. cents may indicate a drop to 47.75 cents in the longer term, also citing technical analysis.'

Note that the recommendation is to sell if something (the Australian dollar in this case) falls very low in price, not the other way around. The Australian dollar peaked at 98.49 (US) cents in mid-July 2008 before the months (September to December) of large fluctuations in currency and share prices. (The fall in housing prices in the USA occurred much earlier.) The global financial crisis around 2008 was triggered by economic and financial problems of the USA (including high government debts and excessive subprime housing loans that led to big price increases and the subsequent collapse over 2006 and 2007), while the Australian economy was in an excellent condition. Despite these, the Australian dollar dropped within weeks to less than 60.5 cents. In my view, investors/speculators made the mistake of habitually taking the US dollar as the safe haven at times of crisis and flocked to it during a crisis.[2] When countries X, Y, or Z trigger a financial crisis, it is correct to take the US dollar as the safe haven. However, when the USA itself triggers the financial crisis, it is incorrect to take the US dollar as the safe haven. It took several months for investors/speculators to correct themselves. The Australian dollar recovered strongly over the second half of 2009 and went on to hit a record high of around 110 cents in mid-2011. This was also clearly excessive in comparison to its fundamental value of purchasing power. After dropping to a low of around 68.5 cents early in 2016, it is now (mid-November 2017) trading at around 77 cents, a value more consistent with its purchasing power.

When the Australian dollar was trading at about 65 cents, I published an article in the *Business Times* in Singapore on 23 October 2008[3] saying: 'I come from Australia and know the Australian economy well. I am confident that the Australian economy is strong and will remain strong. The Aussie dollar should recover soon.' After that, it actually fell much lower to below 61 cents, before recovering as mentioned earlier.

The examples of the two previously mentioned bulleted reports remind me of my experience more than 40 years ago. Only a few years after my PhD and before buying my first share in the stock market (but already with our house to live in), I had an occasion of discussing financial matters with a few friends. A Mr A said, 'They use the rule of 10%.' Mr B asked, 'What is this rule of 10%?' Although I knew next to nothing about finance either in theory or in practice, and that was the first time I heard of this rule of 10%, I thought I was clever and knew the answer. Without waiting for Mr A to reply, I said to them, 'The rule of 10% means that, if you evaluate the share of a company at $100, if the share

---

[2] Although the reversal of the 'carry trade' also had an important role, it should not cause such a large change if people were more rational and took more account of the fundamentals.

[3] 'Anomalies in the unfolding global financial crisis', p. 25.

price decreases to $90 or below, you buy; if it increases to $110 or above, you sell! That is the rule of 10%!' I said this with so much confidence that not only Mr B nodded his head, Mr A also nodded his head apparently in agreement with me.

A fortnight or so later, by coincidence, I read in a magazine an article referring to this rule of 10%. I opened my eyes wide to verify that I was correct in interpreting this rule. I found something like this: the rule of 10% means that, if the share market fluctuates downward, with average prices falling by more than 10%, it means that the bear market has come – quickly sell! If the share market fluctuates upward, with average prices rising by more than 10%, it means that the bull market has come – quickly buy! So this so-called rule of 10% is completely opposite to what I explained to my friends. Haha!

With such rules and advices as the bulleted examples around, and with most, if not all, investors/speculators (myself included) having very imperfect information and imperfect rationality, it is unsurprising that financial markets fluctuate very widely. The largest ever price bubble was probably the Tulipomania of Holland over 1634–1637. The prices of tulip bulbs increased by many thousands of times. A well-to-do person inadvertently ate one while waiting in a friend's house and became bankrupt as a result. More recently, we have the bubble and collapse in the Baltic Dry Index (which gives an assessment of the price of moving the major raw materials by sea), which hit a historical record of 11,793 on 20 May 2008 and dropped to 663 on 5 December 2008, losing 94.38% in a mere few months. It dropped further to 290 on 11 February 2016. Then it climbed back to 670 on 21 April 2016, an increase of more than 131% in 70 days. As of 19 Dec. 2018, it is at 1,378.

On 18 September 2013, the Fed (central bank) of the USA announced that economic recovery was too fragile to cut back on its massive $85 billion-a-month government bond purchase stimulus program. The US share market reacted to this by hitting a record high. This is like a patient, who having been told by his doctor that he has not recovered enough to decrease medication, then goes out to celebrate the 'good' news.

Thus, we see that finance behaves quite differently from the real economy. Half-jokingly, I told the audience at my keynote speech, mentioned earlier, that a university has no need for a finance department. We do economic analysis and just change the sign of our conclusions from negative to positive or vice versa and we get the required results for finance. However, after the election of President Trump, I still lost money in the share market. I did my economic analysis correctly and sold shares. I forgot to change the sign!

Related to the anti-market and anti-money sentiments is the procedural preference that people may have. Probably affected by 'tradition and other cultural influences, people have preferences on the procedure or method of decision making other than their instrumental value in bringing about desired outcomes' (Ng 1988, p. 218). On top of the outcomes, the way or method of the decision making or act itself (like wine versus cash) directly affects people's preferences and feelings. Procedural preferences may partly be due to the indirect effects on future outcomes. To this extent, they are not purely procedural, but affected by the consideration of the effects on future outcomes. However, some purely procedural aspects cannot be ruled out. To the extent that a basis of our procedural preferences such as the anti-market sentiment is partly due to our bias against money and the market, such preferences may decrease in intensity with more information, education, and progress. Are there more fundamental justifications for over-ruling market exchanges and/or economic efficiency?

More than four decades ago, in discussing the big trade-off between efficiency and equity, Okun (1975) argued that the justifications for rights against economic efficiency take three routes: libertarian, pluralistic, and humanistic. 'To the advocate of laissezfaire, many rights protect the individual citizen against the encroachment of the state, and thus convey benefits that far outweigh any cost of economic inefficiency' (Okun, 1975, p. 10). This is quite true, but it only explains the existence of individual rights (against the state) but does not explain the infringement on economic efficiency. For example, why shouldn't individuals be allowed to trade in rights? Some trades in rights may be inefficient due to, for example, the existence of external effects on third parties, undue exercise of monopolistic power, etc. For such cases, limiting trades in rights does not violate economic efficiency, but is in fact justified on grounds of improving efficiency. Thus, this libertarian ground really only justifies limitations on government power against individuals, not justifying limitations on markets and economic efficiency.

Okun's second justification for rights is called pluralism: 'the network of relationships in a viable society had to rest on a broad base of human motives and human interests. Material gain is (at most) one of the many motives propelling economic activity' (Okun 1975, p. 12). However, I fail to see how pluralism justifies rights that infringe on the calculus of economic efficiency, other than the question of procedural preferences discussed earlier. Of course, I perfectly agree that material gain is not everything, that reputation, dignity, friendship, love, etc. are important. However, this only means that we should not ignore the values of these in our calculus of efficiency. In particular, if we use a more extended framework of analysis of costs and benefits as outlined in Chapter 3 and Appendix C, no objection to this wider concept of efficiency is implied.[4]

A third explanation [humanism] for rights stresses their recognition of the human dignity of all citizens. John Rawls ... has developed that rationale brilliantly, deriving a principle of "equality in the assignment of basic rights and duties" from a theory of the social contract. (Okun, 1975, p. 14)

I fail to see how humanism justifies the infringement of the wider concept of economic efficiency that takes into account the importance of non-economic factors including procedural preferences. According to *Encyclopaedia Britannica*, humanism refers to 'value systems that emphasize the personal worth of each individual but that do not include a belief in God' (referenced in Ng, 1988, p. 223). The *Oxford English Dictionary* defines humanism as any 'system of thought or action which is concerned with merely human interests (as distinguished from divine), or with those of the human race in general (as distinguished from individual)' (Ng, 1988). *Webster's Dictionary* defines humanism as a 'doctrine, attitude, or way of life centered on human interests or values' (Ng, 1988). Most people would agree that, ultimately, it is individual welfare (including contribution to other individuals' welfare) that reflects personal worth, interests, and ideals of people. Thus, for society, humanism is not far from welfarism, which is the maximization of social welfare as an increasing function of individual welfares. Then, even in combination with pluralism, it does not justify the infringement of economic efficiency, except for procedural preferences (which may comprise 'dignity'). An important reason for this preference may be due to the following consideration.

> In Rawls' voluntary association, every member wants to ensure the recognition of the principles of self-respect and of fairness for all citizens, because that recognition protects him. The basic liberties are equally distributed because people value equality as a type of "mutual respect ... owed to human beings as moral persons". (Okun 1975, pp. 14–15).

That people value equality and have preferences on procedural 'justice', etc. must be recognized. However, the question remains, why uphold absolute equality in certain spheres (where egalitarian rights prevail) and economic efficiency (with some trade-off with equality) in others? Ethical choice made in the 'original position' under 'a veil of ignorance' (as to which member of society one would become) is not sufficient to answer the question. In fact, this

---

4 Pluralism means that individual welfare is not just a function of economic variables, but also a function of non-economic variables. This generalization does not rule out economic efficiency.

'veil of ignorance' made famous by Rawls is due to Harsanyi (1953, 1955) who used it in conjunction with a number of reasonable axioms of rational choice to obtain the result that we should maximize social welfare as a sum of individual utilities. Unless absolute equality is consistent with the maximization of this utilitarian objective, the veil of ignorance does not justify absolute equality nor the maximin principle of justice (a critique of which is in Appendix B).

More recent objections to the emphasis on economic efficiency and the expansion of the scope of markets focus on the following three issues: inequality/exploitation/fairness, repugnance of certain markets, and the crowding out of intrinsic motivation and morality in market exchanges. These are discussed in turn in the following three chapters.

5

The Inequality/Exploitation Case against Commodification Is Invalid

In this chapter, let us address the apparently most important case against commodification of many things including human organs and sexual services. The main point here is that commodification allows the rich to exploit the vulnerable position of the poor, e.g., the latter would be the main suppliers of kidneys for the benefits of the former. This exploitation/inequality/fairness point is mentioned by almost all anti-commodification advocates and also given the most emphasis by many, if not most, of them. However, as this chapter argues, this important case against commodification is also the least valid, if not outright mistaken. Other cases with somewhat more but still largely insufficient validity, such as repugnance and crowding out (of intrinsic motivation and or altruism/morality), are discussed in the following chapters.

Arguably the most prominent anti-commodification advocate, Professor Michael Sandel of Harvard University, calls the exploitation/inequality case the 'fairness objection' and explains it as such:

> The fairness objection points to the injustice that can arise when people buy and sell things under conditions of inequality or dire economic necessity. According to this objection, market exchanges are not always as voluntary as market enthusiasts suggest. A peasant may agree to sell his kidney or cornea to feed his starving family, but his agreement may not really be voluntary. He may be unfairly coerced, in effect, by the necessities of his situation (Sandel 2012a, p. 11).

Obviously, if real coercion is involved, including by force or by some undue influence, the exchange involved may be condemned. An example of undue influence may be exercised by persons in authority (employers, teachers, officials) against their subordinates. However, the correct objection here is not against the exchange (or market) as such, but rather the coercion. A similarly valid case against certain exchanges is where the relevant parties may be misinformed, especially when the relevant information is held back on purpose. However, again, the objection is not against the exchange as such, but rather against misinformation. If the degree of ignorance, imperfect information, and/or imperfect foresight is high enough, the banning of certain exchanges may be desirable, such as the banning of hard addictive drugs. I am not against the possible desirability of such banning. But the case should be based on coercion, misinformation, and/or serious ignorance or even irrationality. However, these grounds are not widely used against the expansion of markets. Rather, the point here is regarding exploitation/inequality.

The anti-commodification theorists, including Sandel, define coercion here so widely as to include virtually all cases of selling under poverty or the presence of a high degree of inequality. In the absence of real coercion, serious ignorance and/or irrationality, I wish to argue that a poor person's choice to sell her kidney cannot be regarded as being coerced or involuntary.

True, if a poor person has to sell her kidney just to feed her children, this may not be a desirable outcome, especially in a relatively rich society. A case may be argued that society should help her to avoid this dire circumstance, especially if her poverty is not her fault. Few, if any pro-market economists are completely against governmental help to reduce poverty, if done with some degree of efficiency. Also, no one will likely object if someone or some organization came along to help the poor potential kidney seller to alleviate her poverty to the extent that she no longer finds it necessary to sell. However, for any degree of governmental and private assistance to the poor, if a person, in the absence of serious misinformation, after getting all assistance available, still regards selling her kidney as the best option, and, hence, rationally decides to do so, how could the banning of the intended sale help her? This banning may actually take away her only viable option and force her to take the most extreme of measures, including committing suicide.

In the words of Radcliffe-Richards et al. (1998), 'The weakness of the familiar arguments [against kidney sales] suggests that they are attempted to justify the deep feelings of repugnance which are the real driving force of prohibition, and feelings of repugnance among the rich and healthy, no matter how strongly felt, cannot justify removing the only hope of the destitute and dying.' To ensure that the sale does not involve serious misinformation, some regulation of the legalized kidney market will likely be desirable. By legalizing organ sale with appropriate counselling, many misinformed illegal transactions could likely be avoided.

Even with perfect counselling, it is true that it will still mostly be the poor who may decide to sell their kidneys. Also, if the allocation of kidneys is done by the pricing mechanism of the market (but this part of the exchange may be separated from the procurement part, as discussed by Cohen 1989, Hansmann 1989, Robertson et al. 2014, Held et al. 2016, and others[1]), most kidneys would also be bought by the rich. But why should this be a problem? Most cleaning and other low-skilled jobs are also largely performed by those with lower incomes; enormous houses, luxurious cars, expensive wines, etc. are also mostly bought by the rich. Why do we tolerate inequality in these goods and services but not in the sale of kidneys? No convincing arguments have been offered.

If we could have equality in all areas, it would be ideal. As a leading left-wing student activist led by the outlawed Malayan Communist Party for many years from my junior high school days (late 1950s), I have strong credentials to claim that my inborn inclination towards equality and sympathy for the poor is likely as strong as, if not stronger than, most anti-commodification theorists. True, I have become much less left wing after studying economics and after witnessing the failure of the Great Leap Forward and Cultural Revolution in China in the late 1950s and late 1960s, respectively, and the collapse of the USSR around 1989. However, I am now still much more left inclined than most economists, as witnessed by the subtitle of my book in 2000: *Efficiency, Equality, and Public Policy: With a Case for Higher Public Spending*. I am still holding this 'pro-public spending' view, as witnessed in Ng (forthcoming, a). I am not against equality. I am only against inefficient methods to achieve equality, which will lead to LESS equality for any given degree of efficiency. Banning exchanges on the ground of exploitation/equality is a very inefficient way to achieve equality, as argued later.

We may have equality or inequality in many aspects, e.g., height, weight, lifespan, beauty, intelligence, wisdom, etc. However, for the point of exploitation/inequality, the most relevant aspect is the ability to pay. This is mainly affected by the command of financial/material resources. Thus, let us focus on the equality to earn incomes or accumulate wealth, which we may just call 'economic equality' for convenience. (In the largely atemporal framework, i.e., ignoring different time periods, which we largely use for simplicity, the difference between consumption, income, and wealth may be ignored.)

Economic inequality may be caused by a number of factors, classified here mainly on its relevance:

---

[1] On the use of vouchers and barter to mitigate against outright sale, see Cherry (2017). However, see the argument that the 'decentralized control of unregulated markets should outperform government monopolies' (Epstein 2008, p. 87) and the argument that using willingness to pay is more efficient (Ng 1998). Nevertheless, political feasibility and public understanding may be problematic.

A. Different earning abilities affected by both nature and nurture (including investment in human capital), e.g., Yao Ming is born and nurtured to become 2.3 meters in height and a very talented basketball player; Yew-Kwang is only 1.6 meters tall and dare not even dream of competing in basketball.

B. The pricing of different resources and talents in the economy which, together with the possession of these by different individuals, largely determine their incomes. In a market economy, this pricing is again affected by the supply and demand for these factors.

C. Individual choices regarding earning vs leisure; consumption vs saving; effort vs comfort; dull, dirty, strenuous, dangerous jobs vs interesting and safe jobs; healthy vs unhealthy lifestyles; or whether to give donations and gifts, or to leave inheritance.

D. The inheritance (including gifts) of assets (which may be traced back to other factors in the previous generations).

E. The availability and willingness to use certain connections, relationships, methods, etc., including possibly illicit ones.

F. Luck.

If differences in income or wealth are due to personal choices, they may not constitute real inequality. For example, someone deciding to have more leisure (less time working), more consumption (less accumulated wealth), or simple, easy and safe jobs, may have less income now and in the future than a more hard-working, patient, and risk-taking one. If these two persons have other similar factors, their 'full incomes' (as economists call them) should really be regarded as the same over the whole lifespan. It is our imperfect measure of inequality based on current income/wealth that distorts the picture. However, even if we take off the parts of economic inequality attributable to this factor, there are still other factors accounting for large inequality in most cases. Out of these other factors, the inequality caused by factor E probably is the most unjustified and undesirable, and which even causes large negative effects on others. Apart from this one, most, if not all other factors are really different types of luck. Thus, just like one may make a fortune purely by luck instead of acumen or hard analysis in the share market, one may also be fortunate enough to be born into a rich family or inherit a large fortune from a distant auntie. Similarly, whether one is born with and/or nurtured to have a high earning ability may also be regarded as largely a matter of luck. If one has wealthy parents investing in the human capital of their children, this is classified under luck; if one works harder than others to learn more, this is classified under choice (including effort) here. Similarly, the inequality due to the different pricing of factors one owns under point B may also be regarded as largely a matter of luck, if differences in choice/effort are not involved.

While economic inequality due to luck is not as abhorrent as that due to illicit connections and methods, it is still undesirable, especially if excessive inequality and/or serious poverty is involved. Through the government or charity, society may desirably want to reduce the degree of inequality and poverty if the costs involved are not prohibitive. I do not accept Nozick's (1974) point that, as long as no illicit methods are used, inequality itself is not a problem. Equality has at least three important benefits justifying its promotion.

Human beings are not as strong as tigers, and, hence, we rely largely on our intelligence (in its generalized sense of including emotional quotient and wisdom) and cooperation to survive and prosper. Our sense for equality and justice helps us to cooperate better and, hence, we are probably universally born with a preference for equality. This is further strengthened by nurture as our education and culture are also equality friendly. Hence, a higher degree of equality, if not achieved at prohibitive costs, allows society to be better off because individuals directly feel better off with higher equality.

Second, consumption of the poor meets more urgent needs than that of the rich, at the margin. That is to say, a person's last $1,000 would probably contribute little, if anything, to the utility or welfare of a rich person but may mean a lot to one with low consumption. Thus, a higher degree of equality promotes more aggregate welfare, through the differentials in the marginal utility of consumption. I know that this argument is based on the interpersonal comparability of cardinal utility/welfare that many economists frown upon traditionally. ('Cardinal' here means that it is sensible to speak, not only of ranking two alternatives in terms of high/low, but also sensible to speak of the intensity of preference or the amount of welfare and differences in welfare involved.) However, I have argued strongly elsewhere (Ng 1996a, 1997, 2008, 2015a, forthcoming b) in favour of this interpersonal comparability of cardinal utility/welfare, justified by common sense and evolutionary biology. The age of insisting upon only ordinal measurability and interpersonal non-comparability is, or at least should be, over.

Third, equality reduces crimes and promotes social harmony. This has been known for a long time. However, recent research emphasizing the efficiency-promoting effects of equality has shifted economists' view. Formerly, economists (e.g., Mirrlees 1971, Okun 1975) focused on the trade-off between equality and efficiency. That is, if we promote equality, we need to sacrifice a bit of efficiency, e.g., taxing the rich to help the poor incurs, not only administrative costs, but also creates the disincentive effects that discourage the earning of more money. Now, economists focus on the beneficial effects of equality on efficiency and growth.

One important aspect here is related to the shift from physical to human capital being important for economic growth. When physical capital was important, inequality increased growth by increasing savings by the rich and, hence, increased capital accumulation and economic growth; as human capital becomes more important, equality increases the contribution of widespread education and, hence, growth (Milanovic 2011). In addition, 'Economic historians have shown (Solar 1995, Greif & Iyigun 2013) that the net effect of the Poor Law was probably to foster technological progress, because it weakened the resolve of the inevitable losers to resist it and thus reduced social unrest' (Mokyr 2014, p. 192). Also, 'economic historians such as Lindert (2004, 2009) . . . have shown the complex, but on the whole favorable, effect of the Welfare State on economic performance to the point where the full economic benefits and costs may have been roughly equal, making the Welfare State a "free lunch"' (Mokyr 2014, p. 191). This suggests that more equality-improving welfare spending may be welfare improving, since equality also contributes to welfare more directly as discussed earlier.[2] This is consistent with a recent result that 'Tax policy that alleviates poverty improves economic growth in most instances' (Biswas et al. 2017, p. 724).

The pursuit of more equality by a country is subject to a serious limitation in our globalized world. Contrary to popular belief, at least on balance, globalization actually has led to much poverty reduction, better education, less inequality (at least globally, particularly in helping originally poor countries like China and India), more gender equality, etc. (e.g., see Bhagwati 2004, Chotikapanich et al. 2012, Potrafke 2014). However, the limitation to the pursuit of equality is one of the major costs of globalization. If country A were a closed economy with no transaction/migration with the rest of the world, it may be desirable to achieve a much higher degree of post-tax equality, as suggested by the point of the previous paragraph. However, in our globalized world, capital and the rich are very internationally mobile. If Singapore imposes higher taxes on the rich or on capital, they will likely flee to a highly competitive alternative like Hong Kong. Thus, despite some of Piketty's (2014) logical issues (as shown in Ng 2015b) in his analytical argument on the inevitability of increasing share of income going to capital instead of labour, I am in strong agreement with him on the need for government promotion of more equality and for the need for international cooperation. In a recent

---

[2] For studies showing some efficiency-enhancing features of equality see also references cited at the end of chapter 6 of Ng 2000.

interview with a radio station in Hong Kong, I suggested that Hong Kong and Singapore (and possibly Shanghai and the whole of China) should cooperate so that they may raise more taxes and help the poor more without too much fear of capital and talent flight. The interviewer correctly pointed out that this cooperation would not happen. What a pity. This points to the need for a stronger United Nations in our more globalized and more integrated and interrelated world (Ng & Liu 2003). Probably more important than the equality issue is the one on environmental protection to ensure survival (Ng 2016).

While the use of the market and the associated inevitable inequality to some extent has many problems, as discussed earlier, it may also have some merits. One was pointed out by Hayek, and discussed by Brennan & Jaworski (2016, p. 171): 'Our rapid economic advancement is in large part a result of inequality and is impossible without it. Progress at a fast rate cannot proceed on a uniform front, but must take place in an echelon fashion ... At any stage of [the process of growing knowledge] there will always be many things we already know how to produce but which are still too expensive to provide for more than the few ... All of the conveniences of a comfortable home, of our means of transportation, and communication, of entertainment and enjoyment, we could produce at first only in limited quantities; but it was in doing this that we gradually learned to make them or similar things at a much smaller outlay of resources and thus began to supply them to the great majority. A large part of the expenditure of the rich, though not intended for that end, thus serves to defray experimentation with the new things that, as a result, can later be made available to the poor' (with a footnote referring to Hayek 1960, pp. 42–44). As a tiny example, one may recall that, when the Rubik's cube was first available in the market around 1980, a cube was selling for many hundreds of US dollars at present prices. The price fell very rapidly over the years and has cost less than a dollar for the past two decades or so.

To some extent, the rich first defraying the high initial costs of supplying new goods offset their external costs of conspicuous consumption. This was echoed by Deng Xiaoping's call for 'letting some people get rich first' during the initial decades of reform around the 1980s. If a society does not accept some degree of inequality, it will most likely collapse, not only economically, but socially.

While we should pursue equality, we should do so efficiently. In the absence of some specific efficiency considerations (such as environmental disruption), instead of trying to suppress the functioning of the market, it is in general better to follow the principle of efficiency rules (in specific issues, treating a dollar as a dollar whomsoever it goes) and supplement this with a more egalitarian system in the general tax/transfer policy. The validity of this is established in the following proposition (Ng 1984a).

Proposition A (a dollar is a dollar; efficiency supremacy in specific issues):
For any efficiency-inconsistent system (e.g., random allocation by lotteries or a purely equality-oriented preferential treatment between the rich and the poor, or outright prohibition), there exists another alternative, which does not use the efficiency-inconsistent system, that makes no one worse off, achieves the same degree of equality (in real income, or utility) and raises more government revenue, which could be used to make everyone better off.

Even an economist may doubt the validity of this proposition; in fact, I was forced by my logic to this proposition in an attempt to prove that it was false. (The principle of 'a dollar is a dollar' or efficiency supremacy in specific issues was suggested to me in 1974 by Professor Ross Parish during a casual lunch. I then argued vehemently against it.) An economist is particularly aware of the disincentive effects of an income tax/transfer system. She is also particularly aware that, to minimize the disincentive effects for any given degree of equality achieved, it may be better to pursue equality in different specific issues/areas, rather than concentrate in the general tax/transfer system. The reason that this proposition is valid despite this consideration may be explained.

The degree of disincentive effects is not a function of the degree of progressivity in the tax/transfer system and/or in specific issues separately. Rather, it depends on the degree of progressivity in the overall system. If the degree of equality in the distribution of real income or utility is the same, the degree of disincentive effects will be the same. However, the pursuit of equality in specific issues (like suppressing market function or subsidizing goods consumed by lower-income groups on egalitarian grounds) has additional distortion costs, unless they are designed to take into account specific efficiency considerations like external costs or differential degrees of complementarity with leisure (to offset the disincentive effects of income taxation), in which case they are not classified as purely equality oriented or efficiency inconsistent. Recognizing this, we may see that the issue of inequality and/or the exploitation of the poor does not constitute a valid reason for limiting the use of markets. If ignorance/irrationality and external costs are involved, they are different justifications.

An example of efficiency violation in specific issues based on the equality consideration is the common practice of using 'first come first served' and time restriction instead of adequate pricing for off-street parking in city centres.

Many cities charge partial parking fees, but few charge purely efficiency-based full fees to equate supply and demand. The rationale is that such full fees would price the lower-income groups out. Thus, based on equality considera-tion, only very low parking fees are collected, resulting in excess demand in off-street parking, at least in city centres. Thus, one typically has to circle several times around the blocks hunting for an empty space. This leads to inconvenience, wasted time and petrol, more congestion, and more pollution. The efficiency costs involved are very high. Moreover, even after one luckily finds an empty space, one is typically restricted to park only for a limited period. This causes additional inconvenience and costs of changing parking space. Charging adequate parking fees and allowing parkers the choice of any preferred length of parking will save a lot of costs, but this is seldom practiced due to the common belief in pursuing equality in specific issues/areas.

Suppose that for a certain parking lot, efficiency supremacy requires increasing the fee charged from $2 to $10 (per period). For simplicity, suppose the increase prices make less wealthy or less urgent drivers (designated as L) out of parking there, and this makes them worse off by $3,000 in total. The more urgent or wealthier drivers (designated as M) are made better off, and they gain $2,000 as a result (due to the increase in both convenience and fees, this sum may either be negative or positive). Moreover, the city council collects more parking fees by the amount of $5,000. These gains of $2,000 and $5,000 must add up to be more than the $3,000 loss, as we are shifting from an efficiency-violating policy to one consistent with efficiency supremacy. This positive aggregate net gain in money terms needs not imply also positive aggregate net gain in welfare terms. The $3,000 loss of L may overwhelm, in welfare terms, the combined gain of $7,000 by the city council and M. Thus, the pursuit of efficiency supremacy policy alone may not always improve social welfare. However, if the overall equality promotion policy is also strengthened or made more progressive, all groups could be made better off. For example, if the central government collects $2,000 more tax from M and $5,000 from the city council, and subsidizes L by $3,000 more, all groups will be made neither better nor worse off, but the central government will have $4,000 excess, which may be used to make all groups better off. Thus, it is better to pursue efficiency supremacy in all specific areas and also strengthen the general equality policy as needed.

Making the general equality policy more progressive may involve taxing the rich more and helping the poor more and hence may generate more disin-centive effects. If we look at this from the tax/subsidy perspective alone, this is true. However, the more progressive tax/subsidy is used to offset the gains of M and the city council and the loss of L due to the shift of an inefficient but equality-oriented policy (insufficient parking fees) to the efficiency supremacy policy (efficient parking fees). Thus, if the change in tax/subsidy is combined with the resulting changes in gain/loss of L, M, and the city council together, there are no overall changes in the utility levels of people in different income groups. The overall incentives will also be unchanged. Thus, to achieve any degree of equality in real income (utility/welfare), it is better to do so only in the general equality promotion policy, not in any specific area. By pursuing equality in specific areas, we incur unnecessary additional costs (including the time and petrol costs of finding a parking spot and the associated congestion and pollution in the earlier example). Thus, we can only achieve the same degree of equality with higher efficiency costs. Conversely, for any degree of overall efficiency attained, we can only achieve a lower level of equality by trying to achieve equality in specific areas. The desire to do more, but using inefficient methods, actually ends up with less equality overall.

This deplorable outcome is not just a theoretical possibility but has actually happened in the real world for many major countries, including Australia, the UK and the USA. For many decades before the 1970s, the egalitarian movement has been very strong in these countries, resulting in the pursuit of equality in specific areas using inefficient methods, with such slogans as 'first come, first served' and 'equal access'. Together with the fairly progressive income tax/transfer system, the overall system had generated very high degrees of disincentives. A political alliance was thus strong enough to reverse the previous changes towards more progressivity in the tax/transfer system, leading to several substantial decreases in progressivity over several decades since the 1970s. For example, the Australian tax reform announced on 19 September 1985 and effected in 1987 reduced the highest marginal income tax rate from 60 to 49%. The tax reform in New Zealand in 1989 sharply slashed the highest marginal tax rate from 66 to 33%. Similar to the Australian and New Zealand reforms, the 1992 tax reform in Norway substantially lowered the top marginal tax rates but only made small reductions of taxes on lower incomes (see Rubolino & Waldenström 2017; for the case of the USA, see Piketty & Saez 2007).

Thus, in retrospect, the previous movement towards more equality in specific areas, after triggering the progressivity reduction backlashes in the general tax/transfer system, actually fail to deliver equality, but the enormous efficiency costs have incurred both during and after the movement. On top of this, several factors (including globalization, 'winners take all', mass media enhancement of the returns of superstars, price booms of properties in good locations, effects of certain new technologies, etc.) accounting for higher inequality (within each country, not between countries) since around the mid-1970s reinforced the decrease in progressivity to make both pre- and post-tax incomes more unequally distributed. This unfortunate outcome, together with an inadequate understanding of the real factors accounting for it, partly, if not mainly, explained the unexpected results of Brexit and Trump's election. Many people wanted changes, but they chose changes that would probably make things worse.

Had these countries been able to resist the excessive pursuit of equality in specific areas inefficiently, the several rounds of decrease in progressivity in the tax/transfer system might have been avoidable. We could then have had more equality and more efficiency at the same time. For such a policy to be acceptable and, hence, implementable, we first need people to understand the basic economics of equality as outlined earlier. Communitarians, in arguing against commodification on the grounds of inequality certainly fail to understand this basic economics, e.g., such conclusions as 'the commodification of everything has sharpened the sting of inequality by making money matter more' (Sandel 2012a, p. 9) ignore economic factors discussed in this chapter. True, commodification makes money matter more, but then we may also tax the rich and help the poor more for any given level of efficiency. Commodification, when passing the cost–benefit test of efficiency, by increasing efficiency, actually allows us to have higher equality for any given level of efficiency, and make all income groups better off, when appropriate offsetting equality-promotion policies are adopted.

To see the inefficiency of pursuing equality in specific areas, consider the following extreme case. For simplicity, first ignore interpersonal differences like adults versus children. We could achieve perfect equality in the allocation of each and every good by a system of forceful egalitarianism where all goods are allocated equally. However, even if feasible, this is inferior to a system where we allow the market to function in the allocation of resources and goods to achieve efficiency but correspondingly use a system of forceful tax/transfers that equalizes incomes for all persons. The objective of equality in total income is achieved, without the inefficiency of allocating all goods equally. Even with the same total income, Madonna will want to consume more lipstick and less rice than I. Giving me any lipstick is totally useless as I do not use lipsticks. Thus, even if we want and could achieve total equality, we should do that only for total income or consumption in aggregate and allow different individuals to choose different goods according to their different preferences. The same degree of disincentive effects is involved without incurring the additional costs of supplanting the market in the distribution of different goods to different consumers.

Consider another hypothetical choice. For any given degree of equality in the post-tax distribution of total money income, consider two alternative arrangements. Under alternative A, we allow only half of the goods to be available for free market operation and the other half is done by completely equal allocation of each good to every individual. The choice of which goods to be in which set is completely random without any justification. Under alternative B, all goods are allowed for free market exchange. Then, clearly, we have higher degree of equality in real income overall, but lower efficiency under A, compared to B. As both equality and efficiency are desirable, we cannot tell for sure which alternative is better for social welfare. However, we may move from alternative B to B', with B' designed to have the same degree in equality as A, by taxing the rich more and subsidizing the poor more if needed. Then, by design, B' and A has the same degree in equality. Which one is more efficient?

The answer should be B'. We can start from A, then move from A to B by just dismantling the restriction on half of the goods from market exchange. This dismantling must make the rich better off but may make the poor worse off. Although the poor may also have more freedom to buy all goods, they lose the previously equally allocated amounts in half of the goods. With lower money income than the rich, they probably will not be able to buy the previously equally allocated amounts. Depending on their preference between more free choice and more allocated amounts, they may either lose or gain. If they in fact gain, my case is strengthened. Thus, assume that they lose. To make them no worse off than under A, the government has to tax them less or subsidize them more. In fact, we may adjust these (changes in taxes or subsidies) at all income levels, such that all groups will be made indifferent between B' and A. Actually, this change is just a special case of Proposition A. As arbitrarily restricting the operation of the market is inefficient, in changing from A to B', the government must be able to collect more taxes (typically more from those at higher income levels) than having to give more subsidies (typically more to those at lower income levels). Thus, after reaching B', the government may use the excess money either on some useful public goods like environmental protection, and/or distribute to all income groups to make all income groups better off, as Proposition A demonstrates (proved in Ng 1984a).

The point is that arbitrarily restricting the function of markets is not an efficient way to achieve equality. A person is rich or poor not depending on her amount consumed of any specific goods but on her total purchasing power. If we want to help the poor, we should try to increase their total purchasing power. In the absence of some specific efficiency considerations, we should let the market work. Of course, we or governments do interfere with the market.

However, these should be based on some reasonable grounds. Taxing pollution to protect the environment is an obviously reasonable and compelling ground. I would even accept some paternalistic grounds (but preferably soft ones) like banning hard drugs and subsidizing merit goods or even providing them for free. Although particular measures (subsidies) may be debatable, these are at least potentially valid grounds. But equality itself is not a valid reason for restricting the function of the market as equality is more efficiently pursued by the general tax/transfer policy than in specific areas. Thus, the inequality/exploitation or 'fairness' (as Sandel calls it) ground is not a valid ground at all in restricting the functioning of markets.[3]

Similarly, we should not refrain from efficient measures in any specific areas (e.g., taxes/subsidies on health grounds like sugar taxes) just due to their being regressive (suggestions along this line abound; e.g., Muller et al. 2017). Rather, we should go ahead with the efficient measures but undertake more general equality-promotion policies if desired.

One may argue that the general equality promotion policy may not be very effective. We may not be able to achieve a much higher degree of equality just using the general tax/transfer policy. Two points may be made on this. First, if certain persons may be able to use their skills, cunning, connections, power, etc. to evade paying more taxes, they are also likely able to use them to evade restrictions in the equality policies in specific areas. When we take into account the presence of interpersonal differences, including adults vs children, males vs females, the rice-eating southern Chinese vs the bun-eating northerners; etc., equal distribution of specific goods would be impractical, and many special rules, supplements, exceptions, etc. have to be allowed. These make the evasion of the equality restrictions much more difficult to reduce than tax evasion. The administrative costs involved would also be prohibitive. For any given level of total administrative costs, the degree of evasion would likely be much higher than the evasion of general taxes. As argued in my 1984 paper in the *American Economic Review*, when we take practicability into account, my case is strengthened, not weakened (Ng 1984a). For example, if a government is not beneficent or efficient enough to pursue the general equality policies well, it is even less likely to handle the equality-oriented policies in specific areas well.

---

[3] Koplin (2017) makes a distinction between 'fair benefits' exploitation and 'fair process' exploitation; the former may be reduced/eliminated by paying higher prices, while the latter cannot: 'political agents might be thought to exploit the poor by taking advantage of the structural injustices that lead them to consider selling a 'spare' organ in the first place' (last page before references). However, it would be much better changing the initial injustices rather than prohibiting sales.

Second, consider the unlikely cases where the pursuit of equality in specific areas is more effective and less costly overall. The justification must be in combination with this cost effectiveness and/or some other considerations (like serious ignorance/irrationality). Inequality alone is not a valid factor. Moreover, in my knowledge, no anti-commodification advocate has based their case on these grounds. They just use the inequality/exploitation or fairness argument on its own, which is invalid.

The case against 'exploitation' need not be completely empty. A classical case with clearly unacceptable exploitation that most, if not all, persons would abhor is this. You are about to drown after a shipwreck. Mr E happens to pass by with his yacht and offers to save you if you agree to pay him 99% of all your assets.[4] Without any other option in sight, you reluctantly agree (so would I). Obviously, no sane judge in the world would enforce such an agreement. A person in the situation like E has a compelling moral obligation to save you irrespective of any remuneration. The immorality of such an agreement is not its market or money aspect. If E requires you to serve him for life or do a certain big favour not involving money or exchange, it would still be equally bad. Thus, it is his failure to save you unconditionally that is absolutely immoral.

Unacceptable exploitation does happen in the real world aplenty. Just a simple example – trafficking of human persons either for sexual or non-sexual exploitation is very common (e.g., Leun & Schijndel 2016 and references therein). However, what really make such cases objectionable are factors such as the actual or threatened use of force, deception, and the violation of laws, not the monetary exchanges involved. Trafficking in human beings (THB) is defined as 'control over another person for the purpose of exploitation' (United Nations 2000, p. 2), including sexual exploitation, forced labour, slavery, servitude, and the removal of organs. In a mutually beneficial exchange without violence and deception, no 'control' is involved. An Uber driver taking a person from one location to another, even if charging extra fare during peak hours does not commit the crime of THB. Even where smuggling (defined as the procurement of an illegal entry into a country; United Nations 2000) is involved, no violation of agreement and no exploitation needs to be involved; however, some cases starting as smuggling may end up as THB (Campana & Varese 2016). Normal business in perfectly legal goods and services may also involve misleading advertising or deception, and are, hence, correctly regarded as exploitative, undesirable,

---

[4] This is not just a purely hypothetical possibility; a similar case (The Port Caledonia and the Anna) happened in 1903, involving a sum of £1,000 (a very large sum at the time). The judge declared the agreement void but allowed the payment of £200); see Wertheimer (1996).

immoral, and illegal. Thus, although immoral exploitation may exist in the real world, the inequality/exploitation objection against commodification is an invalid argument. If no violence, deception, or serious ignorance/irrationality are involved, a person cannot be made better off by being banned to, say, sell her kidney if she chooses so as her last resort.

We allow people to make money by doing dirty, unhealthy, and risky (to life) jobs. Denying the sale of their kidneys reduces their options, and may actually force them to do jobs even more risky than the sale of one of their two kidneys.

Three more points may be made about inequality.

First, citing the *Ethnographic Atlas* (a database on 1,167 societies) by the British anthropologist George P. Murdock (1967), Alesina (2016, p. 937) notes that 'Anthropological evidence ... clearly shows a high degree of equality of resources in hunting and gathering societies. ... The diffusion of agriculture led to a dramatic change in society by vastly increasing inequality.' Presumably, the industrial revolution and modern technology have led further to the outer reaches of the supremely rich. In considering such conclusions, what is commonly ignored is this – while ancient societies were much more equal, that equality was largely based on every one barely surviving. Those who fell significantly below the average simply died, rather than survive to highlight the inequality. Much of modern inequality is not fatal. It is much better to be the modern poor than the ancient dead.

Secondly, consider the argument by Sandel who argues against higher-paying consumers being accorded better or faster services (like first-class tickets, express-lane entitlements, concierge doctors): 'The drawback, of course, is that concierge care for a few depends on shunting everyone else onto the crowded rolls of other doctors. It therefore invites the same objection leveled against all fast-track schemes: that it's unfair to those left languishing in the slow lane' (Sandel 2012a, p. 27). There may be unfairness in the highly unequal distribution of wealth. However, given this distribution, not allowing the use of pricing for distribution in some areas, while achieving higher equality there, will lead to lower equality elsewhere. If the rich cannot use their money to buy more convenient parking lots, they will buy up other items, with lower efficiency. Thus, an economist would argue that items like first-class tickets and concierge doctors are no different from the fact that those with higher ability and willingness to pay get more expensive items like lobsters, 5-star hotel accommodation, more spacious housing, etc.

Speaking of lobsters, I cannot resist the temptation of a side note before continuing with the main argument. In the nineteenth century, lobsters were so plentiful that they were fed only to the poor and prisoners. Prisoners demanded and servants asked for clauses limiting the feeding of lobsters to them to no more than three times a week. The lobster was considered among the least desirable foods, 'a garbage meat fit only for the indigent, indentured, and incarcerated' (see, e.g., Wallace 2005). In contrast, chicken was a delicacy affordable only by the rich. Now, with lobsters becoming very scarce and chicken cheap, lobsters become food for the rich people and chicken as the food for the poor. To some extent, this suggests that if extreme poverty is avoided (no one is starving), some inequality is probably not too serious a matter. Letting the rich pay high prices for items like lobsters, first-class tickets, and luxury Sky boxes (for watching sports) helps to some extent to pay for the costs of supply and, hence, allows others to pay less for other items.

The communitarians may have some point in worrying about the commercialization of certain items, especially some conspicuous arrangements that are perceived to violate some important principles of equality and that of the first-come-first-served. Such perceptions may be incorrect. For example, not charging efficient parking fees not only causes much inefficiency, but also is not really a 'great equalizer'. It may be an equalizer in causing everyone to have to line up, to search, and to be late for important events, but it is not an equalizer overall. It causes greater inequality elsewhere, for any given degree of overall efficiency. Nevertheless, before more people learn of this more sophisticated argument, people may really feel repugnance at the special arrangements. In this book, I accept that we have to consider these repugnance effects (Chapter 6), and also possible crowding-out effects (Chapter 7). Such considerations provide some limits to the expansion of markets, although this expansion may be desirable overall and is a mark of progress (Chapter 8).

Third, the Marxist theory of exploitation, that all profits, rents, and interests are surplus values based on the exploitation of workers, is largely incorrect, as the fact that the marginal productivity of capital is usually positive is ignored.[5] Instead of exploiting others, savers and entrepreneurs typically contribute positively to others through the promotion of growth, introduction of new products and the associated consumer surplus, etc. Saving facilitates capital accumulation. A higher amount of capital complements labour and, hence, increases the wage rates of workers. Alternatively viewed, more capital chasing after workers is good for workers. Thus, the role of capital accumulation in reducing or moderating the degree of inequality in a market economy has been seriously underestimated by many analysts (e.g., Piketty 2014, Scheidel 2017).

A related point may be raised here. In a paper discussing the limits of the market, Basu (2007, p. 576) argues for the possibility of banning child labour

---

[5] See, e.g., 'the party of free-market liberalism, bent on ripping labour out of its lifeworldly context and turning it into a "factor of production" in the service of profit' (Fraser 2014, p. 550).

being desirable as it increases the wages of the parents by limiting the overall labour supply: 'A single child not being allowed to work will of course hurt the child's welfare, since typically it is poverty that drives children to work and stopping one child from working would have a negligible effect on adult wages and therefore would worsen households' poverty. But when a general legislative ban is put in place, all children will be forced to leave work. The unfilled demand for labor caused by this will push up adult wages and it is entirely possible that in the new equilibrium children will be better off.'

The suggested possibility may well apply. If the degree of substitutability (as measured by the elasticity of substitution) between labour and capital is not high (lower than one), a decrease in supply of labour may push up wages substantially so as to increase the total income of workers as a whole. 'The size of the elasticity of substitution is much debated and still controversial; yet, a preponderance of the evidence suggests an elasticity well below 1' (Grossman et al. 2017, p. 1295; see also references cited in a footnote to this quoted sentence).

Does this possibility of making people better off by banning their individually preferred sale of (child) labour violate my argument for efficiency supremacy? No. In the absence of misinformation and irrationality (and external effects like pollution), it would still be more efficient to allow free trade and then tax the owners of capital to help the workers at low income levels if required. This is especially so if we take into account the adjustments in longer terms. With higher efficiency and production, more capital will be accumulated in the longer run, which will help to increase wage rates as mentioned earlier, a factor much underappreciated, as previously noted. Nevertheless, if we take into account misinformation and irrationality (included myopia and the related under-appreciation of the long-term effects of education), the banning of child labour and compulsory education may well be socially desirable, at least in many cases. But this is not based on the invalid argument of inequality/exploitation as such.

If the inequality/exploitation argument (in itself) against the market is unfounded, as argued in this chapter, cases against cross-border trade in organs, transplant tourism, etc. lose much, if not all, of their validity. Such cases are based partly, if not mainly, on people in rich countries exploiting people in poor ones. In the absence of force, misinformation, and serious irrationality, the exploitation argument is not supportable, either for domestic or international trade. Many countries spend huge sums of money to promote their exports and their tourism services. If certain goods and services are tradable domestically, why should they be discouraged or even banned internationally?

6

Repugnance? Similar to 'Honour' Killing

I have explained in the previous chapter that the communitarian objection to the expansion of the market on the ground of inequality/exploitation is, at least on its own, totally invalid. Let us turn now to two of the more valid objections (but still insufficient in most cases): repugnance and crowding out (of intrinsic motivation, altruism/morality). This chapter deals with repugnance and the next chapter deals with crowding out.

If some people really feel repugnance to the buying and selling of say human organs and sexual services, my welfarism framework requires attention to be paid to this, especially in the short-run practical or political level. However, in the long run, it may be best to disregard repugnance as a relevant factor for serious consideration. Using repugnance as the main grounds for, say, banning organ sales and prostitution is really similar to 'honour' killing in being very illiberal, although this is perhaps at a different degree This so-called honour killing is the killing of close relatives, usually sisters or first cousins, for being in love with men outside of marriage, or even after having been kidnapped and raped (see Friedman & McNeill 2013, p. 22). In 2015, more than one thousand girls/women were killed in Pakistan on this ground alone.

One may go further to say that it is also similar to the suicide killing by terrorists that is common around the world today. Like the anti-commodification theorists, these terrorists also believe themselves to be on the 'moral high ground'; they expect to go to heaven after dying from killing the 'decadent' people. The questionable perception of morality, together with insufficient liberalism, leads to terrible outcomes. It may be thought that banning organ sales on the ground of repugnance is nowhere close to terrorism. However, in terms of the number of deaths caused, the banning of kidney sales alone has resulted in more deaths (between five and ten thousand every year in the USA alone; see Chapter 9 for details) than suicide terrorism. My position here may appear extreme but is fully justifiable, as argued later.

Nobel Prize-winning economist Alvin Roth (2007) brings repugnance into prominence in economic analysis. His table 1 lists many items inducing repugnance and acting as restrictions on markets throughout history. He notes that 'some kinds of transactions are repugnant in some times and places and not in others' (2007, p. 38). Cultures and feelings change with time and situations (see also Gillespie 2017.) If we could learn to avoid or at least reduce our unnecessary biases, our society may progress in liberalism, efficiency and fairness simultaneously, just like more liberal societies do not carry out the horrific act of 'honour' killing.

Why do we have the feeling of repugnance or disgust? This feeling is affected by both nature and nurture. Most people find creatures like lizards and snakes disgusting. My wife would scream at the sight of a gecko. This hard-wired feeling helps us to avoid getting near to such creatures (many of which are poisonous) and hence helps us to survive. It performs the same function as our reflex to withdraw our arm (mediated through our spinal cord, not through our brain) upon touching something very hot. Similarly, the feeling of disgust when it comes to food is a disease-avoidance device (Oaten et al. 2009). Most people find new food tastes off and is not palatable. This protects us from eating too much and, hence, from possible illness or even death from eating something poisonous. After we experience no ill effects, the food gradually comes to taste more appetising. This also explains why most people prefer food from their childhood, hence, the Chinese saying: 'Dishes of one's own village taste the best.' One particular instance is the king of fruits, durians. Malaysians love this fruit so much that there is a saying: 'Even having to pawn my sarong, I must eat durians.' However, quite often, new immigrants from overseas cannot even stand the smell of durians. Professor Max Corden, a well-known economist, told me this story, 'When I first visited Malaysia, my hosts gave me a whole fruit of durian to take with me as something very valuable and exotic. It smelt so horrible that I immediately threw it into the rubbish bin upon leaving the taxi.' I personally find another Southeast-Asian fruit called cempedak (also known as durian cempedak, or baby jackfruit) tastier than durian. Moreover, while the top variety of durian, Musang King, costs around US$60 a kilo (with stone but without husk), cempedak is less than 20% that price. However, for some reason, cempedak is not commonly available inter-nationally. There should be some profitable business opportunity there.

However, in my opinion, the more tasty the type of fruit, the much higher the variation in quality, even proportionately. For example, I find that pear tastes fine but is not exciting, and there don't tend to be horrible tasting pears. To my own taste scale, 99% of the quality ranges from say 5 to 20. However, for durians, the 99% range goes from −3 to 200, for cempedak, from −4 to 250.

Perhaps, this is because, if the average quality is high enough, animals will accept the high variation and still want to eat the fruit and help to spread the seeds. As an aside, the reason why durian is the king of fruits is because it has a thick and thorny exterior husk to protect the fruit inside. This requires it to have a strong smell to offset the thick husk. The smell is so strong that those not used to it find it unacceptable, but those used to it find it irresistible.

Our inborn inclinations are also reinforced/qualified through our actual experience and educational/cultural/social contacts. However, neither nature nor nurture is perfect. 'When we know that a particular object has no chance of causing us actual sickness, when we know that it is not actually contaminated, the presence of the feeling of disgust should be no guide to our action. That feeling, we might say, misfires. Mealworms may disgust us, but they are perfectly healthy to eat. Candy bars do not disgust us, but they're not good for us to eat' (Brennan & Jaworski 2016, p. 215). Our current inclination to eat too much salty and sweet food may be explained by changed circumstances. In our long history of evolution, where there was a great scarcity of calorie and salt, our inborn tastes helped us to survive. With calorie and salt aplenty now, we need to be cautious. Similarly, we should examine our feeling of repugnance against certain market transactions critically.

Consider the feeling of repugnance against markets in human organs, kidneys in particular. Several factors are likely important in generating this. First, in an ideal world, at least at the high average per capita income of the world today, no one should be left poor enough to have to sell her kidney to feed her family. Thus, the mere existence of organ sales triggers the inclination towards objection on the grounds of inequality/exploitation. However, upon closer analysis (see Chapter 5), this ground is conceptually invalid, although emotionally very appealing, including to the present writer. Second, the mental image of taking a kidney from a human body is a very bloody one, again triggering our natural disgust response. Third, most people have some degree of the anti-market sentiment (see Chapter 4). Related to this, an anti-rich (including being envious of the rich) sentiment may also be present. If the rich may use their big purses to purchase kidneys from the bodies of the poor, these several factors combine to become an overwhelming force against legalizing the trade. Thus, with the exception of Iran, no countries in the world legally allow kidney sales. However, what all countries, and even what all individuals, do need not be morally right. For example, the concepts of animal rights and welfare have been popular only very recently. This does not make unnecessary cruelty against animals, even during ancient times, right.

One point that could not be overemphasized is that the kidney, whether donated or sold, is used to save another life. If a person is desperate enough to pay a large sum of money to buy a kidney to save her life or that of her loved one, and another is desperate enough to sell one of her kidneys to meet certain urgent/important financial needs, the correct moral emotion should be that of a high level of sympathy for both sides, not of repugnance. Those who believe that they are on the moral high ground of objecting to legal organ sales should get their morality examined more critically.

If I use my hard-earned savings to save my life or that of my loved one by buying a kidney from a willing seller who is not misinformed and rationally decides to sell to meet some urgent financial needs, how could society decide against this on the ground that some feel repugnant about this mutually agreeable and beneficial transaction? Such feelings themselves should be condemned. At least they should be educated to disown such feelings. A representative sample survey of Americans conducted by Leider and Roth (2010) also suggests that disapproval of kidney sales correlates with other socially conservative attitudes. Perhaps we should learn to be more liberal and be less dogmatic.

If you do not want to buy or sell human organs, no one will force you to do it. But if I have to buy or sell to avoid death or serious problems, why on earth do you or society have the right to deny me of that opportunity? Let us accept the fundamental principle of liberalism, no one should be forced to do something or be denied the opportunity to do something without seriously harming others, in the absence of serious ignorance or irrationality.[1] If you do not accept this, are you that far from those committing 'honour' killings and suicide bombings, in being very illiberal and in helping to cause many unnecessary deaths?

For the promotion of liberalism in the long run, we should probably ignore such feelings of repugnance even if they are currently important. We should also learn from past mistakes to be more liberal. Whenever sacred values, sanctity, and similar terms are used to justify banning some useful activities including exchanges, we have to be very suspicious. We should avoid falling to the low level of illiberalism close to those committing honour killings and terrorism. Most people may think that it is impossible for us to sink to such a low level. However, the very illiberal proposal by a most prominent anti-commodification theorist, Prof. Michael Sandel, does not give us much assurance.

In an article entitled 'If I ruled the world', Sandel (2012b) concludes: 'While revising the economics textbooks, I would issue one modest decree: I'd ban the

---

[1]   I accept this liberal principle ultimately on its utilitarian ground of promoting welfare. Hence, there is no conflict with my ultimate moral ground of welfarism.

use of an ungainly new verb that has become popular these days in the jargon of politicians, bankers, corporate executives, and policy analysts: "incentivise." Banning this verb might help us recover older, less economistic ways of seeking the public good—deliberating, reasoning, persuading.'

His view against prostitution in the absence of coercion, misinformation, etc. is also not encouraging: 'prostitution is a form of corruption that demeans women and promotes bad attitudes toward sex. The degradation objection doesn't depend on tainted consent; it would condemn prostitution even in a society without poverty, even in cases of upscale prostitutes who liked the work and freely chose it' (2012a, p. 112). Similarly, the honour killers and terrorists regard sex before or outside of marriage, and other 'decadent' life-styles, as degrading and promoting negative attitudes toward marriage. However, one may have such 'high-brow' views, but should not force others to observe the same moral standards.

7

Crowding Out or Crowding In?

This is potentially a more valid argument. The main point is that the use of market exchange may crowd out intrinsic motivation, altruism, and morality to result in a worse outcome. A similar or related point is the corruption objection which 'points to the degrading effect of market valuation and exchange on certain goods and practices' (Sandel 2012a, p. 111). The introduction of financial incentives can lead to 'the loss of nonmarket norms and expectations' and thereby 'change the character' of these activities (Sandel 2012a, p. 90). Although it is possible to make a distinction, I will define 'crowding out' widely enough to include the corruption objection.

Crowding out or in may refer either to the intrinsic motivation, altruism, or morals (in the subjective sense), or to the actual behaviour, like the amount of blood or organs donated (in the objective sense). In my view, crowding out in terms of the former definition is more important. For example, it is quite likely that a person is willing to use one of her kidneys to save the life of a loved one, if purchasing a kidney legally is not an option. However, in the presence of this option, she may decide to buy a kidney instead. The number of uncompensated donated kidneys is reduced (crowded out) by the legalization of kidney sales. However, this does not mean that her degree of concern/altruism towards her loved one is correspondingly reduced. This degree may likely remain intact, but the availability of a lower-cost option allows her to opt out of the higher-cost way of saving her loved one. If the seller of that kidney makes the decision under full knowledge and rationality, no one is made worse off. The change is clearly desirable. Thus, the existence of crowding out in the objective sense does not constitute a valid ground against legalization.[1] On the

---

[1] Crowding out in the objective sense, including quality reduction, has also been strongly challenged; re kidney donation, see Ghods & Savaj (2006), Mahdavi-Mazdeh (2012), Beard et al. (2013, pp. 177–182), Rana et al. (2015), Held et al. (2016, supplement 6).

other hand, although crowding out in the subjective sense may also exist, it is much less likely. Moreover, the existence of crowding out in the subjective sense is also not a sufficient condition to justify banning free exchange, as the benefits of the free market must also be taken into account. However, it is a factor that should be taken into consideration.

It may be true that financial incentives and market prices may 'backfire' by crowding out nonmarket norms. Sometimes, offering payment for a certain behaviour gets you less of it, not more (Sandel 2012a, p. 114). I read a story: An old man was disturbed by the noise made by children playing basketball close to his flat. He started paying each child 20 cents each day for playing. After a few days, he claimed insufficient money and paid them only 10 cents each. Then, 5 cents. Then, none. The children stopped playing basketball afterwards. I am not sure about the authenticity of the story, but the point about crowding out of intrinsic motivation is clear.

However, as argued earlier in the case for lateness fees (Chapter 2), back-firing need not be bad. If the fee compensates enough for the additional costs of the day care centres, if more parents turn up late and pay the fees, both sides may be better off, and fewer people may get run down by hasty parents driving fast. More importantly, people feel less guilty and may concentrate on being punctual on really important occasions – a likely all-round gain, as practiced in Singapore, and reported in Chapter 2. However, are there serious crowding-out effects leading to a much worse outcome in other cases?

One particular case that I am largely on the side of communitarians is paying children to read. If monetary payment crowds out their intrinsic motivation, the payment may well be counterproductive. Moreover, children are still in their early stage of learning of how to form the right values and may be more vulnerable to the influence (I hesitate to say 'corruption') of monetary payment. However, perhaps further research may give us more insight.

There is a fairly large literature on crowding out/in. Although many evidences on both sides have been presented aplenty, the jury is still out; a decisive conclusion is not available. For example, in answer to the question 'Does the free market corrode moral character?', the answers from 13 'distinguished scholars and public figures' vary from 'Yes, too often' (Kay S. Hymowitz) and 'Of course it does' (Michael Walzer) through to 'Yes, but' (Garry Kasparov) and 'It depends' (John Gray, John C. Bogle) to 'No' (Qinglian He), 'To the contrary' (Jagdish Bhagwatie), and 'Not at all' (Ayaan Hirsi Ali) (see John Templeton Foundation 2008). Obviously, more studies are needed. A possible position to take is to recognize the existence of both crowding out and crowding in, with the net effects in the objective sense difficult to judge, and the net effects in the subjective sense likely negligible. Thus, the use of crowding out as the major reason to justify banning market exchanges where the potential benefits are clear and important, such as in kidney sales, cannot be justified.

The potential crowding out of intrinsic motivation by financial incentives has been studied as early as Titmuss (1970) and Deci (1971).[2] Titmuss argues that monetary payment crowds out intrinsic incentives and reduces the quality of blood supply, as the intrinsic suppliers are replaced by those aiming for financial rewards. However, Titmuss' study has been challenged, including as being based 'too heavily upon anecdote and incomplete data ... inaccurate and incomplete in many respects', raising 'serious questions about his thesis' (Hippen & Satel 2008, p. 97; see also Starr 1998, Epstein 2008, Mellström & Johannesson 2008, Slonim et al. 2014). Also, evidence from nearly 14,000 American Red Cross blood drives and from a natural field experiment shows that economic incentives have a positive effect on blood donations without increasing the fraction of donors who are ineligible to donate (Lacetera et al. 2012, 2013). Similarly, 'Contrary to the hypothesis of Titmuss, the empirical literature suggests that the total supply of compensated and non-compensated blood donated appears to increase in the presence of compensation, so that non-compensated and compensated plasma donation structures can effectively coexist' (Skinner et al. 2016, p. 161).

One relevant point is the amount of pay/price involved. 'In a real-effort task, individuals indeed work harder for charity than for themselves [suggesting crowding out], but only when incentive stakes are low. When stakes are raised, effort increases when individuals work for themselves but not when they work for others' (Imas 2014). Thus, 'well designed fines, subsidies, and the like minimize crowding out and may even do the opposite, making incentives and social preferences complements rather than substitutes' (Bowles & Polania-Reyes 2012).

The old doux-commerce thesis on the civilizing effects (making people gentle, honest, and peaceful) of market relations also suggests crowding in.

---

[2] See Frey (1997), Deci et al. (1999), Fehr & Falk (2002), Ariely et al. (2009), Frey & Jegen (2001), Janssen and Mendys-Kamphorst (2004), Gneezy et al. (2011), and Festré & Garrouste (2015) for surveys, and Bowles (2008), Chetty et al. (2014), Bartling et al. (2015) for experimental studies. For a theoretical analysis of crowding out from the interaction of 'altruism and greed with concerns for social reputation or self-respect', see Bénabou & Tirole (2006). On the use of moral sanctions and moral rewards (feelings of guilt and virtue) to influence individual behaviour for social welfare maximization, see Kaplow & Shavell (2007). On the crowding out of intrinsic motivation by rewards and punishment, especially in raising children, see Kohn (1999, 2005); for a critic of Kohn that it 'ignores a major body of work' (p. 153) and involves 'biases' (p. 154), see Reitman (1998). On a conceptual analysis of motivational crowding out, see Evren & Minardi (2017).

This was argued from Charles-Louis de Montesquieu, Adam Smith, and Thomas Paine to Albert Hirschman (1982, 1992, 2013) and McCloskey (2006, 2016). 'Capitalism has not corrupted our souls. It has improved them. . . . Love, in short, is arguably thicker on the ground in the modern, Western, capitalist world' (McCloskey 2006, pp. 23, 141). Berggren & Nilsson (2013) and Prasad (2012) also argue that economic freedom, trade openness, and the removal of controls, in particular, foster tolerance and reduce violent crime. Zak (2011) argues that, not only is moral behaviour necessary for the proper functioning of markets, but markets also strengthen moral values. Cowen (1998) traces the positive impact of commerce on arts. In particular, commerce produces Mozart, Beethoven, Michelangelo, and Shakespeare – each of whom, Cowen shows, was a businessperson trying to make money. The case of Shakespeare seems to be supported by the fact that one of his plays is titled 'As you like it.' Shakespeare was asked by his publisher about the title. Being unable to think of an appropriate one, Shakespeare said, 'As you like it', and the publisher took that as the title. This suggests that Shakespeare was not very serious in thinking about an appropriate title, and just ask the publisher to use any one they like.

> 'After extensive research, Cowen concludes that there's little evidence that the market is dumbing down people's tastes in art and music. Rather, at worst, it's supplying philistines with the culture they already want. And, at its best, the market is producing plenty of high culture. It's no coincidence that a society's commercial centers tend to be its cultural centers as well, and no coincidence that if you want a good philosophical critique of commercial society, you'll find that these are being produced in Boston, New York, and London, not Pyongyang, Moscow, or Havana. You might lament that as Hollywood tries to reach a broader audience, movies are being dumbed down. But, at the same time, for-profit premium channels such as HBO and Showtime are producing the best film drama available' (Brennan & Jaworski 2016, p. 131).

Markets serve people of different preferences largely without discrimination and economizes on shared fixed costs where relevant.

Nearly two centuries ago, Mill (1848, III.17.14) regarded the moral benefits of commerce as more important than its economical ones:

> But the economical advantages of commerce are surpassed in importance by those of its effects which are intellectual and moral. It is hardly possible to overrate the value, in the present low state of human improvement, of placing human beings in contact with persons dissimilar to themselves, and with modes of thought and action unlike those with which they are familiar.

Commerce is now what war once was, the principal source of this contact. Commercial adventurers from more advanced countries have generally been the first civilizers of barbarians. And commerce is the purpose of the far greater part of communication which takes place between civilized nations. Such communication has always been, and is peculiarly in the present age, one of the primary sources of progress. To human beings, who, as hitherto educated, can scarcely cultivate even a good quality without running it into a fault, it is indispensable to be perpetually comparing their own notions and customs with the experience and example of persons in different circumstances from themselves: and there is no nation which does not need to borrow from others, not merely particular arts or practices, but essential points of character in which its own type is inferior. ... And it may be said without exaggeration that the great extent and rapid increase of international trade, in being the principal guarantee of the peace of the world, is the great permanent security for the uninterrupted progress of the ideas, the institutions, and the character of the human race.

This old view of Mill still applies in our modern world, as testified here: 'Over the past several centuries, the world has seen the many ways in which an active free market spurs material and social progress while at the same time strengthening moral character. By contrast, people who have lived under the free market's primary modern rival, the ideologically-driven planned economy of state socialism, have suffered as economic performance stagnated, civil society withered, and morality was corroded' (He 2008, p. 8). And, 'To appreciate just how effectively the free market strengthens moral character, it is helpful to glance at economic systems that undermine or openly reject it. Everywhere Communism has been tried, for instance, it has resulted not just in corruption and sub-standard products but also in fear, apathy, ignorance, oppression, and a general lack of trust. The Soviet Union and pre-reform China were morally as well as economically bankrupt' (Ali 2008, p. 22). Also, 'the moral attractions of markets are clear. Consider immigration. Across the world, people tend to migrate to market-friendly societies and away from market-unfriendly societies—and money is not the only motivating factor. They are also drawn by the opportunity to live under a system that offers a better quality of life, and especially by the opportunity to escape from the morally degrading favor-seeking of many other [non-market] economic arrangements' (Cowen 2008, p. 18).[3]

Eisenberger & Cameron (1996) question the validity of the argument that rewards the crowding out of intrinsic motivation. Schnedler & Vanberg (2014) argue that, instead of really crowding out intrinsic motivation, the individuals

---

[3] On the pros and cons of the doux-commerce thesis, see also Oman (2016) and Movsesian (2018).

involved may just be 'playing hard to get' in order to obtain higher prices for their services. Elías et al. (2015) show that cases against organ sale are much affected by the lack of relevant information. 'The estimated approval rate for organ payments increased from a baseline of 51.8 percent to 71.3 percent when information was provided—a 19.5 percentage point increase ($p < 0.01$), or about 38 percent of the baseline' (p. 363).[4]

The existence of some crowding out in certain circumstances cannot be denied, and this is intuitively unsurprising. One remarkable case is that of nuclear waste siting in a Swiss town. When people were asked to vote on their agreeability for the use of a location in their town as a waste site without compensation, a lesser proportion of voters were against than when financial compensation was mentioned. Without payment, people have higher willingness to sacrifice for the greater good (Frey et al. 1996). At least to some extent, the existence of public spirit which was crowded by the offer of financial compensation likely played a role. However, while communitarians may hail this as demonstrating the limit of markets, economists may also suspect a high degree of expressiveness in the voting.[5] The vote was not decisive in the actual choice but was only a tool for opinion sounding. Also, a single vote will almost never change the decision. Thus, many voters may vote to show that they are good citizens and not money-hungry persons. The use of experimental choices with actual reward-related consequences may help to complement the inadequacy of actual public voting.

Gagnon & Goyal (2017) also show that markets may either reduce or increase social ties (networks); markets and networks may either be complements or substitutes. As both crowding out and crowding in may happen, a decisive conclusion is difficult. At least our knowledge now is inadequate to use crowding out as a solid ground to limit the expansion of markets. A more balanced position is that markets and morals are mutually reinforcing and mutually limiting, as expressed by Friedman & McNeill (2013, p. 6), quoted in the displayed passage in the Preface.

Differences in views about crowding out or in are related to the following difference between economists and communitarians. Economists focus on scarcity, not only scarcity in resources proper, but also in time, effort, attention, and the capacity for altruism and morality. Communitarians focus on the point that this capacity is not fixed, but rather grows with more usage. For

---

[4] See also Heath (2012).
[5] The main point is that as the vote of any single individual has negligible influence on the outcome, one may vote mainly to express one's own view rather than voting to try to affect the outcome; see Brennan & Buchannan (1984). For experimental evidence, see Tyran (2004), Tyran & Wagner (forthcoming).

example, in the case for lateness fees, as discussed in Chapter 2, most economists probably agree with me that if we do not always have to be punctual in
matters of our routine life like picking up children, we may be able to focus
our time, effort, attention, and moral capacity on matters that are more
important. We will then likely be able to avoid being late for more important
appointments, and be able to be nicer to friends or a passer-by, for example.
On the other hand, the communitarians may worry that, if we could just pay
a small fee for being late in picking up children, we will be corrupted into
thinking that punctuality is a matter of just a few dollars. Worse, such disregard
for the morality of punctuality may further corrupt other aspects of morality,
making us less moral. Both sides may argue like this without a decisive
conclusion. However, if we look at history, with economic growth, more
division of labour, and the use of markets in wider scope, have people become
less moral? Another more objective indication is that donations for charity and
other altruistic purposes have increased substantially, whether as an absolute
amount or as a percentage of total income.[6]
Some authors claim

> 'that markets corrupt politics, but in fact the most marketized societies are
> also the least corrupt. On the contrary, one of the most consistent findings of
> public choice economics, the subfield of economics that studies government
> behavior, is that politics corrupts markets. The more politicized an economy
> becomes, the more private actors try to rig regulations and the law to cheat
> consumers and competitors. [Footnote reference to Mueller 2003,
> pp. 333–358.] Instead of trying to keep the nasty market away from pristine
> politics, we should be trying to keep nasty politics away from the market.
> In fact, whenever political scientists or economists plot trustworthiness, lack
> of corruption, trust, or citizens' generosity against economic freedom, they
> find a very strong positive correlation. So, for instance, people in market
> societies give more to charity and volunteer more than people in non-market
> societies. [For example, market-oriented societies tend to be the most giving
> and charitable. See the Charities Aid Foundation 2016]. Part of the reason
> they do so is that they are richer and so can afford to do so. (We don't know if
> that's supposed to be an objection or a point in our favor.) But even control-
> ling for income, they still give more' (Brennan & Jaworski 2016, p. 99).

This is discussed further in the next chapter.

[6] World Giving Index 2017: a global view of giving trends. Retrieved from the Charities Aid
Foundation website: www.cafonline.org/about-us/publications/2017-publications/caf-world-
giving-index-2017.
   Giving USA 2018: The Annual Report on Philanthropy for the Year 2017. Retrieved from the
Giving USA website: https://givingusa.org/.

8

Market Expansion Is a Mark of Progress

The phenomenal success of many market economies, the failure of communism in China, USSR, and other countries, and, to a lesser extent, the teaching of basic economics over the last century or so, have convinced most people, including communitarians, on the efficiency and necessity of using the market in the traditional scope of goods and services. However, the communitarians deplore the continuing expansion in the scope of market usage, threatening to turn a market economy into a market society. They want the market to be confined within its traditional spheres, not expanding into other spheres of life where the market principle should have no role to play. In this chapter, I argue that the expansion of the market is a result and indication of progress and will in turn contribute to more progress. Within limits, we should allow, if not promote, this expansion, including the dismantling of unnecessary legal restrictions on markets, such as the cases of kidney sales and prostitution, as discussed in the next few chapters.

What is the main basic principle of the market? The absolutely essential element (*sine qua non*) of a market is exchange. Normally, this refers to mutually agreeable exchange. If I break into your flat tonight and take away valuables, and I call it an 'exchange', because I leave you with a broken window; this is not really an exchange but a theft. Apart from being mutually agreeable, we may also want to add additional qualifications on what kinds of exchanges qualify. One possible requirement is the confinement to items of material value rather than of emotional value. You invite your friends to dinner this week and they invite you next month. Or you help your neighbours in some occasions and they help you on others. We may not want to include such social interaction as market exchanges. However, I think the main difference is that, in the case of dinner invitation and mutual help, no requirement of reciprocation is needed. Friends may also give each other material goods of value like wine and chocolates. Even if reciprocation is usually practiced but not required for any particular instance, we normally do not regard it as exchange but as social interaction. Market exchanges need not be in material goods, but may also be in services and even in information of value. If you just share your grief with your friend/neighbour and get much emotional relief, it is not exchange, but a social activity. However, if you have to pay her $x per hour, it is not an activity of friendship but market purchase of emotional support. Even if you ink a contract or make an agreement with her to pay you back not in money but in emotional support in the future, it still looks more like exchange than social interaction. Thus, it is not whether the item is of material or emotional value that is important, but the requirement for reciprocation.

'We think of *markets* as representing anonymous and monetized exchange, while *community* refers to personalized and non-monetized interaction in social networks (e.g., Gudeman 2008; Parry & Bloch 1989)' (Gagnon & Goyal 2017, p. 1, n. 1, italics original). While whether it is anonymous and monetized or not is certainly relevant, the requirement for reciprocation seems more important. Thus, if two neighbours or friends who know each other exchanged their respective cars for mutual convenience without using money but with full requirement for reciprocation, it looks more like a market exchange than a social or community activity.

Of course, we may have different degrees and grey areas here. For a very good friend, one may not care much about how many times in a row one has been paying for the dinners. However, who counts as a 'very good friend' may largely depend on how much un-reciprocated help he has given you before and how much you enjoy his company. Mutual benefits are not only essential for most friendships but also most marriages. With few exceptions, the only important loving relationship (with 'love' interpreted in a wide sense) without the requirement of mutual benefits is probably parental love for their own children, which is largely dictated by our nature (although also influenced by education and social interaction), selected to ensure survival over generations. Even here, nature ensures survival partly by rewarding parents with positive emotions and partly by making them take into account directly the welfare of their children, over and above the emotional effects. Few, if any parents are willing to sacrifice for their children only for the emotional effects.

We also have some (much lower) degrees of affective and non-affective care for others other than our own children. The affective one refers to the emotional effects (warm glow) and the non-affective one refers to those over and above the emotional effects.[1] Many economists doubt the possibility for non-

---

[1] For an analysis of warm glow, see Andreoni (1990).

affective altruism, but I have argued for it compellingly (Ng 1999). Both types of altruism exist even in our dealings in market exchange. However, since market exchanges are mutually agreeable and mostly mutually beneficial, the reliance on altruism is not very important, although some degree of trust may still be essential. Some degrees of altruism are more important in social interaction. However, the differences are largely a matter of degree. As noted earlier, even marriages depend much on being mutually beneficial, at least in the long term. Viewed in this perspective, the difference between market exchange and social interaction is not that large. This consideration makes the expansion of the market beyond its traditional scope unlikely to be a serious negative, especially in terms of the possible crowding out of altruism or morality.

Even without studying economic history (which will reinforce our points here) in detail, we may use common sense and common knowledge to see that the following is true. After the evolution of *Homo sapiens*, we went through a long period of living in small groups as wandering hunter-gatherers, barely surviving. Not much division of labour was involved beyond that between men and women due to biological differences and between the head person and the rest, due to the usefulness of having a commander. This period is known as the Paleolithic era, covering the long period before 10,000 BC. This was followed by the Mesolithic era over 10,000–7,500 BC with the domestication of animals and gradual rise of agriculture, giving rise to settled groups. The following Neolithic era over 7,500–3,500 BC saw more division of labour within and between tribes, giving rise to exchange and the use of money (which is a medium of exchange) (Lannoye 2015).[2]

The use of money overcomes the difficulty of addressing the double coincidence of want. If you want to use a dozen eggs to exchange for one kilogram of apples, you have to find someone who happens to want to use one kilogram of apples to exchange for a dozen eggs. This is quite difficult except by unlikely coincidence. Thus, money facilitates exchange enormously and promotes the division of labour further. The division of labour in turn gives rise to economies of specialization and great increases in the wealth of nations, as Adam Smith (1776 [1982]) analyzed. True, the great increase in wealth, especially during and after the Industrial Revolution (around 1760–1830) was also facilitated greatly by technological progress and the use of institutions allowing and facilitating exchanges. However, scientific and technological progress itself depends much on the division of labour. Without elaborate exchanges

---

[2] For the detailed history of the relevant periods, see Christian (2015) and Barker & Goucher (2015).

facilitated by the use of money, a tribe in autarky could only barely survive, not capable of devoting time and resources to the pursuit of knowledge. Modern civilization, including science, technology, literature, music, etc., depends much on the use of money. Should we feel so negative about the use of something so productive? True, the pursuit of money may also give rise to something very wicked. However, this is true of everything useful. A knife is very useful in the kitchen but may be used for murder. We should be wise enough to separate the wicked aspect (malice aforethought) from the purely instrumental aspect.

In a primitive society without much division of labour and without specialized professions like medical doctors, much medical treatment was done within a family or tribe, without payment. Thus, it was natural to regard medical treatment as altruistic help one should offer to others for free. Charging a fee would thus be regarded as immoral, just like charging a fee for saving a shipwrecked person now, as remarked earlier. 'In less developed societies, people consider more acts wicked' (Friedman & McNeill 2013, p. 23).[3]

Around the time of Socrates (469/470–399 BC), people made the distinction between arts and crafts and believed that people should only charge for crafts but not for arts. The practice of medicine was initially regarded as an art, not a craft. The Hippocratic Corpus advised practicing medicine without receiving payment. Fee charging for practicing medicine was much frowned upon but was gradually accepted by necessity (cf. Schiedermayer & McCarty 1995). Treating and caring for the sick without charges are admirable and honourable acts. However, if we refuse to pay for our medical doctors and nurses, the objective of treating and caring for the sick would be seriously curtailed, not encouraged. Had we persisted in our objection to paying for practicing medicine, we certainly would not be able to enjoy the very high standard of specialized medical care we enjoy now.[4] The same is true for the provision of education, entertainment, and other services. At the time of Adam Smith (undisputed father of economics), people viewed selling one's service of singing in the public as a 'discredit' and Smith cited this to explain the higher pays needed (Smith, 1776 [1982], p. 209). We now not only regard this as acceptable, but as honourable.

---

[3] On the dynamic balance between the market and the government, see de Grauwe (2016).
[4] This does not imply that imperfections do not exist. Nevertheless, despite many imperfections and increasing problems like environmental disruption that we face, our life expectancy has increased very substantially and continuously.

Similarly, when life insurance was first introduced in the nineteenth century in the USA, many people regarded it as an 'unacceptable gamble against God' (Taylor 2014; cf. Zelizer 1978). People admonished, 'You want to set a *price* on your life, and then place a *bet* on your date of death?' Now, virtually everyone regards taking life insurance as a prudent and perfectly acceptable measure. As noted by Kessler & Roth (2014, p. 426), 'repugnant transactions have a long and varied history that changes in time and place (e.g., charging interest on loans, indentured servitude, selling horsemeat for human consumption, and same-sex marriage all have been repugnant transactions in some times and places and not in others)'.

The feeling of repugnance is also related to misconception. Charging interests on loans (regarded by the Catholic Church as a sin until well into the thirteenth century, and also by many other religions) is a good example. For simplicity, assume that there is no inflation (general increase in the average price level). Then money interest also equals real interest. Repayment more than the principal borrowed is then mistakenly seen as exploitation. The mistake is due to ignoring the positive marginal productivity of capital (i.e., the productivity of an extra unit of capital). Labour is more productive if complemented with more land, materials, machines, etc. Loans allow one to use more capital-intensive or more roundabout methods of production with higher productivities. As this involves time, $100 today is more valuable than $100 next year. The difference is due to the marginal productivity of capital. If the marginal productivity of capital is 5%, the $100 this year, when invested, will become $105 next year. Thus, charging an interest rate of 5% just equates the $105 next year to the $100 this year. No exploitation is involved. One may also view the difference between $100 this year with the same $100 next year from the perspective of the preference for present versus future values. However, when the market for funds is in equilibrium (i.e., supply equals demand[5]), the rate of time preference for present consumption/income/wealth should be equated with the marginal productivity of capital. (The complications of uncertainty, taxation, etc. are ignored for simplicity.)

As Berggren & Nilsson (2013, p. 181) argue, for both the market institutions and the market process, 'the dynamic functioning of the market economy . . . can stimulate tolerance in three ways: first, by people internalizing a positive outlook on others through transactions that demonstrate that those who are different can be trusted; second, by a conscious desire to better one's situation and by realizing that this entails treating others, not on the basis of

---

[5] To be pedantic, one should say 'the quantity supplied equals the quantity demanded'.

characteristics such as race or sexual orientation but on productivity; and third, by enabling a transformation of society from the small, closed group (that exerts pressure on people to conform to one way of life) to the great society, where people need not try to control and dislike those who deviate from majority practices and characteristics.' Berggren & Nilsson (2013) also recognize the possibility of a negative relationship, when markets bring about greed, anonymity, and deceptive behaviour. However, according to their overall cross-sectional regression analysis for 69 countries, the 'results indicate that economic freedom fosters tolerance' (p. 181). As also mentioned by Berggren & Nilsson (2013), Rode (2013) shows how to access to sound money, free trade, and freedom from regulation seems positively related to subjective well-being, while Frey & Stutzer (2002) demonstrate more generally how institutions affect happiness levels.

Comparing different countries, we see that the USA, a country with one of the highest per capita incomes and a liberal use of the market, actually tops the world in terms of the charitable giving by individuals as a percentage of GDP (Charities Aid Foundation 2016, p. 3). Comparing different times, 'A widely shared view is that the more a society relies on the market, the larger is its economic freedom' (Prados De La Escosura 2016, p. 438). Also, 'more economic freedom fosters economic growth' (De Haan & Sturm 2000, p. 238). Moreover, 'An expansion of economic liberty, nearly three-fourths of its possible maximum, has taken place in the OECD [Organization for Economic Cooperation and Development] [countries] during the last one-and-a-half centuries. Its evolution, however, has been far from linear. After a substantial improvement from the mid-nineteenth century that peaked in 1913, the First World War brought with it a major setback. A postwar recovery up to 1929 was followed by a dramatic decline in the 1930s and, by the eve of the Second World War, economic freedom had shrunk to its 1850 levels. Significant progress in economic freedom during the Golden Age (1950–73) fell short of the pre-First World War peak. A steady advance since the early 1980s has resulted in the highest levels of economic liberty in the last two centuries.' (Prados De La Escosura 2016, p. 466; see also figure 4 on p. 451.)

'Also, economic development typically implies an increasing role of markets in society, possibly reducing the repugnance of trades in previously unacceptable areas' (Elías et al. 2017, p. 79). 'In the case of abortion, higher income per capita is strongly associated with the adoption of formal legislation with increasingly permissive rules. Similarly, for prostitution there is an association between higher income per capita and the adoption of formal legislation legalizing the (non-organized) exchange of sex for money' (Elías et al. 2017, pp. 77–78). However, 'The positive relationship between income and formal legislation, as well as the liberalization of non-organized forms of prostitution is absent or even reversed in the presence of a nondemocratic regime, of limited economic and political rights for women, and in countries where Islam is the prevalent faith' (Elías et al. 2017, p. 79). This points to the importance of progress in both income and liberalism for the higher acceptance of markets.[6]

In the presence of markets and free trade, not only do markets promote economic growth and vice versa, one also benefits from others (especially your neighbours) getting richer. In a paper entitled 'The enrichment of a sector (individual/region/country) benefits others' (Ng 1996b), I show that, at least in the benchmark case, the enrichment of one benefits others, by providing the latter with a larger sector to trade with and to learn from. This is consistent with: 'For people living in small, warlike hunter-gatherer communities, it really is a disaster if the tribe across the river is stronger and smarter than you. But for people living in market societies, it's not only not a disaster, but good to encounter people who are stronger and smarter than you' (Brennan & Jaworski 2016, p. 172).

We may thus conclude that, when a society becomes more advanced, with higher per capita income, higher degrees of specialization and division of labour, better legal systems, better transfer of incomes from the rich to the poor, better education, and better understanding of the function of the market, more liberal attitudes, etc. then an increasing number of activities may be subject to market exchange with gradual popular acceptance. This higher acceptance and broader scope for the market in turn promotes efficiency and economic growth, if not also morality. In general, this is an applaudable, not a deplorable development. In other words, in terms of three common Chinese proverbs:

习以为常，
近朱者赤，
平心接受。

In English, when read horizontally, this says: [As people] are used to it; and are in close proximity to it; they will accept it with equanimity; and when read vertically, this says: [As] Xi Jinping (Chinese president), [testifies] with red heart, as something normal and even communists would accept.

---

[6] The economy, institutions, and values co-evolve with complicated interactions; see, e.g., Alesina & Giuliano 2015, Bisin 2017.

9

The Case for Legalizing Kidney Sales

The sale of body parts may be defined to include blood, bone marrow, milk, sperm, surrogate motherhood, kidney, liver or parts thereof, etc. In this chapter, the focus is on the sale of kidneys. Blood donation is discussed in the next short chapter.

Nearly 65 years after the first successful kidney transplant in 1954, the monetary selling and purchase of kidneys are illegal in virtually all countries. This results in waiting lists for kidney transplants that extend into years in most countries, with many dying while waiting (Lim 2008), leading to 'a disaster of our own making' (Beard & Osterkamp 2014). As of May 2018, the National Kidney Foundation of the USA listed some 121,678 individuals waiting for an organ transplant in the USA, including 100,791 seeking kidney transplants.[1] In 2016, more than 4,500 candidates waiting for kidney transplants in the USA alone died. (See also the website of the Organ Procurement and Transplantation Network: https://optn .transplant.hrsa.gov/.)

A notable exception is Iran where regulated legal markets exist with the volume of annual sales between one and two thousand per year. This method has avoided many problems (including the reduction of 'coercion' on unpaid related donors) associated with the inadequate black-market kidney trade and all other systems that are used in other countries which have failed to solve the worsening kidney transplant queues (Ghods & Savaj 2006). It is true that some ex post regrets exist (Cohen 2014). However, this is true for most, if not all, other legal or illegal transactions and decisions. The existence of substantial regrets may warrant more pre-sale counselling, but no system can ensure the complete absence of regrets. Obviously, the costs of some regrets may be overwhelmed by the large surpluses for both the selling and purchasing sides.

---

[1]   Figures as of 11 January 2016.

What about crowding out? I already remarked earlier (Chapter 7) that crowding out in the subjective sense is unlikely while that in the objective sense need not be undesirable. Moreover, empirical evidence seems to suggest little to no crowding out even in the objective sense; 'after the legalization of the sale of kidneys in Iran in 1988, the annual rate of (uncompensated) living donation remained stable at 11–13 percent. . . . Altruistic behavior turns out to be more resilient than its defenders suppose' (Hippen & Satel 2008, pp. 107, 109). Comparison with the blood plasma case also suggests no significant, if any, crowding out (Epstein 2008, pp. 92–95).[2]

One may cite cases in China where someone wanted to sell his kidney just to finance the buying of an iPhone to show the silliness of the transaction, at least from the perspective of the kidney seller. However, this silliness was a problem involving that particular seller, not that of the legality of kidney sales. Kidney sales are illegal in China. In fact, with legal status and appropriate regulation, the tragic case of an illegal kidney sale that results in serious injuries (see the footnote to this paragraph) would most likely be prevented. Such cases in fact illustrate the serious problems of illegality, not of legalization. Legal prohibition does not stop transaction and trafficking but creates many problems (Hippen 2005). Also, one may also cite the case of a person in Tianjin in 2003 who, in order to buy a mobile phone, borrowed and skipped meals to save money. He succeeded in buying a mobile phone, but ended up in the hospital while cycling to show off his newly acquired phone to dozens of friends, fainting in the process partly due to undernourishment. The purchase was certainly silly, but no one suggested banning mobile phones. Similarly, one cannot reject the legality of kidney sales based on some silly transactions.[3]

While there are similarities for different forms of organ sales, a big difference between blood and kidney sales is this. Voluntary donation, especially with adequate education of its benefits (Chapter 11), is likely to provide adequate supply in the case of blood, but not in the case of kidneys. Also, while blood donation is actually good for the donors even without compensation, the same cannot be said for giving away one of your only two kidneys. Our bodies can replenish blood but cannot regrow kidneys. Risks to donors are not negligible; see Eghtesad et al. 2003. The risks involved are not enormous either. 'Increased risk of death to a healthy 35-year-old from giving up a single

---

[2] See also Berggren & Nilsson 2013 and Prasad 2012 on the point that economic freedom fosters tolerance and reduces violent crime; Levitt & List 2016 on the use of extrinsic rewards to foster intrinsic motivation and habit formation; Zak 2011 on the morality-strengthening effects of markets; and Goette et al. 2010 for a survey.

[3] See http://news.sina.com.cn/o/2015-09-16/doc-ifxhxzxp4388159.shtml and http://news.sohu.co m/20120406/n339897086.shtml.

kidney is about the same as that involved in driving a car sixteen miles every workday' (Hamburger & Crosnier 1968). Another more recent reference from 2016 projects that end-stage renal disease risks after donation among kidney donors in the USA are about 3.5–5.3 times as high as projected risks in the absence of donation (www.nejm.org/doi/full/10.1056/NEJMoa1510491). In other words, even without donation, potential donors still face a substantial risk of around 20–30% of developing end-stage renal disease. Other studies have shown no increased risk for other major chronic diseases such as type 2 diabetes or adverse psychological outcomes; see a 2018 review of existing literature from 1964 to 2017 that use observational studies (https://annals.org/aim/article-abstract/2671305/mid-long-term-health-risks-living-kidney-donors-systematic-review). (On estimates of the risk of live organ donation, see also Schold et al. 2013 and Muzaale et al. 2014.) 'Many individuals willingly (and most of us would probably conclude, reasonably) incur risks in order to achieve savings in personal expenses or to obtain higher wages' (Hansmann 1989, p. 72; see also: www.ncbi.nlm.nih.gov/pmc/articles/PMC2831347/; https://papers.ssrn.com/sol3/papers.cfm?abstract_id=2468503; http://ftp.iza.org/dp6693.pdf). Why the inconsistency between different areas?

As discussed earlier, we accept the possible case for regulation/restriction of markets based on generalized external costs, including the feeling of repugnance which seems to be the main form of external costs for the case of organ sales. Someone may genuinely feel repugnant that a rich person may purchase a kidney and prefer that kidney sales be illegal (Roth 2007, Elías et al. 2015). However, for those ill and on their deathbed, and for those who have to painfully watch their loved ones suffer or pass on, their sorrows which partly stem from denied opportunities, must be incomparably more important than the feeling of repugnance by the unrelated others. Moreover, this feeling of repugnance is partly based on the misconception of equality/poverty as explained in Chapter 5, and partly based on questionable morality (Chapter 6). What is the ethics of feeling repugnant against people desperate enough to sell kidneys and people desperate enough to buy kidneys to save lives? Sympathy should be directed to both sides.

What about the point that compensating organ donors financially is against human dignity? As argued by Satel (2008, Chapter 5), this moral view is too narrow, and that 'dignity can be preserved when donors' safety is protected and they are treated with respect and gratitude' (p. 7). Indeed, 'just as "dignity" is invoked as a reason to oppose donor compensation, it can be seen as a potent justification for supporting it, because compensation promotes vital features of human dignity as commonly understood: the advancement of freedom, the amelioration of suffering, and the preservation of human life' (Satel 2008, p. 78).

Although I will not go as far as saying that 'Human dignity is a useless concept' (Macklin 2003, title), it is quite true that it has been used to oppose many changes/innovations that may greatly improve social welfare overall.[4] If we stick to the old concept of dignity, all teachers, nurses, medical doctors, all service providers, etc. have to reject receiving their salaries and work voluntarily only. We would have to go back to a society with less than 5% of our current incomes and with 99% of our output consisting of agricultural products only (see Chapter 8). In any case, I find the position of Cherry (2017, p. 504) compelling: 'insofar as the living donor's consent morally authorizes organ procurement in the case of uncompensated donation, it morally authorizes such surgery in the case of compensated donation' (see also Taylor 2017).

Decades ago, Hansmann (1989, p. 76) observed that, 'after several decades' of experience our society has accepted a thriving market in human sperm brokered by proprietary firms . . . there was substantial ethical resistance to this market when it was first introduced. Yet over time we have chosen not to so characterize such transactions . . . so that market transactions in human sperm are not perceived as undermining non-market norms'. Similarly, the market for kidneys should be accepted in time. If some people or society as a whole feel sympathetic enough for the poor who are desperate enough to sell kidneys, they should help them sufficiently to relieve them of the need to sell their kidneys. Few, if any, economists are against such help. However, if this help is not forthcoming, and if some individuals are desperate enough to be willing, after adequate counselling, to sell their kidneys, how could prohibiting them from doing so help them?

Out of many attempts to provide a justification for prohibition, I find the one offered by Rippon (2014) to be more persuasive conceptually, but still not quite enough. Rippon's point is that, if a person can legally sell her kidney, she may be under more social pressure or moral obligation to repay her financial debts by selling her kidney. However, such pressure pales in comparison to the importance of saving lives. Also, as argued earlier (Chapter 5), we should tackle the issue of poverty by improving equality rather than by the prohibition of market exchange.[5]

---

[4] See, e.g., Pinker (2008) on how far unreasonable proposals have been made on the shallow ground of dignity, to the extent that he finds dignity almost a useless concept.

[5] A somewhat similar point is: 'Philosopher Debra Satz (2008) has pointed to the challenge of morally good exchanges taking place where there are conditions of inequality. Can people freely choose the limits of an exchange if they suffer under extreme inequality? Is choice an

If a person, rich or poor, is willing to use one of her kidneys to save another life without compensation, she is allowed to do so; if done with compensation, irrespective of the monetary amount, she is not allowed to do so. And the main reason justifying this banning is that of exploitation. Isn't this ironic? Many examples are available to question this banning. We allow people to earn more money by taking riskier jobs. Certainly, if they are paid too little despite the high risks, exploitation may more reasonably be alleged. How could banning payment altogether reduce exploitation?

Also, the 'examples, of firefighters and military, pump the intuition that while of course U.S. society pays both of them, there is nothing that lessens the danger of the task, nor our admiration for them, by the presence of money. "Of course, one reason we admire firefighters, salaried though they are, is that they put themselves at some inconvenience or even grave risk for the sake of others. The same extends to the compensated kidney donor" (2008, 68).[6] Organ sellers, like firefighters, should be financially compensated for their heroic acts' (Gillespie 2017, p. 5).

Around five to ten thousand kidney patients die prematurely in the USA alone each year, and about 100,000 more suffer the debilitating effects of dialysis, because of a shortage of transplant kidneys.[7] In addition, there are many other advantages of transplantation, e.g., 'Transplantation is superior to dialysis in terms of potential to return to work as well as in terms of labour income' (Jarl et al. 2018, abstract). To reduce this shortage, some scholars advocate having the government compensate kidney donors. One study presents a comprehensive cost–benefit analysis of such a change. It considers 'not only the substantial savings to society because kidney recipients would no longer need expensive dialysis treatments—$1.45 million per kidney recipient —but also estimates the monetary value of the longer and healthier lives that kidney recipients enjoy—about $1.3million per recipient. These numbers dwarf the proposed $45 000-per-kidney compensation that might be needed

---

individual decision if there are collective spillover effects? In other words, if a person lives in a community where people have decided to sell their kidneys for money, it may be harder for individuals to obtain a loan if they themselves are not willing to make similar sales' (Wherry 2015, p. 2). This is not a valid ground for banning or other intervention, because it is just a pecuniary external effect, rather than a real one like pollution. A pecuniary external effect works through affecting market prices/terms (the higher interest rates or terms of getting loans in the case here); a real external effect affects others directly. For example, pollution damages our health directly without having to affect prices. Normally, a pecuniary external effect does not affect the efficiency of the market system, while the question of equality should be dealt with through the general equality promotion policy, as argued in Chapter 5.

[6] The quotation within the quote comes from Satel (2008, p. 68).

[7] On the committing of suicide by patients under dialysis, see Epstein (2008).

to end the kidney shortage and eliminate the kidney transplant waiting list. From the viewpoint of society, the net benefit from saving thousands of lives each year and reducing the suffering of 100 000 more receiving dialysis would be about $46 billion per year, with the benefits exceeding the costs by a factor of 3. In addition, it would save taxpayers about $12 billion each year' (Held et al. 2016, abstract, p. 877; see also Matas & Schnitzler 2004).

Indeed, these researchers further argue:

'Finally, some argue that compensating kidney donors will lead to body parts being bought and sold like commodities. But kidneys are already bought and sold. When a kidney is delivered to the operating room of a transplant recipient, it is not provided free. The patient is charged about $50,000 (which may be passed on to an insurance company or taxpayers) that reflects the costs of recovery, testing, and transporting the kidney. Indeed, everyone involved in the procurement process – doctors, nurses, hospitals – are paid the going market rate for their services – everyone except the person who donates the kidney. Why is it considered "commodification" to compensate kidney donors, but not to compensate everyone else involved?' (Held et al. 2016, Supplement 6).[8]

Refusing to legalize kidney compensation 'imposes an intolerable burden on thousands of very ill individuals who suffer and sometimes die' as they await a transplant (Becker & Elías 2007, p. 22). These researchers also estimated that an amount of about US$75,000 (at current prices) would be enough to have sufficient donors to eliminate the shortage. This figure pales in comparison to the huge costs of dialysis and the importance of saving a life. Any 'practice that augments the number of kidneys available for transplantation must be ... regarded as beneficent unless it carries with it overriding bad consequences that outweigh its benefits. The *onus* falls on those who oppose a specific to increase the supply of organs (for example, the sale of organs) to produce convincing arguments that this would be so' (Cameron & Hoffenberg 1999, p. 725, italics added). Thus, even if the arguments and evidence on crowding out and repugnance are inconclusive, we should not ban organ sale, especially for kidneys.

In fact, Beard et al. (2013) went so far as to regard the failure to legalize kidney sales as a serious government failure largely caused by the collusion to erect 'barriers to entry ... [to protect] a global cartel of transplant surgeons

---

[8] As reported in *China Daily* on 16 May 2017, 'in China a kidney transplant costs more than 300,000 yuan (about $46,000) and a liver transplant about 630,000 yuan' and that 'cost is a major barrier for people wanting access to transplants'. One yuan equals about 15 US cents in foreign exchange.

supported by allied specialized personnel that benefits greatly from exercising the right to allocate organs for transplantation' (Zweifel 2014, p. 258; reviewing Beard et al. 2013). This government failure is particular remarkable as according to 'Gallup poll, Americans overwhelmingly support organ donation' (Robertson et al. 2014, p. 103).[9]

A misguided objection to kidney sales may be partly based on an exaggerated estimate of the costs or risks faced by the seller/donor. Instead, recent research in Singapore reported on 30 November 2016 (www.straitstimes.com/singapore/health/living-donor-not-at-higher-risk-of-kidney-failure-study) shows that: 'In fact, donors lead healthy lives and are not at a higher risk of kidney failure or dying compared to the general population, according to a new study conducted by researchers from Singapore General Hospital (SGH) and Duke-NUS Medical School – believed to be the largest of its kind in South-east Asia. ... Internationally, the statistic for the risk of death from a donor surgery is one in 3,000 which is considered to be very low, as low as going for an appendix operation ... Researchers say one in 2,000 people are born with one kidney – a condition known as renal agenesis, and yet they lead a normal life and have a normal lifespan."[10]

Even if certain markets (such as kidney sales and prostitution) should ideally not exist for some reason, legally banning them usually just drives them underground with worse consequences. We have an obvious experience in the prohibition of alcohol in the USA from 1919, as ably summarized by Friedman & McNeill (2013, pp. 65–66):

> 'The result was a classic of morals [perhaps not morals but bad laws from questionable morals – Ng's note] leading markets awry. Prohibition cut consumption by perhaps 25 to 50 percent but tripled the average price. And enforcement turned out to be far harder than Prohibitionists had predicted – but that really wouldn't surprise anyone who does the math. The estimates imply a doubling, more or less, of industry revenue, and windfall profits for suppliers. ... The new profit opportunities degraded morals. Illegal brewing, distilling, importing (bootlegging), and sales (in speakeasies) become widespread and condoned by local norms, encouraging a general disrespect for the law and hypocritical authority. Organized crime got a major boost, and homicides and police corruption increased. Consumption shifted toward drinks with higher alcohol content (easier to smuggle) and greater health risks. Government revenues from alcohol taxes vanished while enforcement

---

9   In addition, certain market designs may make them more acceptable politically; see Vulkan et al. 2013, Roth 2015, and Glaeser 2017.

10   On the relatively low risk and health costs to donors, see also Schold et al. 2013.

expenses increased. .... Public support collapsed after 1930, and in 1933 the Twenty-first Amendment ended the "noble experiment".'

Another argument on the undesirability of legalizing organ sale is based on the increased danger of ordinary people. 'The commodification of human organs may lead to uncontrollable social danger. Once human organs may be turned into cash, how much attention from robbers would they attract?! If my daughter were to carry assets of millions of U.S. dollars on the road, I would feel very scared' (Sang in Ng & Sang, 2016).

This argument is unconvincing. The legalization of organ sales does not legalize the robbing of organs. In fact, under illegality, the prices of organs are much higher, motivating the theft of organs even more. For those criminals daring to steal your organs, they are more motivated by the high prices of the organs than the consideration of legality; stealing organs is illegal whether organ sale is legal or not. Thus, the higher prices under illegality should contribute more to the danger to ordinary people. Hence, legalization actually reduces this danger. Moreover, legalization entails more regulated and controlled transactions almost exclusively in hospitals, reducing much danger and other hazards under illegality.

While the legalization of kidney sales would have many benefits, including the saving of many lives, the monetary payment for blood donations should usually not be needed. It is not that the monetary payment for blood donation is bad and should be made illegal. Rather, as discussed in Chapter 11, it would not be needed if people know the beneficial effects of blood donation. For now, we will first discuss the issue of presumed consent.

10

Making Presumed Consent the Default Option

Not only is the legalization of kidney (and possible other organs) sales desirable, I believe that for cadaveric donation/sale after death, the default option should be that of presumed consent. Unless a person has explicitly registered her unwillingness to donate her organs upon death, the law should allow organ transplantation should she die in circumstances that allow it. However, the establishment of death should be quite strict to avoid premature transplantation.

Many countries have adopted the legal position which takes the default to be non-agreement. A person has to explicitly register her agreement. In fact, even for people who have explicitly opted to donate, organ procurement organizations often follow the negative wishes of the families of the deceased (Healy 2006, Thaler & Sunstein 2008, Glazier 2011, Dalal 2015). This is rather unfortunate. Many savable lives have been lost due to such laws and practices. Making presumed consent the default not only saves lives and the huge costs of dialysis (both the financial costs and the debilitating effects on the patients), but also saves a lot of unnecessary transaction costs. Most people are not against the donation of their organs upon definite death, but have not taken the trouble of registering their agreement.[1] Even I, who have long been a strong supporter of presumed consent, only registered my consent three decades ago; I should have done so more than five decades ago. My initial failure to register was due to ignorance (not knowing that one has to register), then followed by years of procrastination.

While letting people sell their harvestable kidneys in future deaths through the reduction of insurance premiums (Hansmann 1989) has its merits, the effectiveness in increasing the supply is questionable. The effectiveness of compensating the next of kin is even more doubtful.

---

[1] More than 70% of people in a public poll in the USA had a positive view towards organ donation after death; see Koop (1984).

If my next of kin passed away without leaving consent, I would be willing to agree to the donation on her behalf. However, if I stand to benefit, especially financially, this would almost certainly preclude my agreement. (Yes, I have anti-money sentiment here.) The law should adopt the default of presumed consent (unless the individual involved registered objection before death, the organs after death may be used to save others). Next of kin should not be given the right to object. I would prefer that the law does not give me this right to object on behalf of my next of kin. I would prefer that the organs could be used to save the lives of others, but I would prefer to not have to make and shoulder the decision of doing it for my next of kin. If my loved one passed on, I would not want the additional distress of having to think about having her organs taken. Society should just do it without even consulting me. This is similar to a real-world case involving the excavation of tombs discussed here.

This case where the violation of the preferences of people actually improved their welfare happened half a century ago (in the mid-1960s) in Singapore under Lee Kuan Yew's government. Lee decided to expropriate a piece of land used as a cemetery for certain public development without sufficient compensation. Existing tombs there had to be excavated for reburial elsewhere. Such an excavation is regarded as an extreme disturbance of the peace of the dead and most surviving children would not take millions of US dollars to accept such excavation. Even if the government had only to pay a small fraction of the willingness to accept, the public development would certainly turn out to involve negative net benefits. However, I certainly agree with Mr. Lee that the government should look after the welfare of existing (and future) people rather than that of the dead, even if this has to be in violation of the preference of the people now. This welfare-improving decision in favour of development would not only certainly fail to pass the traditional cost–benefit test based on preference, it would also likely fail to pass the public choice test of democratic voting (also based on preference).

It is interesting to examine why preference fails in this case. First, it is partly due to the external costs created by the tradition of excessive respect for the 'peace of the dead'. An individual failing to show due respect would run the risk of social disrespect. Some due respect for the dead may serve some useful function but has become excessive due to a complex process of interaction, including the individually rational but socially harmful strategy of pretending to be very respectful. While this failure can be explained via the traditional analysis of external costs, the same cannot be said for the second source of failure, as discussed in the next paragraph.

Second, even abstracting away the danger of social disrespect, individuals may have genuine preference for showing extremely high respect for the peace of the dead due to cultural influence. They may genuinely feel the importance of avoiding the excavation of the remains of their ancestors (and similarly for not taking their organs upon death). However, if the decision for compulsory acquisition was made by the government, they would accept it as unavoidable and beyond their control and hence would suffer little loss in welfare. It is thus more than a publicness problem, but also a problem related to a divergence between preference and welfare discussed in Appendix A. If the decision were put to a vote, most of them may feel compelled by the respect for the dead to vote against excavation and development. However, if the decision were made for them by the government, most of them would not feel too distressed and would not blame the government, provided it was really done for public interest. Thus, Lee's decision almost certainly increased social welfare despite being against the preferences of the people. However, this example has some degree of exceptionality and does not justify autocratic decisions against the will of people in most cases. Many such decisions disregarding both the preference and the welfare of people have resulted in many tragedies, including the Great Leap Forward and the Cultural Revolution in China. However, given that development was desirable, Lee's decision certainly relieved many people of their dilemma or decision burden, at least to a large extent. Thus, the example certainly suggests that making the default presumed consent for organ donation after death without allowing the next of kin the right to object is similarly most likely to improve welfare.[2]

Another publicly imposed choice of default that will likely be desirable is health related. It is probably a good policy to have all canteens, especially those in schools, sell healthier food as the default. As an example, when a student asks for bread, only wholemeal bread should be sold. Less healthy options like white bread should only be sold if the consumer explicitly asks for it. I am not in favour of a stronger paternalistic policy of making these less healthy options unavailable. Consumers are still allowed to buy them, but they should be given the healthier options as the default.

I have a personal story to tell. In the year 1968, while doing my PhD at the University of Sydney, I decided to shift from eating white to wholemeal bread

---

[2]　Economists may wish to note the big divergence between the willingness to pay (WTP, which is limited by one's wealth/liquidity) and the willingness to accept (WTA, which may truly be infinite). In the presence of such a huge divergence, what is the sensible efficient option? In Ng (2004b, appendix 4A), I propose the use of the 'marginal dollar equivalent' to replace WTP and WTA or compensating variation and equivalent variation in income, to make the appropriate cost–benefit analysis.

for health reasons. As wholemeal bread is tougher to chew, during the first fortnight of shifting, I kept doubting my decision and was tempted to shift back to white bread. I was a bit doubtful whether the health benefits were worthy of the costs of taste reduction. Nevertheless, I persisted and got used to eating the tougher wholemeal bread. About six months later, I once failed to get any wholemeal bread on sale and ended up buying white bread instead. After I ate one slice of that, I said to myself, 'How could this stuff be edible? It tastes like flour! Horrible!' After getting used to eating wholemeal bread which is more chewy and tasty, it is a much better choice both health wise and taste wise. Those who have not shifted to healthier food (not just bread) on taste grounds should do so as soon as possible. After a period of adjustment, the healthier choice is likely also the tastier choice.

In fact, wholemeal bread is not only healthier, it is also likely to be less costly. True, a loaf of wholemeal bread costs more than a loaf of white bread. However, the same amount of wholemeal bread lasts longer until the next meal/snack is needed. Thus, it does not really cost more and it will likely help us in preventing excessive weight gain. In addition, one of the main reasons that wholemeal bread costs more is because it is less popular, and hence costlier to stock. In the retail industry, items that sell fast cost less to stock due to a lesser need for shelf space and time, and faster capital turnover. If the policy of having wholemeal bread in school canteens is followed, it will become much more popular and the cost advantage of white bread will be largely reduced, eliminated, or even reversed.

Apart from the default option in school canteens, another way to help the transition to healthier eating is to tax the less healthy options more. White bread, sugar, cigarettes, etc. should all be heavily taxed. Do not object to such measures. In fact, research by Gruber & Mullainathan (2005)[3] shows that higher taxes on cigarettes actually make smokers happier. The higher taxes induce them to smoke less and hence make them become healthier and happier. This result may not be consistent with the simple and narrow economic analysis, but is consistent with my allowance for the possible divergences between preference and welfare (Appendix A). This also shows that my case for market expansion within limits is not based on simplistic market ideologies, but on rational analysis, although certainly imperfect (but still much more adequate than most anti-commodification theorists).

While simple economics may not be sufficient to tackle some problems involving more interdisciplinary factors and hence need to be extended (as discussed in Chapter 3 and Appendix C) to include the use of interdisciplinary

---

[3] Also available as chapter 6 in Ng & Ho (2006).

knowledge, it may be largely sufficient for tackling certain problems without complicated factors involved. For example, consider the problem of allocating a limited number of COEs (certificates of entitlement for car ownership in Singapore). The determination of the appropriate numbers of certificates to issue may involve more complicated factors, including congestion and pollution, and, hence, knowledge of environmental sciences would be useful. However, for the narrower problem of distributing a *given* number of certificates, simple economic analysis suggests that auctioning is usually both efficient and fair (especially if the question of equality has been taken care of in the general equality promotion policy, as argued in Chapter 5). More specifically, if auctioning is already accepted, and the problem is only which type of auctioning method should be used, it is an even simpler question of technical economic efficiency.

An auction may be done by open or sealed bidding. In either option, the winning bidder may pay the price she bids ('pay as you bid' or 'first-price' auction; equivalent to the Dutch auction, which starts from a high price going downward until some buyer accepts) or may just pay the price of the highest losing bid ('second-price' auction; equivalent to the English auction, which starts from a low price going upward until no one bids higher). In 2013, there was a public debate in Singapore, with many calling for a change from the second-price auction to 'pay as you bid'. This was obviously caused by the popular mistake in thinking that the second-price auction led to higher COE prices, and in not knowing the efficiency of the second-price auction, as explained in Appendix E.

When we want to build houses, bridges, etc., we may suggest our budgets and general preferences, but we leave the technical details to the architects, engineers, and builders. Similarly, if the public does not know why the second-price auction is much more efficient than 'pay as you bid', they should leave the choice to economists. For such narrower issues, economists have the consensus opinion and simple economics alone is largely sufficient.

11

Blood Donation

In most countries, blood is supplied mainly by voluntary donation with only symbolic recognition and minor in-kind rewards instead of by monetary payment. Although some shortages still occur from time to time, this is usually solved by donation campaigns. For example, as reported in the media in Singapore, Minister for Health Mr. Gan Kim Yong called upon more blood donations while presenting awards to champion blood donors on World Blood Donor Day (10 June 2017). The National Blood Programme is jointly run by the Singapore Red Cross (SRC) and the Health Sciences Authority (HSA). The Red Cross also cooperates with the Ministry of Education and the Ministry of Defence in promoting blood donation. Nevertheless, blood donation still falls short of demand. The situation is made worse with an aging population and an increasing demand for blood, while the donation rate of the younger population continues to decline. This situation is similar in most countries, necessitating frequent donation drives.

At least, where this method largely works, even if imperfectly, keeping the system of voluntary donation has some advantages.

- First, using monetary payment for blood may crowd out voluntary donation and attract unsafe donors, as analyzed from Titmuss (1971) to Costa-Font et al. (2013); but see Slonim et al. (2014) for the many complicated factors involved, as discussed in Chapter 7.
- Second, and relatedly, the financial payment of donors may decrease the warm-glow effect of voluntary donation. In contrast, receiving payment may generate some sense of desperation, having to sell blood to make ends meet.
- Third, monetary payment necessitates substantial financial costs on the blood collection side. Although this is offset by the financial gains of the

donors, the social importance of both sides may not be exactly equivalent, depending on each case.

- Fourth, financial payment may result in very unequal incidence of donation among the population, with much higher incidence for the lower income groups.

In itself, this last point of unequal distribution may not be much of a problem. However, some donation, whether paid or unpaid, is actually good for the donors, while excessive donation may be undesirable. This is so because, in our long history of evolution as hunters-gatherers, we faced frequent blood loss in our daily life. Thus, we are programmed to replenish our frequent blood loss. However, modern living makes blood loss almost non-existent. This unhealthy situation is improved by undertaking frequent but not excessive blood donation (e.g., Salonen et al. 1998, Fernández-Real et al. 2002, Meyers et al. 2002, Edgren et al. 2007, Zacharski et al. 2008, Vahidnia et al. 2013). The problem is more serious for men than for women; the latter have their normal monthly loss of blood. On the other hand, due to this monthly low, women are more capable of replenishing blood in their bodies. Thus, women also do not have to worry about moderate blood donation. An adequate education on this simple point of the desirability of blood donation for the donors will likely make voluntary donation more than sufficient to ensure an adequate blood supply in most countries.

This is particularly relevant for a culture like that of the Chinese, although not just confined to China. The traditional belief in China is that any part of the body, including even hair and skin, not to mention blood, is from the parents and should not be discarded. Thus, in the widely read historical novel *The Three Kingdoms*, when a captain had an eye shot by an arrow, he pulled out the arrow, with the eyeball attached. Instead of throwing it away, he said 'stuff from parents; must not be thrown away' and swallowed the eyeball.

Another belief is that blood is the essence of life and losing blood will weaken the body significantly (Zaller et al. 2005, Tison et al. 2007, Lownik et al. 2012). This half-truth ignores the point that our body is programmed to replenish blood loss. If we have a lesson at secondary school on the biological basis of healthy blood donation, voluntary donation will increase at least ten times in China, without payment. If we could have an adequate and safer blood supply with just some simple education, there is no need to shift to a system of using financial payment to induce blood donation.

12

Prostitution[*]

Prostitution has some specific features. First, most prostitutes are female. Even male prostitutes mainly serve men. Female clients exist, but are rare. Second, in most countries, more men are sympathetic to the legalization of prostitution than women. In fact, 'women are less accepting of the purchase [of sex] compared to men in all countries' (Jonsson & Jakobsson 2017, p. 63; see also Petersen & Hyde 2011 for a survey.) Why are there such big differences? The main explanation lies in evolutionary biology.

In evolutionary biology, the deciding factor is survival and reproduction fitness. To be able to pass on her genes to the next and future generations, a woman has to undergo nine months of pregnancy, a few years of breastfeeding, plus more years of bringing up the child to be capable of independence. During the years of breastfeeding, the mother typically does not produce eggs anymore to allow the body to concentrate on producing milk to feed the current child. Also, a woman typically stops being fertile after around her early forties, again to allow sufficient remaining years to concentrate on bringing existing children to adulthood. Thus, the number of children a woman can bring up to adulthood is limited by her years of fertility. Her strategy (evolutionary biology wise, not conscious planning wise) for success is largely in attracting a strong man to stay with her and help in protecting and providing for both her and her children. Flirting with many men does not help much, if at all. On the other hand, a man needs only half an hour to pass on his genes to the next generation. Thus, all men are born with an inclination to sleep with many fertile women. Their higher demand for more sex explains why most prostitutes are female; men's intrinsic understanding of their inborn

---

[*] This chapter is jointly written by Ms Yan Wang and Prof. Yew-Kwang Ng, both of Nanyang Technological University.

inclination explains their more liberal attitude towards the legalization of prostitution.

In this connection, the story of President Calvin Coolidge (the 30th US President from 2 August 1923 to 4 March 1929) may be retold. The President and Mrs Coolidge were being shown (separately, due to the busier schedule of the President) around an experimental government farm. When Mrs Coolidge came to the chicken yard she noticed that a rooster was mating with a hen. She asked the attendant how often a rooster mates with a hen and was told, 'Dozens of times each day.' Mrs Coolidge said, 'Tell that to the President when he comes by.' Upon being told, the President asked, 'Same hen every time?' The reply was, 'Oh, no, Mr President, a different hen every time.' To which the President replied: 'Tell that to Mrs Coolidge.'

This story explains the term 'the Coolidge effect' which refers to a phenomenon in many animal species, including chickens, where males exhibit renewed sexual interest if introduced to new receptive sexual partners, even after cessation of sex with prior, but still available, sexual partners. The evolutionary benefit to this phenomenon is that a male can then fertilize multiple females, giving rise to more offspring.

Peter Singer (2016), one of the most influential and wise moral philosophers of our time, comments: 'In species that reproduce sexually, sex is, for obvious reasons, one of the strongest and most pervasive desires. Humans are no exception in this respect. In every modern society, humans exchange money or other valued items for things that they desire and could not otherwise obtain. For various reasons, a significant number of people cannot get sex, or sufficient sex, or the kind of sex they want, freely. Unless at least one of these conditions changes, demand for paid sex will continue. I find it hard to see how any of them will change sufficiently to eliminate that demand.'

Two important lessons may be learned from this. First, for women, they should recognize the natural tendency of men already discussed. If they do, they should not feel so sad as to commit suicide after discovering the infidelity of their husbands, as done by a famous Hong Kong movie queen, Lin Dai, at the age of 29. Second, for men, they should learn that this natural tendency mainly helps them to pass on their genes; it does not maximize their welfare. Although they may not be able to completely reverse the tendency, they may try to reduce its influence to increase their welfare instead of the number of their offspring.[1] These two most important lessons do not seem to have been taught at all, at any level.

---

[1]   On the divergence between biological fitness and welfare, see Ng (1995).

TABLE 12.1. *Ratio of Number of Prostitutes to Adult Males*

Country	Number of prostitutes	Number of males (aged 15 to 64 years)	Ratio (prostitutes:males)
China	5,000,000	511,975,905	0.009766
USA	1,000,000	106,908,102	0.009354
UK	58,000	20,966,117	0.002766
India	3,000,000	452,880,598	0.006624
Germany	400,000	27,429,770	0.014583
Thailand	250,000	24,053,844	0.010393

Data Sources: number of prostitutes are retrieved from the website www.havocscope.com/prostitution-statistics/ and number of males (aged 15 to 64 years) in the year 2016 are retrieved from the website https://data.worldbank.org/indicator/SP.POP.1564.MA.IN.

As reported in *Zaobao Weekly*, p. 6, 26 March 2017 (*Zaobao* is the major Chinese daily newspaper in Singapore): 'Mary who has worked as a sex worker for more than ten years has lost all confidence in men. She said sarcastically, "There is no more good men in the world; all good men have visited me. My clients include the religiously pious, professionals, and policemen who looked down upon us"' (our translation). Comparing the estimated number of practicing prostitutes to the adult male population in a city or country (see Table 12.1), we see that there is about one prostitute for everyone hundred adult males. Since a prostitute probably serves several clients a day, roughly speaking, an adult male buys commercial sex about once a month. Whether prostitution is legal or not, we must conclude that either a significant proportion of men visit prostitutes very frequently or an overwhelming majority visit quite occasionally, or, more likely, a combination of both. The majority of clients are not sick or abnormal. They are normal men. Also, 'Respondents tended to regard prostitution as a permanent part of the Macau community and believed that the likelihood of the government being able to eliminate prostitution through legislation was extremely low' (Yan et al. 2018, abstract).

Most modern societies have a legal system of monogamy, which has many advantages. However, this does not quite square with men's inborn inclination towards sexual variety. Legal prostitution is the least costly way of solving this contradiction while maintaining the stability of families under monogamy. Making prostitution illegal increases the incidence of infidelity, bigamy, rapes, and other crimes. One may argue that a married man buying commercial sex is also being an infidel. However, would most wives find the emotional infidelity of their husbands with non-prostitutes much less tolerable?

The case against the moral acceptance of prostitution is partly based on some form of extreme egalitarianism that ignores gender differences. We truly believe in the equality between females and males, but we should recognize the substantial differences between them. One example of extreme egalitarianism is the provision of female and male washrooms of equal space in most public places. However, women have a higher demand for washroom usage. We, thus, typically, see long queues during intermission breaks of performances for women's washrooms, but not in men's washrooms. We should increase the size of women's washrooms, even if this could only be by reducing that of men's washrooms. Men have a lesser demand for washrooms and usually could make do with smaller ones. On the other hand, men have more demand for sex. If the system of monogamy is not complemented by legal prostitution, worse outcomes like sexual harassment, extramarital sex, rapes, bigamy, etc. will be the result. As reported by Ms Jane Li of the *South China Morning Post* for *Business Insider* on 12 March 2017, many angry wives in China are paying 'mistress hunters' to end their husbands' affairs, at a standard charge of ¥50,000 each (about US$7,500). The legalization of prostitution would not eliminate such problems, but would likely reduce their magnitude.

Recognizing the different needs of men and women in different areas, we reject the banning of prostitution on the ground of 'gender equality, concerning men's violence against women' (Jonsson & Jakobsson 2017, p. 64). Rather, we should regard legal prostitution as just the provision of a sexual service similar to any other service, such as hairdressing. However, the positive contribution of a legal sexual service to society could be a thousand times more than that of hairdressing.

'Consider the character Belle in the TV series Secret Diary of a Call Girl. [The show is based on a real person, Brooke Magnanti, who is now a research scientist at the University of Bristol.] Belle is a college graduate. She chooses to be a high-class prostitute because it pays well and she enjoys sex. She isn't desperate and could get another job. Belle hasn't been beaten, raped, enslaved, or exploited. She hasn't experienced mental illness, addiction, or childhood trauma. Selling sex does not traumatize her; rather, she enjoys it. Some people might find her behavior distasteful, repulsive, or undignified, but that doesn't make it wrong. Buying sex from someone like Belle isn't inherently wrong. ... It's a mutually enjoyable, mutually beneficial exchange with an autonomous, consenting adult. Buying sex from Belle is roughly on par, morally speaking, with paying a musician to play you a song' (Brennan &

Jaworski 2016, p. 151). We would go further than this. If the prostitute is desperate to earn money, it would be even more acceptable to buy sex from her, at least in the absence of serious misinformation. A poor farmer is more desperate to sell his produce than a rich one. Other things being equal (including information), most people would rather buy from the poor farmer to help him to relieve his poverty a little than from the rich farmer.

Prostitutes 'are harmed, not because prostitution is harmful, but because society at present seriously wrongs prostitutes' (Moen 2014, p. 80) by making prostitution illegal, and hence practiced 'in conditions of near-slavery, marginalization, and stigmatization' (Vicente 2016, p. 476; on the effect of stigmatization in prostitution see also Benoit et al. 2018). On the other hand, under legalized conditions, Rössler et al. (2010) found that about 40% of the prostitutes they studied declared that they actually liked the job. Similarly, Abel (2010, p. 183) comments that 'some participants in this [New Zealand] study spoke of being naturally promiscuous and therefore argued that the transition into sex work was unproblematic', as quoted by Vicente (2016, p. 478), who is in favour of a 'policy of vigilance [but legal], complemented by a policy of support of prostitutes who want to leave the sector'.

> 'Apparently, many people do not have any kind of problems with having sex for money. They do not experience it as a form of dominance, they do not feel objectified by it (or if they do, they are able to circumscribe such feelings within the practice itself), they do not care much and overall are very happy with the money they make. It is not sensible to accuse such people of false consciousness; and it would certainly seem grossly unfair to tell them that they are not allowed to exercise the trade they have chosen to make their business ... [However] we should offer prostitutes who want to leave the job realistic options, realistic help and proper integration' (Vicente 2016, pp. 482, 485).

This position appears sensible to us.

Much objection to prostitution is based on obvious biases, for example: 'When men use women in prostitution, they are expressing a pure hatred for the female body. It is as pure as anything on this earth ever is or ever has been. It is a contempt so deep, so deep, that a whole human life is reduced to a few sexual orifices, and he can do anything he wants' (Dworkin 1997, pp. 144–145). Just some common knowledge of normal human nature allows us to see that this is just about the very opposite of the truth. For the overwhelming majority, it is unfulfilled desire, lust, etc., not hatred.

Even if the moral acceptability of prostitution is debatable, making prostitution illegal still makes the situation worse. No society has been able to stem out prostitution completely. When China almost eliminated prostitution under Mao's rule from 1949 to 1976, the abuse of power for sexual advantages still prevailed, including most prominently by Mao himself. For the majority, the suppression of human nature may partly explain this; when the Cultural Revolution was launched in 1966, we witnessed the worst kinds of cruelty and sadism ever, practiced almost by all for many years. Although the connection might be complicated and might involve many other factors, some influence was likely.

After studying the situation of prostitution in 21 European countries, Wagenaar (2017) finds it 'safe to conclude that in terms of influencing the prevalence of prostitution in a country, prostitution policy is largely ineffective. ... Perhaps the most obvious conclusion from our research is that all countries under study have—and throughout history, have had—a prostitution market. No matter what legal regime the government adheres to or has adhered to in the past, prostitution is of all times. The number of sex workers in a country might fluctuate, but this is usually the result of extraneous forces outside the purview of policy makers'. Wagenaar also believes that legalization may not be enough, a 'collaborative governance' approach working with some sex worker advocacy organizations may be needed (see also Jahnsen & Wagenaar 2017, Wagenaar et al. 2017).

There is a study[2] showing the percentages of men (by country) who paid for sex at least once. Interestingly, among 15 countries for which men paid for sex at least once in their lifetimes, in the top two countries, Cambodia and Thailand, prostitution is illegal, but prevalent. Although there are many other factors involved, to some extent, it demonstrates that simply banning prostitution is unlikely to significantly decrease the consumption of commercial sex. Research also gives a (probably highly understated) figure of 20.6% of self-identified men who have previously purchased sex (Maszak 2018).

Banning prostitution can only drive it underground, with even more severe problems associated with black markets, including:

- Making the control of sexually transmitted diseases (STDs) much more difficult. The illegality of prostitution could prevent sex workers from accessing human immunodeficiency virus (HIV) information and services. Lower sexually transmissible infection (STI) rates were reported by clients and sex workers from licensed brothels (Seib et al. 2009).

---

[2] ProCon.org. 'Percentage of Men (by Country) Who Paid for Sex at Least Once: The Johns Chart'. Retrieved on 1 June 2011 from https://prostitution.procon.org/view.resource.php?resourceID=004119.

- Increasing the scope of activities for the criminals. Concerns about exploitation and objectification are behind much of the continued support for keeping prostitution illegal. Recent research indicates that a prostitute has a 45–75% chance of experiencing workplace violence at some point, and a 32–55% likelihood that she or he was victimized in the past year (Deering et al. 2014). However, to incorporate what we know about the black markets, much of the violence associated with sex work is exacerbated by its illegality. Sex workers who are preyed on won't report to police and have no choice but to rely on pimps and madams for protection, which usually leads to more violence. 'In New Zealand, prostitutes say legalized brothels are "fantastic," with sex workers free to report harassment and violence. Whereas in the U.K., where it is still illegal, they had a case of a violent robbery and the poor old brothel operator reported this to the police and the police arrested her', said Catherine Healey, national coordinator for the New Zealand Prostitutes' Collective. Indeed after the practice of legalizing prostitution, Germany and New Zealand observed a decrease in violence against sex workers (Tyler 2010). Similarly, after studying legal indoor prostitution in Rhode Island, researchers found that 'while the size of the indoor sex market in Rhode Island increased, reported rape offenses and female gonorrhea incidence declined' (Gunderson 2018). From these facts, making prostitution illegal cannot stop it but only promotes an unsafe environment for sex workers. It should be admitted that a better way to protect sex workers is to make health and safety laws for them, rather than forbidding prostitution and driving it underground.
- Increasing corruption in the police force. Abuse from police is not a rare situation in a country where prostitution is still criminalized. In a study 'Crime and Abuse Experienced by Sex Workers in Ireland', 18.4% of participants reported having encountered corrupt police while working as an escort (Uglymugs.ie 2013). Some estimate that police actually abuse American sex workers more often than clients do (Reisenwitz 2014). 'The original impetus for the legalization of the sex industry in New South Wales was an inquiry into police corruption that showed that the sex industry was a major source of police bribes. Legalization ended that in a single stroke' (Singer 2016).
- Increasing the other costs of transaction involving sex.
- Reducing the general respectability of the law and, hence, reducing the degree of general law observance.

The problems created by prostitution being illegal are particularly acute in China, with its distorted and very high boy/girl ratio at birth, and the large influx of temporary urban workers from the countryside. Many millions of men of marriageable ages in China are destined to be unable to find wives. The legalization of prostitution would not completely solve, but would certainly reduce, many serious problems substantially.

The Chinese government's birth limitation policy and the cultural preference for sons created a skewed sex ratio of 122 boys to 100 girls in China (Zhu et al. 2009, Wei & Zhang 2015).[3] This serves as a key source of demand for the trafficking of women as brides and for forced prostitution. Chinese women and girls are subjected to sex trafficking within China; they are often recruited from rural areas and transported to urban centres. China is also a destination for women and girls from neighbouring countries, who are sometimes subjected to forced marriage and forced prostitution upon arrival (US Department of State 2013).

Other things being largely equal, the rural–urban migration and the skewed sex ratio have led to a big increase in demand for prostitution services in China. With so many migrants on their own for long periods and with dozens of millions of men destined to be unable to get a wife, making prostitution illegal is a gross violation of their human rights.

The legalization of prostitution would help decrease the following costs:

- Health effects, mainly the spread of HIV/acquired immune deficiency syndrome (AIDS) and other STDs. Worries about more widespread sexually transmitted infections account for an essential part of the banning of prostitution. Globally, female sex workers are 13.5 times more likely to be living with HIV than other women (UNAIDS 2013). Researchers at the 20th International AIDS Conference in Melbourne, Australia, presented a new paper in which they studied HIV among female sex workers in Canada, India, and Kenya. They found that infections could be reduced by 33–46% in those countries if prostitution was made legal (Shannon et al. 2015).
- Crime (especially rape) rates. It has been estimated that if prostitution were legalized in the USA, the rape rate would decrease by roughly 25%, or a decrease of approximately 25,000 rapes per year (Cundiff 2004). A study conducted in Queensland showed a 149% increase in the rate of rape when legal brothels were closed in 1959, while other offences

---

[3]   China recently (November 2015) moved from a one-child policy to a two-child policy. However, Xu & Pak (2015) argue that 'the gender imbalance need not improve under the two-child policy'.

against the person by males increased by only 49% (Barber 1969). In 1980, Rhode Island effectively legalized prostitution by accident when lawmakers deemed the state statute on prostitution to be overly broad. They accidentally removed the section defining the act itself as a crime while attempting to revise it, although lawmakers did not realize the error until 2003. Over the next six years, new cases of gonorrhoea among women state-wide declined by 39%. Interestingly, reported rapes also declined by 31% (Buggiano 2015).

- Information and transaction costs will be drastically reduced for both prostitutes and their clients.
- Moral externalities. It is difficult to carry out a cost–benefit analysis which compares the increase in the utility levels of prostitutes and their clients, vis-a-vis the higher social costs imposed on those who feel offended by this 'immoral' behaviour. However, the result that 'permissive laws liberalize attitudes toward partakers while increasing utility' (Chen & Yeh 2014) is supportive of legalization. Moreover, it is notable that people, especially women, can accept if their neighbour is a beggar but cannot stand prostitutes, as prostitutes are less likely to be accepted by the public than beggars. People who have a prostitute as a neighbour seem to be adversely affected by public views. Hence, it increases their disutility more than having a beggar as a neighbour. There is no doubt that the higher the degree of public acceptance, the less disutility they get of having a prostitute as a neighbour. The legalization of prostitution may decrease the degree of repugnance and, hence, to some extent, decrease the moral external costs; legalization significantly causes a higher degree of acceptance. While it could go in the complete opposite direction, that people feel more repugnant towards prostitution when it is legalized, the data are pretty clearly in favour of the positive effects of legalization. Assessing attitudes in eight European countries using newly collected survey data, Jonsson & Jakobsson (2017, abstract) show that 'Citizens in countries where the purchase of sex is criminalized are less tolerant toward the buying of sex compared to citizens living in countries where the purchase of sex is legalized. Also, people viewing gender equality as important are less accepting of the purchase in countries where buying sex is prohibited, but more accepting in countries where buying sex and running a brothel are legal.'

We also did a similar analysis using data from 1995 to 2014 from the World Value Survey. Our results consolidate the positive causal effects of the legalization of prostitution on the overall social acceptance of prostitutes. Meanwhile, the degree of acceptance also depends on the degree of economic freedom. Prostitution is more likely to be accepted in countries which have higher indices on the economic freedom index. However, which way the causality mainly runs, i.e., whether policies cause attitudes, or attitudes affect policies, is more difficult to establish. Likely, both ways of causal direction are important.[4] Also, factors affecting people's attitudes to issues involving morality are very complicated (Heidt-Forsythe 2017).

- Legal resources freed from the unnecessary and ineffective eradication of prostitution may be used to reduce human trafficking and forced prostitution. Thus, from a costs perspective, legalization is also likely to be efficiency improving.[5] Obviously, if force and misinformation are involved, whether in prostitution, human trafficking, or what not, legal sanctions may be justified. Human trafficking involving prostitution often involves international border crossing (Cho 2016). The existence of trafficking does not imply the use of force. In fact, the association with migration from less to more developed countries strongly suggests that many, if not most, of those that are allegedly 'trafficked' are actually seeking migration voluntarily. Even if they are couched into prostitution, provided no force and serious misinformation are involved, no serious undesirable results may be involved. Unfortunately, the use of force and misleading information exists aplenty, especially under conditions of illegality. Legalization may offer a better approach (cf. Jonsson & Jakobsson 2017).

In addition to this, it may also be mentioned that the legalization of prostitution allows the government to tax it appropriately. If the moral case against prostitution can be sustained to some extent, a case for higher taxes on it may be entertained. This will allow the government to collect a very substantial source of revenue which may be used to reduce taxes elsewhere and/or to provide more public expenditures in desirable avenues.

Our support for the legalization of prostitution also comes from the consideration for the children of prostitutes. There is no doubt that lives of children born to prostitutes are greatly affected. In addition to nutritional deficiencies, minimal health care, and non-availability of basic needs, they have to live with the social stigma that comes with their mother's profession.

---

[4] Cf. Kotsadam & Jakobsson (2011), Immordino & Russo (2015a).
[5] On the likely effects of different methods of regulating prostitution, see, e.g., Immordino & Russo (2015b).

The case may become even worse if their mother's work is not recognized as legal. Under these conditions, schooling is not easily available to these children because of their family background. Eventually, these children are likely to follow in their mother's steps and end up as a part of the sex trade. Although we cannot claim that the situation of these children would become much better when prostitution is legalized, at least some improvements are likely.

The enormous benefits of legalizing prostitution may also be seen by comparing different countries. Prostitution in Ireland is dangerous, this is fairly uncontroversial. Prostitutes are forced to work alone or else face charges of running a brothel. They feel alienated from the law because they work outside it. Illegality attracts further illegality. Client abuse of sex workers is prevalent (Behan 2013). A Colorado study for the American Journal of Epidemiology (Potterat et al. 2004) suggests prostitutes are roughly 18 times more like to be murdered than otherwise similar groups of women. Many of these sad incidences would be reduced with legalization. In May 2016, Amnesty International urged governments to repeal laws criminalizing the exchange of sex for money by consenting adults. We hope to see that many governments will respond positively to this call.

13

Conscription

The military draft or conscription (called 'national service' in some countries, including Singapore) has been very commonly used throughout history all over the world. Economists, recognizing both the inefficiency and inequity involved in forced conscription, are generally in favour of 'paying the soldiers their hire'. This chapter shows that the issues involved are much more complicated, even if we are only confined to the purely economic factors, and disregarding possible effects on the morale of soldiers, patriotism, and the morality of all of society. There are factors both against and in favour of conscription.

While the factors involved are complicated, generally speaking, there has been a gradual replacement of conscription by the payment of volunteer soldiers. As a rule, poorer countries practice conscription more often. In 2015, out of 170 countries, there were 66 countries practicing conscription, and 51 of them had a per capita GDP (PPP adjusted) of less than US$1000 per month. Of the available data, 39% of 170 countries practice conscription, and 62% of the 100 richest countries do not.[1]

In 1970, US President Richard Nixon appointed Milton Friedman (1976 Nobel laureate in economics) to a commission on moving to an all-volunteer force (AVF). Initially, the commission was evenly split between supporters and opponents. During a Congressional Testimony, General William Westmoreland, the then army chief-of-staff, stated that he did not want to command an army of mercenaries. Friedman countered: 'General, would you rather command an army of slaves?' Westmoreland drew himself up and said,

---

[1]   Sources: http://chartsbin.com/view/41609.
      www.statista.com/chart/3907/the-state-of-military-conscription-around-the-world/.

'I don't like to hear our patriotic draftees referred to as slaves.' Friedman replied, 'I don't like to hear our patriotic volunteers referred to as mercenaries.' Friedman went on, 'But if they are mercenaries, then I, sir, am a mercenary professor, and you, sir, are a mercenary general; we are served by mercenary physicians, we use a mercenary lawyer, and we get our meat from a mercenary butcher.' Thus, Friedman secured 'a unanimous vote for the volunteer army, and for freedom' (Buchholz 2007, p. 252).

The USA moved from conscription to an AVF in 1973. Its defence budget did not increase very much because of this move. More importantly, its military capabilities did not decrease, but rather strengthened. In this era of high technology, specialized professional volunteers are much better soldiers. The performance of the US military in Afghanistan and the two Gulf wars are testaments to its strength. In the words of a Nobel laureate: ' ... a voluntary army is very professional and fights harder under difficult circumstances (think of Afghanistan and Iraq), that many young men and women from middle-class families, and even upper-class families, do volunteer, and that instead of exploiting minorities it provides some of the best opportunities for their advancement (Colin Powell is just one prominent example)' (Becker 2012, p. 2). Also, not to forget the huge amount of hardship saved by not having yourself or your son conscripted against your will. Similarly, the expansion of the market in many other spheres will likely contribute to social welfare.

Now, consider the opposing factors for and against conscription. First and foremost is its disregard of individual preferences and its violation of freedom. As practiced in most cases, conscription only recognizes the difference between females and males, and, to a lesser extent, age; usually only men of a certain age group (16.5–40 in Singapore) are subject to conscription. For this 'eligible' group, no differences and choices are entertained, with rare exemptions under permanent disabilities. Person A may positively enjoy his service as a soldier; person B may absolutely dread the years of compulsory service/ training. For the compulsory part of national service, no account for such differences is allowed. The fact that there are not too infrequently cases of self-mutilation to qualify for exemption from national service shows the size of the costs imposed on the compulsory nature of conscription. Such cases are seldom, if ever, reported. One gets to know of them from acquaintances. When I was about 8 in 1950/51 in Malaysia (then Malaya), my third eldest brother, who was 15, was about to reach the age for conscription. My father sent him to China to escape being drafted. At that time, Malaya had several times the per capita income in comparison to China and was a dream migration destination for people from China. The reverse migration involved very high costs.[2] Early contributions in the analysis of conscription (e.g., Oi 1967, Hansen & Weisbrod 1967; Friedman 1967, Altman & Barro 1971) concentrated on these very high costs of conscription and hence were 'virtually unanimous in their belief that volunteer military forces would have lower social costs and be more efficient than conscripted forces' (Warner & Negrusa 2005). Later authors (Lee & McKenzie 1992, Ross 1994, Warner & Asch 1996) allow for the factor discussed in the next paragraph and, hence, accept that it is possible for a conscripted force to have a lower total social cost.

This opposite consideration is that, especially if the demand for military service is high, the pay sufficient to attract enough volunteers may require high taxes to finance the expenditures. Economic analysts focus on the distortion-ary costs or excess burden of taxation. Typically, raising $100 million of taxes imposes a combined burden on consumers and producers of about $130 million, even before counting the administrative costs of tax raising. Thirty percent is the average percentage that economists estimate in terms of the extent of excess burden. For taxes on specific goods, this may consist mainly in distorting consumer choices between different goods. For general income or consumption taxes (including goods and services taxes, or GST), the costs manifest in the distortion between income/consumption versus leisure. That is, taxation encourages people to have more leisure and earn less income for consumption. In other words, the costs are disincentive effects.

The excess burden of taxation to finance public spending (including, but not confined to, military spending) is one factor behind most economists' case for 'big society, small government'. Another factor is the inevitable inefficien-cies in spending the money of other people (i.e., the public). While both of these factors have some validity, I happen to place much less emphasis on them than most economists, for the following reasons.

- First, the analysis of excess burden of taxation starts from the assumption that the initial situation without taxation is efficient. However, since most production and consumption involve many external costs like pollution and the emission of greenhouse gases, the situation without taxation is really inefficient. Taxes of about 30% of GDP may actually serve to correct for the excessive environmental disruption. They gen-erate positive corrective effects, not negative distortive effects.
- The analysis of the disincentive effects of taxation focuses only on the side of taxation, failing to account for the side of spending. Consider the following situation: A. No taxation, no public spending. If you earn an

---

[2]   On the high costs incurred for evading conscription, see Warner & Negrusa (2005).

extra $1,000, you keep all of it. However, with no maintenance of law and order, your $1,000 has a high chance of being robbed soon after you leave the cashier. B. You pay 30% tax and keep only $700, which is nevertheless protected. Most people may find that incentives for earning extra should be higher under B instead of A (Kaplow 1996, Ng 2000).

- Much of private consumption is motivated by the relative competition effect. While each individual may compete to perform relatively better than others in having a larger house, a more luxurious car, etc., for the whole society, on average, the relative position cannot be improved. Effort spent on relative competition is a complete waste at the social level. Considering the importance of relative competition, taxes of about 30% of GDP may be justified on this ground of checking wasteful relative competition alone.[3]

- Taxes on diamond goods (goods, like diamonds and gold, valued for their market values rather than for their intrinsic consumption effects) impose not only no excess burden, but no burden at all. A tax of $100 million imposes not a burden of $130 million, not $100 million, but $0 million, as I argue in *American Economic Review* (Ng 1987).

- After the levels of survival and comfort, higher consumption leads to virtually no increase in happiness. Thus, public spending may be very costly in monetary terms, but may be virtually costless at the fundamental welfare level. If spent in areas really important in increasing social welfare, like environmental protection, poverty reduction, education, research, etc., even very costly items of public spending may still be worthwhile.

Accordingly, the case for 'big society, small government' may not be valid. It focuses on the inefficiency of public spending but ignores the possibility of even grosser inefficiency of private consumption. Taxes on private consumption/income/production may be more corrective than distortive. If so, then the point regarding the excess of burden of raising government revenue to pay for voluntary soldiers, possibly offsetting the inefficiency of conscription (as emphasized by economists in the 1990s mentioned earlier) may not be applicable. Nevertheless, there is a different generalized 'cost' that most economists largely ignore, due to their professional focus on traditional economic efficiency instead of equity.

If we have to raise a lot of taxes to pay for voluntary soldiers, the post-tax incomes of civilians may be much lower than those of soldiers, driving the

---

[3] See, e.g., Blanchflower & Oswald (2004) and Ng (2015a).

marginal utility (and hence also the marginal social welfare) of the income of the soldiers to a very low level in comparison to that of the civilian population, thereby violating the requirement of equity (in the sense of the equality, or at least no big divergence between the marginal social welfare values, of the incomes of different persons). Thus, there may exist an conflict between equity and efficiency on the one hand and freedom (free choice of what occupation to take) and fairness on the other, making them not simultaneously completely achievable.[4] Here, equity is defined by the equality of (or at least not too much disparity in) the marginal utilities of income of different persons (roughly speaking, not too much of a rich–poor disparity), and fairness by the equality of (or at least not too much disparity in) total utilities, ignoring initial differences between persons. They are thus quite different concepts (details in Ng 2009, chapter 3). As these desirable factors cannot be met simultaneously, the maximization of social welfare may require sacrificing a bit of each. This is a potential justification for conscription at the fundamental level.

A closer analysis suggests that the existence of important increasing returns (doubling all inputs more than doubling output) is essential for this E-F conflict. If there are no increasing returns, and, for simplicity, ignoring interpersonal differences to focus on the aspects under consideration, everyone should serve both the same fraction of time as a soldier (and the rest of the time as a civilian), thereby achieving equity and fairness. The existence of important elements of increasing returns and learning by doing in military services may, at least in some cases, make conscription welfare improving even at the costs of violating free choice and fairness. Basically, the high costs of training and the importance of experience make it efficient for a soldier to serve a long time. Thus, except for the case of a very threatened country, it is generally desirable to confine military service to a fraction of the population. On the other hand, unless this desirable fraction is very small and/or unless the supply price of voluntary soldiers is relatively low (as may be the case when patriotism is high), very high levels of payment and revenue may be needed to call forth the required number of volunteers. This high level of required revenue may then give rise to the two problems of the excess burden of taxation and inequity between soldiers and civilians discussed earlier.

In the presence of significant increasing returns (including the need for minimum basic training and the presence of learning by doing) in military training and service, it may be desirable to have selective conscription where a fraction of the population are required, perhaps by a random draft, to serve in

---

[4] For a more general and detailed analysis of this E-F conflict and its implications beyond the issue of conscription, see Ng (2009, chapter 3).

the armed forces. Although this almost unavoidably creates inefficiency, violates free choice, and creates unfairness, its efficiency in taping the increasing returns in military service more may yet offset its costs. Nevertheless, the efficiency costs of forced conscription may be very high, both in its violation of freedom and in its resultant misallocation. The ex post unfairness involved may also be undesirable. Thus, despite its popularity, conscription may well have been used to an excess in most cases. Where an AVF is adequate, conscription may well be an inferior choice. Nevertheless, where the degree of increasing returns is high and the required amount of military service is large, such as for a country at war or when very threatened, the desirability of conscription cannot be completely excluded. Economists largely miss out on this fundamental potential justification for conscription partly due to their focus on efficiency (less on equity), and partly due to their abstracting away of increasing returns in much of their analysis.

On top of the economic factors, the use of conscription may also be conducive to the promotion of a general sense of comradeship on the battlefront and, more widely, a sense of patriotism. This is similar or related to the issue of the crowding out of intrinsic motivation and morality in using the market, as discussed in Chapter 7. Here, we may note that an army of volunteers may also have some advantages in morale and motivation. Thus, the contrast of 'mercenaries' versus 'slaves' in the exchange between General Westmoreland and Professor Friedman mentioned earlier. There are different and complex factors affecting morale and motivation here. Conceptual analysis alone is an inadequate guide.

Empirical evidence shows an overwhelming support for an AVF. The USA has good experience in this, as it moved from conscription/draft to AVF in 1973. 'Despite a rough start, the AVF has been a brilliant success. Quality is far better than under a draft. A volunteer military can be choosy and set higher standards. Even when the army was reducing its requirements during the worst of the Iraq years, its quality standards remained well above those of conscript forces. ... The end of the draft also has dramatically improved commitment and morale in the armed forces. The difference is simple: recruits who want to serve and succeed are likely to perform better than draftees who want out, the sooner the better' (Bandow 2012).

The 'America's military leadership is adamantly opposed to instituting a new draft. The generals and admirals argue that a draft would weaken mission capability and create enormous structural and management problems. Morale and force cohesiveness would suffer intensely' (Kane 2006). 'The military itself, having tried it both ways (i.e., all-volunteer and conscription), strongly prefers an all-volunteer force. It allows for a far greater level of professionalism and efficiency than a conscript army. Also, morale is far better when all involved feel strongly that they are engaged in a noble and chosen pursuit than when they are forced to participate in an activity they would not choose. (As a professor for three years at the U.S. Military Academy at West Point, I had occasion to discuss this with dozens of officers and hundreds of cadets. That's not a scientific sample, but all the ones I spoke to said it was their perception that the dominant view favored an all-volunteer force.)' (Skoble 2003, p. 12).

The case for AVF, especially in terms of morale, is not just confined to the USA. 'The Israeli Defense Forces (IDF) has always monitored the changing attitudes of its troops and has recently concluded that the IDF will have to eventually drop conscription and go to an all-volunteer force. The most obvious sign of the declining morale is the growing number of young men and women who are avoiding service (draft dodgers in U.S. parlance)' (StrategyPage 2015). Similarly, past Taiwanese premier, Yu Shyi-kun (You Xi-kun) said that an AVF is 'the wave of future for Taiwan'. To deal with the lasting morale, retention, and recruitment difficulties, the government of Taiwan hopes to transit from conscription to an AVF (see Chase 2008, p. 126, Shih 2016). As reported in the newspaper (*Zaobao*) on 9 October 2017, p. 13, Taiwan will join Australia, the USA and the UK in having an AVF.

Although volunteers have to be paid more than the usually low pay for conscripts, the pay needed to attract sufficient volunteers is surprisingly moderate. One reason is that there are people who prefer military careers. The pay only has to be comparable to those of other occupations of similar qualifications to attract them. Thus, unless a country has to attract a very high proportion of people to serve in the armed forces, the pay does not have to be very high. For example, according to the comparison shown on the US Army website[5], the pays for volunteers in the USA are significantly less than comparable civilian pays, but, when considering the additional benefits of the soldiers, the overall remuneration is slightly more (less than 10%).

With progress, especially when a country becomes larger and richer, the need for conscription decreases on several counts. First, with a larger population, we need a lower proportion of people to be in the armed forces to defend the country. Second, as we get richer, the hidden costs of conscription become much bigger when converted into money equivalents. Third, we also have more money which could be spent on the higher pay needed to attract volunteers. Moreover, with the increasing importance of technology, the defence capability could be raised more by having a voluntary and professional armed forces than by training conscripts.

---

[5] www.goarmy.com/benefits/total-compensation.html.

14

Profiteering

There are many different types of profiteering, some of which are condemned even by efficiency-conscious economists. If someone profits from some activities (including selling goods) by providing misleading information, purposefully withholding relevant information, restricting competition from others, etc., it can be shown that such activities may likely harm others and are likely inefficient from a social perspective. Economists are generally against such profiteering. However, there are also a host of other activities regarded as profiteering and frowned upon by the public or even made illegal. In many such cases, they are really efficient and should be made legal, especially if the public can see the efficiency involved and therefore do not have feelings of repugnance against them.

A commonly condemned form of profiteering is speculation. There are also many different forms of speculation, some of which may be questionable and may even do large harms in certain circumstances, including those involving financial crises (which usually also involve many other factors, including information imperfection, not just speculation). For simplicity, let us consider the simplest case where the profiteering speculation is actually efficient but is still condemned and made illegal in many cases. This is buying something (at a place or time) at a low price and selling it (at another place or time) at a much higher price, making big profits.

China started its reform and opening up from December 1978 under Deng's leadership. Before that, not much private commerce went on. Thus, many goods had huge differences in their scarcity values. During the first few years or even a decade of reform, many acute traders bought goods where they could be bought at low prices and sold them at other places at much higher prices, making huge profits. In those years, the media in China was full of condemnation of those profiteering speculators. Such 'speculation' (投机倒把) was regarded as illegal and immoral. Only economists defended such activities.

Simple economic analysis shows that, in the absence of misinformation and artificial monopolization, such speculation is socially efficient and beneficial. If good X is priced at $10 per unit at place A, and at $30 at place B, a trader who buys X at $11 at A, transports it to B at a cost of $3 (all per unit) to B and sells it at $29 there will have made a profit of $15 per unit, at a profit rate of more than 100%. This is clearly profiteering. But who has she harmed? She makes the sellers at A better off; she makes the buyers at B better; she pays sufficiently for the transportation costs. She has caused no harm. Such speculation or profiteering is efficient and should not be frowned upon or made illegal. If there are significant pollution costs involved in the transportation, a case for taxing pollution or petrol may be made, but no case for banning such speculation is valid.

Similarly, a trader may buy a good in summer when it is supplied abundantly at a low price. She may then store or can it and sell it at a higher price in winter. Thus, we have fruits to eat all year long, and even low-middle-income persons in Singapore may eat lychees produced in China, thanks to free trade. In ancient northern China, only the emperor and his concubines were lucky enough to eat lychees transported from southern China non-stop by fast running horses one after another. By the way, although lychee is much more well known internationally, longan (smaller in size and with brownish instead of red skin) is much better tasting than lychee.

Profit-making free trade and production eventually made the price differentials between different places and times disappear, apart from the possible transportation/storage costs. Thus, while trade and speculation are still going on, the opportunities for clear, quick profits have largely disappeared, and high profits now depend more on useful innovations (except for some monopoly power enjoyed by some state enterprises). Thus, we no longer hear media condemnation of profiteering speculation. The cure for profiteering speculation is free trade, not banning speculation.

Another type of profiteering frowned upon by the public is benefiting indirectly from doing good deeds. An actual example may illustrate this; on 28 September 2016, the leading Chinese daily in Singapore *Lianhe Zaobao* carried an opinion article entitled 'Never use the name of environmental protection to really seek profits.'[1] The editor of that column also wrote in support of this article. Before that, the Automobile Importer & Exporter Association of Singapore recommended to the government to charge additional fees on old cars in the renewal of COEs on the grounds of higher pollution levels. Presumably, if the continued use of older cars carries additional fees, this would encourage more car owners to shift to new cars,

---

[1] LING Qing Rong 凌庆荣

increasing the business of the importers. Thus, the article condemns the Association of using the pretext of environmental protection to suggest something which would benefit their business. The article alleges 'Some organizations or enterprises with ulterior motives may cleverly use the issue of environmental protection as a cover to achieve agenda and motives that they cannot openly disclosed.' The column editor supported this with: 'The public is very concerned that some organizations use the pretext of a concern for the environment and public charity to make profits, using the work of environmental protection as an instrument for making money. Environmental protection and charity activities easily attract the engagement of people. However, when the public contribute their kindness, they should have a clear understanding and judgment of the whole activity, to avoid being used.'

Is using environmental protection (or any other noble cause) to make money immoral? If, in such an activity, serious harm on others and/or the environment is made, it is bad. However, the reason this is bad is due to the harm, not because she is making money. We all have to make money to survive. Making money itself is OK; it is harming others that is bad.

I am a full-time professor at Nanyang Technological University. One may correctly claim that I am (and any other paid teacher is) using the sacred causes of truth finding and educating the young to make money. We do receive salaries from our universities/schools. However, if we do not plagiarize or concoct our research results and are not irresponsible in our teaching, we contribute to knowledge and education and earn our salaries; there is then nothing wrong in using the sacred work of truth finding and education to make money.

In ancient times before the high degree of a division of labour, many things beneficial to the whole of society probably had to rely on the public spirit of people. Such altruistic activities, which still exist now, certainly are worthy of admiration and encouragement. However, if we rely only on altruism, but do not use any rewards, many useful services will be seriously under-supplied. If we do not pay salaries to those who treat the sick, look after the disabled, educate the young, etc., will we have enough specialized and qualified doctors, nurses, and teachers? Thus, by letting people get benefits, including making money, in doing good things, we can get many more good things done. Moreover, providing services to get good things done and getting rewards for such services are mutually beneficial; there is nothing bad in this.

If someone makes money in charity by stealing the money for charity, this is of course extremely immoral and should be seriously penalized. The cost is not just the stolen money, but more in discouraging future charity contribution. A person may also gain from charity by:

- Making his company popular with consumers through contributions to charity, thus making more profits in the future.
- Making him personally well known as a philanthropist, gaining in reputation although not in money.
- Benefiting from the warm-glow feeling in his own heart for doing something good for others, even if neither making money nor gaining reputation.

If he does not cause any harm to others, we do not want to discourage his charitable donation on the grounds of his benefiting from either one or more of these sources. Getting benefits, including making money, for oneself is not bad; it is harming others that is bad.

For another example, suppose someone invents a technology that will cut pollution enormously and uses it to make a huge sum of money. If she does not use devious methods and causes no harm unto others but helps to reduce pollution substantially, this must be hailed as a noble achievement. However, it is also the exact case of 'using environmental protection to make money'. Thus, making money, even using something, including people, are not themselves bad; it is causing harm that is bad.

The objection of most people for being 'used' is at least partly based on some misinterpretation of or being misled by Kant's case against treating a fellow human being as just an instrument. (This is further discussed in Appendix B.) Using others or being used without harm cannot be bad. It is the harm caused that is bad. We use things and people all the time. We use each other, usually for mutual benefits. I will be very glad if anyone uses me as an instrument to gain something for himself, provided no harm is made to me or others. I want to help others, if the costs to me are not too high. As a high school student, I participated very actively in clandestine left-wing activities that were trying to establish a communist society. We undertook enormous risks of being expelled, imprisoned, or even killed. I was a lucky one, but two sisters of my wife were imprisoned (one for many years) and some of my friends were shot dead. The reason was that we (mistakenly from the current perspective) believed that a communist society would bring happiness to most people and, hence, was worth the personal sacrifice. Thus, if I and others suffer no harm and you can just use me to achieve some gains, you are very welcome.

Decades ago, my late colleague Xiaokai Yang and I established a new academic journal. We invited some prominent economists, including some Nobel laureates, to be on our board of editors, without having them do any real editorial job. We just used their names to promote our journal. Now, I also sit on the editorial boards of a number of journals and do not do any editorial work. This is a common practice of academic journals. Usually, academics on the board of editors are honorary only: no job, no pay. Unless you know that the true editor inviting you to sit on the board is a crook, or that the journal will be used for some illegal or immoral motives (never so known), you take such an invitation as an honour and accept accordingly. No one minds being used in this manner.

Long-lasting friendly or loving relationships are usually mutually beneficial. In some sense, both sides are using the other for their own benefits, and possibly that of the other. Thus, use itself is not a problem, it is harming others that is the problem. If no one is hurt, you may bang on the table to let loose your anger without worrying about the feeling of the table, because it has no feeling. However, you must not slap any person just to express your anger, because an individual has feelings. Thus, for a person (and more generally for all those with the capacity for happiness and suffering) you must not use her merely as an instrument without considering her feelings. This is the correct part of Kant's philosophy. However, in using Kant's teaching, many people go to the excess of condemning all instrumental use of people even when no harm is made.

For the case of the Automobile Importer & Exporter Association of Singapore discussed earlier, their recommendation to charge extra fees on old cars might be motivated more by making more profits for themselves than stemming from a concern for environmental protection. However, if the extra fees do benefit the environment (almost certainly so), and no other serious harms are involved (not known), they should not be accused of using environmental protection as an instrument for making more profits. Instead, the recommendation of charging the extra fees should be supported. Environmental protection benefits the whole world and for a long time. Each person shares only no more than 0.0000001%. Thus, many people do not have enough motivation to promote environmental protection. At least to some extent, we may have to rely on those with 'ulterior motives' like the Automobile Importer & Exporter Association to help.

I spent years doing research and writing this book. Many of my fellow assistant professors in our Division of Economics typically come back to the office to work after dinner and on weekends. We are partly motivated by curiosity, truth finding, and contributing to a better society. However, the personal reasons of maintaining our jobs and pays, our reputation, and our own enjoyment may be much more important, at least in many cases. Again, self-interest and instrumental use are no grounds for condemnation if no harm to others is involved. In fact, a good society is one in which its economic, legal, political, social systems, and customs are beneficial to the cooperation (also reads 'mutual utilization') of its members for mutual benefits. By allowing the use of market exchange to expand, we can generally promote more cooperation, as discussed in Chapter 8.

Why do many people condemn self-interest, profiteering, and instrumental use then? First, in order to make profits, many do use means that harm others, resulting in a worse situation for the whole of society. It is true that we should then focus on the harm done. However, often we may not have enough evidence for this. Thus, many people are suspicious of possible harm to others when some are profiteering and/or engaging in the instrumental use of some good causes. However, I think that some reasonable grounds are needed before we should be so suspicious. Like the Automobile Importer & Exporter Association case, no presumption for accusation seems to be available. That they were in fact so strongly and openly accused suggests that there is a further reason. This second reason, I suggest, is the anti-market, anti-money, anti-profiteering sentiment of the public, as already discussed in Chapter 4.

15

Water: A Typical Case of Under-Pricing

Unlike the legal prohibition of such market exchanges like kidney sales and prostitution, as discussed in previous chapters, the market and monetary payments are legally used for some goods; however, the use of the market mechanism is seriously inhibited because the prices are controlled by the government at levels different from their free market levels. There are two opposite types of such price controls. One is where the controlled prices are above the market levels; a typical example is minimum wages legislation. The opposite case is where the controlled prices are below the market levels; typical examples include car parking in city centres, rent control, and water pricing. The case of car parking has already been discussed in Chapter 5. Here, we focus on water pricing.

In February 2017, the Singapore government announced a scheduled increase in water prices for 2017 and 2018 of 30% in total. As I strongly supported the increase in water prices in subsequent media interviews, I received several emails strongly condemning me, including accusing me of being 'unfeeling' and 'disgusting', and one that said 'I absolutely detest you.' Some inadequate understanding must be involved, partly because media interviews are not fully reported/televised due to space/time limitation. However, there are also deeper issues involved.

Since I joined Nanyang Technological University in Singapore in early 2013, I have frequently heard suggestions on the need and the methods to save water on radio and newspapers. I seldom or never heard of the need to save other goods. Why?

A likely reason is that water prices do not adequately reflect the costs of supply. This is consistent with the fact that water prices have not been adjusted since 2000 in Singapore. Although Singapore has not had much inflation in the last few years, the general price level has still increased by more than 30% over the last 17 years. Considering inflation, the announced 30% increase in water prices does not actually catch up with the rise in price levels. Also, according to Mr Heng Swee Keat, Singapore's Minister of Finance (from his Parliamentary debate reported in newspapers on 3 March 2017), revenues from water pricing only cover operating costs, but are insufficient for infrastructure investment. This also suggests under-pricing.

Singapore gets some of its water supply from Malaysia. The costs of this supply have been low. However, Singapore also supplies water by producing new water and by desalination (converting sea water into drinkable water). The costs of these supplies are much higher. At least from the viewpoint of economic efficiency, a good should be priced at the cost of the highest cost source to encourage efficient saving. If the government makes money by this policy, such as it has in its COE auctioning, it could then levy lower taxes on other areas, or have higher government spending on worthy avenues. As long as the government is reasonably efficient and not too corrupt, the overall result should be better.

According to basic economics, if we want to encourage people to consume a good less, the simplest and most effective way is to increase its price. So, why are the prices of water typically too low for this purpose, necessitating encouragement of water saving and even water restriction in many cities, including Melbourne, where I lived for 38 years between 1974 and 2012?

Water is regarded as a necessity. If we do not have water, we will die. Thus, most people think that water prices should remain low. True, everyone has to drink about 1–2 litres of water every day. However, this represents roughly only a fraction of 1% of domestic water consumption in most cities and countries including Singapore (this fraction is even smaller if commercial, industrial, and agricultural consumption is included.) The remaining 99% or more is used for less essential purposes, including cleaning and gardening, and non-domestic usages, not to mention much wastage. The proportions of the more essential parts of our consumption of food, living space, transportation, etc. are probably higher than that for water. Should we suppress the prices of all these goods?

To avoid wastage and encourage efficient conservation, each and every consumer should pay a price reflecting the costs of supply. In the presence of significant external costs like pollution, the environmental costs should also be included, possibly through taxation like the proposed carbon tax. Consumers may then decide how much consumption is worth. This principle should apply to all goods and services, including water. We may then save the costs of artificial encouragement and the inconvenience of restriction.

Apart from inconvenience, restrictions could also be quite counter-productive. During my 38 years of residence in Melbourne, water restrictions were imposed several times. Once, the restriction was that one may water the garden only two days a week and only during 6–8 am and 7–9 pm. The reason is that watering over the sunny times involves much more waste due to evaporation. I remember distinctly that I ended up doing much more watering than the periods without any restriction. The psychology is that if I do not water in this limited and allowable period, (1) I miss out on something scarce; and (2) if my garden needs watering in the next few days, I will not be able to do so, so I better water it sufficiently in the allowable periods to avoid this. I was not the exception; my neighbours told me the same thing.

Some extreme egalitarians may think that we should just impose an absolute restriction so that everyone consumes no more than the same average quantity. This is almost always impractical. For example, for food consumption, we certainly have to allow for different needs between children and adults, females and males, the growing young and the elderly, etc. For petrol, there is the distinction between those with and those without cars. Even for those with just one car, there are big differences between different sizes of cars (with different petrol requirements per kilometre driven), different numbers of family members served by the car, different distances of residences from places of work, schools, etc. Obviously, it is much more efficient to let different consumers with their different needs or preferences choose their own quantities, as long as they pay for the costs of supplying the goods.

The same price may be trivial to a rich person but a substantial burden to one on lower incomes. True, but this is a problem of income distribution, not of pricing certain goods. In the presence of large inequality, as is usually the case, helping the lower income groups and lowering the degree of inequality may be desirable. However, a person is rich or not depending on her total income or wealth, not on her consumption or the affordability of some particular good such as water. We should try to increase the incomes of the lower income groups rather than let them face low water prices, as the latter option leads to wastage.

I agree with one email commentator that people at my income level should pay higher taxes. Singapore has scored well in efficiency policies, including almost an 'A+' for its second-price auctioning of COE for owning cars, in comparison to a 'fail' for Beijing's system of lottery and using plate numbers to restrict driving. However, Singapore has not done quite enough for improving equality. Possibly following the call to action on this front by my predecessor Professor Lim Chong Yah around 2011, the government has done more over the past few years. However, he faced strong opposition in the initial periods after his call.

True, taxing the rich and helping people of lower incomes may involve disincentive effects. Despite this, it is still better to increase equality through general equality promotion, including tax/transfer, instead of pursuing inefficient policies in specific areas like water pricing. This is so because such inefficient policies also have disincentive effects, on top of their distortive effects, as I argued in *American Economic Review* in 1984 (Ng 1984a), and also discussed in Chapter 5.

As a rule, we should not only use the market to allocate goods efficiently, we should also let the market prices reflect the relevant scarcity and costs, instead of artificially trying to control prices to be either below or above their market levels. This does not rule out the need to tax important external costs like pollution to make the market prices reflect not just private costs of production, but also the social costs of environmental disruption. Car park fees, water prices, rents, etc. should all be allowed to reflect their long-run social marginal costs. If society feels that some people do not have enough income to pay for essential goods at these prices, society should help to increase their total purchasing power, not let them face artificially lower prices.

The under-use of efficient pricing occurs very widely. For example, as reported in *Telegraph Travel* by Hugh Morris on 11 August 2017, the Croatian city of Dubrovnik will drastically cut the number of visitors allowed into its ancient centre in an effort to prevent ruinous overcrowding, as announced by the new mayor. An economist would wonder, instead of using number limitation, why not use pricing to cut down the number of visitors, resolving the associated overcrowding and/or ruinous effects? The revenue collected could be used to better maintain the site or could also partly be used to help the poor. The poor would find it more important to reduce their poverty than to get 'equal access' to exotic sites. Perhaps the mayor is worried about making future tourists unhappy about fee charging. If this is correct, it is the public who fails to appreciate the role of prices in allocating scarce goods. Paying higher prices for scarcer goods is both efficient and equitable. Perhaps the very high degree of inequality is inequitable, or caused partly by some inequitable factors. However, it is these factors that may be inequitable, not the need to pay higher prices for scarcer goods.

The insufficient use of pricing in legal enforcement or punishment is discussed in the next chapter.

16

Fines, Imprisonment, or Whipping?

Another case of the under-use of the market or pricing system is the tendency to use imprisonment instead of higher fines.

There are different methods of penalizing criminals. Here, only the three more commonly used methods of fines, imprisonment, and whipping are discussed, ignoring some other methods like hard labour, deportation, and capital punishment (the death sentence). I discuss the problem generally, and not directed at on any specific cases.

Comparing fines and imprisonment, most economists are in favour of using the former as far as possible. Professors A. M. Polinsky and S. Shavell of Stanford University believe that fines should be used until the wealth of the convicted have been exhausted before imprisonment may be considered (Polinsky & Shavell 1984). The reason is simple (but some complications are discussed later). If we can use higher fines instead of imprisonment to achieve the same degree of penalty, society will not only save a lot of the costs of imprisonment, but will also obtain the resources of the fines. If so, why is this fines-first policy not practiced in any country in the whole world? The inadequate use of fines is partly due to the largely misguided anti-market sentiment discussed in Chapter 4. However, is the simple economic argument in favour of fines-first watertight?

Most people regard the economic argument as considering only efficiency while ignoring equity or equality. However, we have already discussed in Chapter 5 that if the efficiency supremacy policy in specific areas is supplemented by a stronger equality promotion policy, people in all income groups will be made better off, effectively nullifying the counter argument based on equality.

Most societies not only fail to follow the fines-first policy, but also impose strict time limits on off-street parking. Even if the parking lot is available for legal parking 24 hours a day, seven days a week, no one may park for more than a short, specified period each time. Because of its scarcity? Lobsters and expensive hotels are also scarce, but we do not mind using higher prices to allocate those goods. Why do we not do the same for scarce parking space? Most economists (myself included before I wrote the 1984 paper; Ng 1984a) do not fully understand the logic of efficiency supremacy policy for specific areas. Thus, it is not surprising that the general public, with their anti-market sentiment, do not like to see the rich being able pay their way out of violating regulations, while those who cannot afford to pay may have to go to jail. Such preferences make judges and societies opt to use imprisonment well before the scope for fines has been exhausted.

We see quite often that, when both fines and imprisonment are simultaneously imposed on a convicted person, it is typically along the lines of: 'Five thousand dollars in fine plus five months of sentence.' The cost of one-month imprisonment, even to a person on average to below average income levels, is well over $1,000. Such combined sentences could be improved by increasing the fine component by many times and reducing the imprisonment component to a small fraction, with roughly the same deterrent effects, but at a small fraction of the total cost to society. There are many cases where the maximum fine for an offence is $5,000, while the maximum prison sentence is 5 years. The serious under-utilization of fines is clear. A case reported worldwide on 3 August 2017, including by the *Washington Post*, typifies the point.[1] A Cambodian court sentenced an Australian woman to 18 months in prison and a US$1,000 fine for providing commercial surrogacy services in the country. Not only is the banning (done in Cambodia in 2016) of commercial surrogacy questionable, given the ban, the cash fine of US$1,000 is disproportionately too small in comparison to the imprisonment of 18 months, even to a local Cambodian. (Cambodia has a per capita GDP of well over US$1000 a year.)

Similarly, when Hasmiza Othman (nick name, Datuk Seri Vida) was convicted of failing to pay a GST of RM$4.2 million in late 2016, she was fined only RM$80,000 (without any other penalty) which is less than 2% of the evaded amount (see the report in *Lianhe Zaobao* on 20 September 2017, p. 12.)[2] The maximum fine for such a conviction of 'RM50,000, three years jail, or both' is also biased in the leniency in the fine amount, while severe in the imprisonment term. Another report on 21 August 2017 in *Lianhe Zaobao* mentions the maximum penalties for a certain crime (taking photos of girls under their skirts) being S$10,000 or 5 years imprisonment, or both.

[1] 'Australian nurse jailed in Cambodia for running illegal surrogacy clinic.'
[2] '浴"在钞票珠宝浴缸 马国女商人拍炫富MV遭抨'

Again, the fine is much less severe when compared to the imprisonment. As Singapore has a per capita GDP of over S$72,000 per year, the amount of S$10,000 is less than 3% of the per capita GDP for 5 years. Also, in Singapore, the maximum punishment for the crime of operating brothels is S$10,000 and/or 5 years imprisonment (*Lianhe Zaobao*, 30 September 2017, p. 14). The degree of under-utilization of fines versus imprisonment is phenomenal.

Crimes involving money, including theft, tax evasion, corruption, etc., should mainly be penalized with large enough fines to make the convicts face a negative expected value for committing such a crime. A rough convict may not be very scared of imprisonment. If we fine him a relatively small amount, but send him to jail for some years, he may still be a rich man after coming out of jail. The deterrence effect may be weak. Such inadequate use of fines in comparison to imprisonment is most inefficient in both wasting resources (imprisonment is very costly to the society) and in the deterrence effect. Convicts should be fined to bank-ruptcy before being sent to jail.

In contrast, when courts are awarding damages for individuals against commercial enterprises, they tend to over-award. For example, as reported in the mass media on 22 August 2017, the Los Angeles Superior Court has ordered Johnson & Johnson to pay US$417 million to a Californian woman who claimed she developed ovarian cancer after using the company's talcum-based products, such as Johnson's Baby Powder for feminine hygiene. Such excessive amounts of awards are partly due to the anti-market (and by relation, also anti-commercial enterprises) sentiment discussed in Chapter 4. Another contributing factor could be the following consideration. If a person is ser-iously harmed, it may be true that no amount of financial payment will be able to fully compensate for the damage. Although US$417 million may well be insufficient for full compensation, the hundreds of millions of dollars in excess of the first or first few million dollars are of very low marginal utility to the person involved. There is not much point in making that person a billionaire overnight. The US$417 million paid by Johnson & Johnson will eventually fall upon persons of only moderate income and wealth levels.[3]

Consider the very serious crime of murder. Most people agree that such a crime cannot be penalized by a fine alone, no matter how high it may be, but must also be supplemented by at least imprisonment, if not capital

---

[3] When willingness-to-accept figures are infinite or close to infinity, it is more sensible to figure in terms of 'marginal dollar equivalent' as discussed in Ng (2004b, Appendix 4A).

punishment. Many economists will probably agree. But as an economist, one should ask: Why is a fine not enough?

One possible answer is that life is invaluable or that the value of life is infinite. This answer is suspicious. True, for most people, if you are killed, no matter how much money is paid to your surviving family members, the compensation is not sufficient to offset your loss. However, no one (even Bill Gates) is willing and able to pay an infinite sum to reduce the probability of death. Whether you agree or not, in accordance to the maximum amount of money you are willing to pay to reduce the probability of death by a small amount (say 0.1 in a million), which may be revealed in your choice of a safer airline, economists may calculate the dollar value you place on your own life. According to Viscusi & Aldy (2003), the average value of a life for the USA was US$10 million, or perhaps about $13.5 million at current levels of prices and incomes. This is a large sum, but certainly finite (see also León & Miguel 2017).

If someone is convicted of a murder, is fining him the sum of $13.5 million enough? For simplicity, we assume here that the probability of successful conviction is one. If the probability of successful conviction is less than certainty, say only 0.5, the fine is adjusted to make the expected fine still the same. Society is faced with one more death. However, if we use this $13.5 million to invest in public safety measures, many more deaths will be averted. Research shows that the marginal costs of reducing one death in many public safety measures are hundreds or even thousands of times less than $13.5 million. We use one death to achieve a reduction of many deaths. It seems worthwhile, doesn't it?

If one may just pay $13.5 million to murder a person, the power of a billionaire will be enormous. He could threaten anyone willy-nilly. According to the argument discussed in Chapter 5, it seems that we may just tax the rich more, while allowing them to use money in a wider scope. However, there are further complications for extreme cases like murders. First, my 1984 paper really only shows that 'a dollar is a dollar' whomsoever it goes (Ng 1984a). Each marginal dollar should be treated equally for specific issues. But it does not show that a billion dollars is a billion dollars; a billion dollars for one person does not equal the sum of a thousand dollars for each million persons. Second, it only shows a quasi-Pareto improvement: individuals within each income group are made better off as a group. If individuals in the same income group differ in preferences, some may be made better off and some worse off. For small changes, these may be ignored as insignificant. However, for huge changes, including murders, they may be too big to be ignored. If there are some potentially dangerous individuals in the group, the desired extra tax on the group may be too large (disincentive-wise) for others with no dangerous tendencies. In addition, with tax evasion, the extra taxes may not be effective for all. Also, some individuals get their wealth not from working, but from inheritance and even devious sources. All these considerations make the use of imprisonment or even capital punishment possibly justifiable in serious crimes.

Nevertheless, two conclusions remain valid. First, as most people have some degree of anti-market sentiment and do not understand the general superiority of the efficiency supremacy policy (in specific areas), fines have been inadequately used in almost all societies. Second, as the taxation efficiency of a country improves, problems of tax evasion decrease, illicit sources of incomes decrease, and, as people's understanding of economics improves, more and more penalties may take on the least costly form of fines. However, the amount of fines must be sufficient, taking into account not only the damages inflicted, but also the possibly low probabilities of conviction. The actual optimal fines depend on circumstances and require careful analysis. However, casual empiricism suggests that the fines of most societies probably should be increased by at least ten times and prison sentences reduced to none or only a tiny fraction, for most crimes. For example, sometimes we see that a crime involving ten thousand dollars is sentenced to a fine of only several thousand dollars. As the probability of conviction for such a relatively minor crime is usually only a small fraction, the optimal fine should be at least several dozen thousand dollars.

Compared to imprisonment, whipping involves fewer material costs to society and has very high deterrent effects. For a tough repeat criminal, he may even bully other inmates if imprisoned; the deterrent effects of imprisonment may then not be very high. Supplementation with whipping may be needed, as is actually done in Singapore and some other countries. However, many people regard whipping as an uncivilized form of punishment and should not be used. Is this right?

Looking at, or even just imagining, the situation and pain of whipping is repugnant. However, if we have to use penalties beyond fines, whipping is better than imprisonment in some important aspects. Apart from much lower material costs, whipping is more (although not perfectly) focused on the criminals themselves, while imprisonment usually imposes higher costs on the family members of the criminals. As imprisonment penalizes the innocent more (relative to whipping), is it really more civilized? Perhaps those insisting on no whipping may be thinking like an ostrich, at least in some sense.

However, if many people find whipping repugnant, this may be regarded as its non-material cost; similarly, the feeling of repugnance against kidney sales should also be taken into account (but trumped by the higher importance of life saving and the promotion of liberalism), as argued in Chapters 6 and 9. Thus, whipping should be reserved for serious crimes, especially repeat criminals. For less serious crimes, especially for the first-time convict, more reliance should be placed on fines.

17

Some Specific Areas

In this chapter, we discuss a number of different areas where the market is typically limited or not used at all. Each topic is only briefly discussed, focusing on what I see as the essential elements, without necessarily covering all relevant points.

17.1 FROM SLAVERY TO SURROGATE PREGNANCY

Slavery or life servitude is a clear example that currently has little, if any, objection to its universal illegality from even strong free-market supporters. I also do not object to the banning of slavery. Why the difference between kidney sales and slavery?

First, I concede to the banning of slavery largely on the importance of imperfect information in the real world. People may make mistakes. 'Not only does an individual lack complete knowledge about her future self, but also her conditions are likely to change in ways that she cannot now predict' (Satz 2009, p. 102). In a world of absolutely no mistakes and irrationality, the banning of voluntary slavery is not necessary. The use of force of course justifies banning virtually all market exchanges; no one should be allowed to force anyone into an exchange of anything. However, mistakes may also be made in a kidney sale. So why the difference between the two cases?

Several important points are relevant. While losing a kidney is not a small matter, servitude for life is a much bigger one. Slavery is too big a mistake to make. To protect the very small percentage of people who would make such a mistake, this has to be done, even if at some significant cost. Second, in the case of kidney sales, the benefit to the recipient is that their life is saved; the benefit-to-cost ratio is enormous, overwhelming the possible costs of a mistaken sale. Therefore, adequate counselling, instead of banning, should usually be the appropriate solution for the case of kidney sales. Third, we want to promote more equality between individuals; having some individuals owning others is too unequal and against the spirit of mutual equality and respect. Thus, the banning of slavery is justifiable.

Apart from mistakes, there is another potential benefit to banning slavery due to the divergence between preference and welfare, similar to the case of Lee Kuan Yew's expropriation of cemetery land for public development discussed in Chapter 10, on presumed consent. In ancient China (less so now, but still to some extent), it was a compelling duty of children to give a deceased parent a decent burial. Thus, one often reads in novels or watches in films how a poor man willingly sold himself to become a slave in order to give his deceased parent a decent burial. If the prevailing law does not allow slavery, such a person will not become a slave, improving his welfare, if not his preference.

If it may be justifiable to ban selling oneself into slavery, it should be even more justifiable to ban selling one's children. This is because a third party, a child, is involved. Parents should love and care for their children. Selling one's child violates this responsibility. Using the logic of Brennan & Jaworski (2016), if we ban the selling of children, we should also ban the giving away of children for free. The problem of selling children is not that it 'places a price' on them. In fact, I have placed a price on myself; I am for sale (see the end of Appendix B). Rather, it is the failure to perform the responsibility of being a parent. While this may be so for most normal cases, some exceptions may have to be allowed. If an unmarried teenage mother is willing to give up the baby for adoption to caring foster parents desperate to have a child, perhaps permission might be a better alternative in some cases. As a welfarist, I do not have a strong stand on cases where there are welfare costs and benefits of ambiguous magnitudes. It is dependent on the situation. Situations of desperation (such as extreme poverty and teenage pregnancy) and those of normalcy may have to be treated differently.

The case of surrogate motherhood/pregnancy is different. This is not selling your own baby, but providing a service to help others have babies. Creating a new life is a wonderful thing. Thus, with sufficient counselling to avoid decision making under serious misinformation, I am strongly in favour of allowing surrogate motherhood/pregnancy. Many people may think that having more people makes existing people worse off through resource competition, congestion, and pollution. Such a belief is usually based on mistakes, as discussed in Appendix D. With appropriate taxes on congestion and pollution, a larger population, through either immigration or more births, typically makes existing people better off economically, and if no serious disharmony is created, better off overall.

17.2 FROM VOTE TRADING TO CORRUPTION

There are different forms of vote trading. One case is where a member of congress/parliament or a senator enters into an agreement with another, typically in the same or different committees where they cast votes to make decisions, to have some exchange of votes. For example, member A may find issue X not important for voters in his constituency, but issue Y important, while member B finds the reverse to be true. Then, A may agree to support B's preference for issue X in exchange for B's support in issue Y.

Vote trading may also happen for the same issue at the same time/vote. Consider a voting method whereby the full ordering of all alternatives of each voter is taken: first preference, second preference, third ... to the last. (In British general elections, a voter only chooses the top preferred candidate; in the Australian ones, a voter lists first, second ... to the last preferred candidate, revealing the full ordering.) Now suppose member A slightly prefers alternative X to Y, and strongly prefers either X or Y to Z. Even in the full ordering system, a voter cannot distinguish between strong and weak preference. Thus, A cannot report his preference as: X, Y, ..., Z. He can only rank: 1. X, 2. Y, 3. Z. Only the ordering is revealed, but not the intensity of preference.

Now suppose member B prefers alternative Y moderately or strongly to Z and prefers Z slightly to X. Then, A and B may agree to the following trading arrangement. A agrees to change his ranking to: 1. Y, 2. X, 3. Z in exchange for B's agreement to vote also: 1. Y, 2. X, 3. Z. In other words, A agrees to rank B's top preference, Y, top (actually A's second preference), in exchange for B's ranking A's worst fear, Z, last (actually B's second preference). Then, A gets the benefit of reducing the chance of his worst fear happening, and B gets the benefit of increasing the chance of her top choice winning.

If we compare the vote ordering and the actual ordering of voters, this vote trading actually distorts the true ordering of each voter. This looks bad. However, if we look at the orderings of both individuals together and recognize the intensity of dis-preference of A for Z, we may see that vote trading allows the intensity of preference to be disclosed somehow, although not perfectly. Thus, such vote trading has at least some beneficial effects in allowing the intensities of preferences to be somewhat accounted for in a voting system that uses rankings only.

A very different type of vote trading is typified by a candidate or his party paying voters to vote for him. Most, if not all, people, myself included, condemn such practices. An election is a democratic, although imperfect, mechanism where individuals express their preferences to help elect candidates who, hopefully, may serve society well in making political decisions. The reason that vote trading here is bad is because it differs from the exchange of goods (or services) in the marketplace in at least two very important aspects. For the case of market exchange in private goods, a seller/producer sells his own good (which may be produced) and a buyer/consumer buys for her own benefits. Where important effects on some third parties are involved, such as pollution, in the process of production or consumption, then, ideally, taxes should be imposed in accordance to the damages involved. Then, market exchanges are mutually beneficial and efficient. As a rule, they should be allowed, not banned.

For political elections, we do not have exchanges of private goods. Rather, we are to choose decision makers on behalf of the whole of society to make public choices which affect all individuals. The vote of each individual, in combination with those of others, helps to choose politicians who will make important public choices. Having general elections achieves several important functions, including getting people interested in politics, having a sense of participation and responsibility, and, most importantly, helping to select better politicians and making politicians responsible to the people. A Chinese proverb says roughly something like: Three fools are better than a wise person. Everyone makes mistakes. Combining the votes of many individual members (including in committees) generally helps to reduce mistakes. Selling one's vote violates this citizen's responsibility. In this important aspect, I agree with Sandel (2012a, p. 10) that 'civic duties should not be regarded as private property but should be viewed instead as public responsibilities'. Frey & Stutzer (2000) also show that voting, especially direct democracy, is positively associated with happiness. This 'positive effect can be attributed to political outcomes closer to voters' preferences, as well as to the procedural utility of political participation possibilities', p. 918.

One complication is, especially in elections involving large numbers of voters, the probability that the vote of a single voter, by itself, will be decisive in affecting the election outcome is extremely small. This reduces the incentives of each voter to get information and to vote correctly. It also makes the material costs to the seller of the vote negligible and smaller than the price paid in buying votes. The price is pocketed by the seller alone, but the costs are imposed on thousands, if not millions, of others. The purchase and selling of votes should thus be illegal and immoral.

While the vote of a single individual has a negligible chance of changing an election, those of many individuals combine to have an important outcome. This is witnessed by the Brexit referendum on 23 June 2016 on whether the UK should exit the European Union (EU). From the reports, both before and after the referendum, it appeared likely that a majority was in favour of remaining in the EU. As it actually turned out, a slight majority (51.89%) voted to leave. This was probably due to the fact that a sizable proportion, being confident that the outcome would be remaining anyway (thinking 'my own vote will not change this result'), decided to vote to exit as a protest vote against the government. That this was likely the case was suggested by the reports of many voters regretting voting to exit (Dearden 2016). While democratic voting is imperfect, without the check and balance of voting and other democratic elements, we run the danger of a bad dictator with possibly far worse outcomes, such as the Great Leap Forward and the Cultural Revolution in China.

If the purchase and selling of votes should be banned, it is even clearer that corruption should be banned a fortiori. Corruption is unduly benefitting privately from abusing one's power in office; bribery is unduly purchasing private benefits through the abuse of power of some officials. The serious damages to the public are obvious. Some commentators see some benefits of corruption in lubricating an otherwise bureaucratic system (the greasing effect). However, such short-term benefits incur high costs on third parties (e.g., those not paying bribes get a longer delay in being served) and will also lead to more bureaucratic inefficiency and further corruption and, hence, create a vicious cycle.

Consider: 'when a judge accepts a bribe to render a corrupt verdict, he acts as if his judicial authority were an instrument of personal gain rather than a public trust. He degrades and demeans his office by treating it according to a lower norm than is appropriate to it' (Sandel 2012a, p. 46). The point about degradation may be valid. However, the more important reason against such corruption is the distortive effects of the verdict. The distorted verdict not only compromises justice and impartiality, they will also have longer run effects of reducing confidence in the system, and, consequently, making people undertake reduced cooperation and socially useful activities. Research shows that corruption is the most important factor impeding economic growth (e.g., Easterly 2001, pp. 241–252).[1]

17.3   FROM FRIENDSHIP TO NOBEL PRIZES

It is not that you should not buy friendship; rather, you cannot buy true friendship (similarly for true love and other relationships). Once you pay,

---

[1]   The effects of corruption on growth is complex, with the greasing effect also applicable to some extent; see, e.g., Campos et al. (2016) and Chang & Hao (2017).

you really only buy paid companionship or paid assistance, which may be quite fine. You may only get true friendship by 'being friends' with others, not by paying money. Thus, the point that you cannot buy true friendship neither supports nor negates the case for using markets more broadly where beneficial. True friendship is not something amenable to the use of markets. However, I do not think we should ban paid companionship. On the other hand, wise persons do not try to enhance friendship by paying money to friends. Nevertheless, mutual help, including financial help where needed, is fine.

Nobel prizes and similar awards should clearly not be sold. Their function is to recognize outstanding contributions to knowledge (or some other socially worthwhile causes). This serves to confirm existing contributions and also to motivate future contributions. If these awards could be bought for money, the function of recognition would be lost. Naming a building, a chair, etc. after either a person who has made important contributions or donated a huge sum of money is a different matter. Such practices have been used for both purposes (recognizing donation and recognizing other contributions) for a long time and largely regarded as acceptable. Why the difference between Nobel prizes and naming rights? An important, but simple, reason is that Nobel prizes are restricted to a contribution to knowledge in certain areas only. If someone established a prize or an honorary award in charitable contribution, then winning such an award by making huge contributions is possible and acceptable. Having such an award may also be desirable, as charitable contributions are useful. Also, no confusion will likely be involved.

On the other hand, paying to pass an exam or to get an academic degree is different. This seriously confuses and even misleads others and should be banned. An example deserving of a definite ban and heavy penalty is the selling (even if disguised) of illicit 'awards'. As reported by *The Times* on 24 July 2017, some businessmen have been accused of exploiting the reputation of the University of Oxford to sell millions of pounds worth of fake awards. They advertise opportunities to get 'boosts' and 'recognition from Oxford' and invite people to apply for awards that cost many thousands of pounds each, under the pretence of administrative costs. They also use images of Oxford colleges in their advertisements and use a similar typeface to that of the university on their logo. The University of Oxford has confirmed that it has no affiliation to the organization set up by these businessmen. Such fake awards do not just involve mutually agreed selling and buying of something, but also provide misleading information. This is costly both to the misled public and to the genuine awards. Even if they do not misuse the name of the University of Oxford, just the effective selling of awards is already misleading, making the public less clear about, for example, which city is more deserving of 'Best city'.

17.4 PAYING OTHERS FOR LINE STANDING/SITTING

At least in the USA, it is known that rich lobbyists, lawyers, and contractors pay someone to hold a place in line so that the payer can get admittance to some important Supreme Court case or a congressional hearing (also some free performances, like the Shakespeare performances in Central Park by the New York City's Public Theater; see Sandel 2012a, p. 21ff.). Sometimes, people camp overnight or pay someone to camp overnight, paying many thousands of dollars to ensure admittance, such as in the case of the same-sex marriage ruling. Should the limited seats be auctioned off in advance to avoid such huge wastages in time and trouble?

It may be argued that a democratic society wants individuals from different groups to be able to attend those hearings, not just from those who can afford to pay. If so, then two different aspects need to be considered. Is the person getting admittance to a hearing: A. Satisfying her own preference to attend the hearing? and/or B. Performing a function as a citizen of a certain group to attend and react to the hearing? If only aspect A is concerned, we may use the argument of Chapter 5 to prefer auctioning the scarce seats to the highest bidders and take care of equality in the general equality promotion policy. However, if aspect B is also important, the pure auctioning system may miss out on something.

Due to the simultaneous existence of both the private and public aspects, a perfect simple system may not be possible. The current first-come-first-served system makes sure that those with a low ability to pay may also be represented. However, it is somewhat biased against those with a high opportunity cost of time. Thus, I suggest a combined system. A proportion (perhaps half) of the limited seats is auctioned to the highest bidders to cater to those with money, but no free time, and the rest is rationed by lottery or queuing to cater to those with free time, but low paying ability. We save a lot of time for those with a high opportunity cost of time, and we still get some cross-sectional representation. Moreover, we generate more money which could be used perhaps for expanding the seating capacity.

Is the proposed dual system acceptable? In fact, the US Supreme Court is already using a form of dual system. Two different lines are used, one for the public and one for the members of the Supreme Court bar. One has to be a lawyer in good standing for three years and pay a fee of US$200 to be a member of the bar. Even if this dual line system is kept, it is still desirable to introduce the dual auction-plus-lining system, at least for those hearings expected to be in high demand.

17.5 SELLING PERMITS FOR HUNTING RHINOS

As mentioned by Freiman (2015, p. 346), 'Michael Sandel talks about the South African government's decision to sell permits to hunt black rhinos – an endangered species. The decision has a cold, calculating, consequentialist rationale: if you let people sell, in effect, the lives of these rhinos, they can profit from producing more of them and thereby stave off their extinction. Think of it this way: chickens, pigs, and cows aren't in any danger of dying out.'

'If you believe it's morally objectionable to kill wildlife for sport, the market in rhino hunts is a devil's bargain, a kind of moral extortion. You might welcome its good effect on rhino conservation but deplore the fact that this is achieved by catering to what you consider the perverse pleasures of wealthy hunters. It would be like saving an ancient redwood forest by allowing loggers to sell wealthy donors the right to carve their initials in some of the trees' (Sandel 2012a, p. 80). Several comments may be added to this observation. First, from the rhinos' perspective, whether their preservation will be desirable depends on whether a life of being hunted has positive net welfare. If not, preservation is no good for them. It may be useful for us humans, but that has to be balanced with the costs imposed on the rhinos. Second, carving initials (or even full names) on trees is quite different from shooting rhinos, as trees are not sentients.

Third, Freiman (2015, p. 347) is correct in noting: 'But I do not see why the blame rests with the market. If trophy hunters are wrong to treat wildlife as sport, it's wrong for them to hunt the rhinos for free.' This is consistent with the position of Brennan & Jaworski (2016). It is hunting itself that should be discouraged/banned, not the market itself. The justification for this is both to reduce the imposition of suffering on animals, and to promote the sentiment of kindness instead of an inclination towards killing. Similarly, human dwarf tossing and similar activities may be banned without incriminating markets as such.

17.6 EDUCATIONAL EQUALITY, UNIVERSITY ADMISSION, HOSPITAL PRIORITY, JURY SERVICE

'Universities typically admit students with the greatest talent and promise, not those who apply first or offer the most money for a place in the freshman class. Hospital emergency rooms treat patients according to the urgency of their condition, not according to the order of their arrival or their willingness to pay extra to be seen first. Jury duty is allocated by lottery; if you are called to serve, you can't hire someone else to take your place' (Sandel 2012a, p. 41). These non-economic, if not anti-efficiency methods of allocation appear reasonable and widely practiced, largely without objection. However, they, apparently, are inconsistent with my case for efficiency supremacy in specific issues as discussed in Chapter 5. Why the divergence?

A number of factors may be relevant for each of the aforementioned cases; I will focus briefly on the more important ones. For university admission, an overwhelming consideration is that the more talented are more likely to benefit from a university education. True, if we consider the simple (but unrealistic) case of perfect information, perfect rationality (no myopia, etc.), no liquidity constraint (anyone can borrow against her future incomes) etc., people who will benefit more from higher education will also be willing to pay more.[2] However, for the case of education, the assumption of perfect information and rationality is particularly suspect. Before being educated, people are typically not informed and rational enough to make the relevant judgement, even with the advice/decision of parents. There may also be important parental inadequacy of knowledge and a divergence of interest. For example, one reason for the excessive pressure to perform in examinations is the emphasis (by students, parents, and society) on certificates/degrees than on true knowledge and wisdom. By admitting students mainly, or even purely, in accordance to talent may cause some inefficiency in ignoring the willingness to pay, but may avoid much more inefficiency due to the combination of imperfect information, imperfect rationality, liquidity constraints, etc.

In addition, educational equality is very important. 'Sahn and Younger (2006) argue that reducing educational inequality is so powerful that it benefits well-being even if income inequality in a nation is still growing. For example, within Latin America the income gap between top and low earners is increasing, however educational inequality is shrinking and therefore well-being in the nation remains at least static' (McInerney et al. 2017, p. 211). Also, inequality perpetuated through generations may be perceived as particularly unacceptable.

For the case of hospital emergencies, the urgency of the condition should be the overwhelming consideration, while the consideration of the willingness to pay may cause fatal delays and perceived unfairness (even if based partly on some incorrect reasoning). Despite some inefficiency in ignoring the

---

[2]   On the importance of credit access to college enrolment, see, e.g., Solis (2017).

willingness to pay (Ng 1998), using the urgency criterion may be the appropriate way overall, at least for cases of emergency.

The case of jury service is mainly due to the desirability of having a representative sample to serve as jurors. If one may buy a replacement, most jurors will likely come from those with low values of time, and, hence, are not quite representative. However, for those with very high values of time and have some particular dislike for being a juror, fulfilling the jury service may be very costly. As representability in jury service is a desirable public good with positive, but not infinite, benefits, allowing the opting out at a high fee may be a better compromise, especially if the public finds it acceptable.

18

Concluding Remarks

It should be conceded that the communitarians have some valid concerns when they raise questions about the possible crowding out of intrinsic motivation and morality in the expanded use of the market. We should examine the relevant issues closely.

Consider the distinction between fees and fines by Sandel:

> It is worth considering the difference between a fine and a fee. Fines register moral disapproval, whereas fees are simply prices that imply no moral judgment. When the government imposes a fine for littering, it makes a statement that littering is wrong. Tossing a beer can into the Grand Canyon not only imposes cleanup costs. It reflects a bad attitude that we want to discourage. Suppose the fine is $100, and a wealthy hiker decides it is worth the convenience. He treats the fine as a fee and tosses his beer can into the Grand Canyon. Even if he pays up, we consider that he's done something wrong. By treating the Grand Canyon as an expensive dumpster, he has failed to appreciate it in an appropriate way (Sandel 2013, p. 128)

I quite agree with Sandel here. I morally disapprove of the hypothetical can tosser. However, the difference between fees and fines is not that large if both are set at their socially optimal level. Whatever one does, if she does not impose some costs on others, we (the society) do not want to charge her either a fee or a fine. We let her do what she wants. If she consumes an apple, she has to pay a price. Ideally, this price should reflect the full social costs of supplying an apple, including costs of growing, transportation, and environmental disruption, if any. The use of such an adequate price leads to social efficiency such that people will not over or under consume. In this function, a fee and a price are similar. In normal usage, a fee is a payment made to a professional person or to a professional or government body in exchange for services; the payment for goods is normally called a price. However, 'price' may also be used more generally.

A fine is quite different and usually carries both legal and moral sanctions, as Sandel correctly notes. Another difference between a fine and a fee/price is that the latter is normally paid for each and every transaction, but the former (a fine) is imposed only when the violator is caught. Given this likely much lower probability of payment, a fine should be much higher in amount to make the expected amount of payment (the amount of the fine times the probability of being caught) no smaller than the damages caused. Ignoring this difference in probability and, hence, the amount, are there other differences between a fee and a fine?[1]

Consider fees/fines for off-street parking in central business districts. Typically, a small fee is charged per quarter of an hour or per 5 minutes, up to a maximum time limit of, say, an hour. If you park for more than an hour, you may incur a fine of a much larger amount if caught. Here, we have a clear distinction that fees are charged for the legally stipulated parking time (like an hour), and fines are imposed for the violation of the legally imposed limit. Thus, the presence or absence of sanction, as noted by Sandel. In this normally practiced case, the distinction between a fee and a fine is quite clear. However, when I say that the difference between the two, if any, is not large, I am referring to the situation of socially optimal practice. I already argued in Chapter 5 that parking fees should be high enough to reflect the full opportunity costs. At the full-cost prices, people should be allowed to purchase however much parking time they like. Then, under this efficient arrangement, we only have parking fees, but no fines; the difference between fees and fines vanishes due to the absence of fines in this case.

Why does society want to charge people fees or impose fines for longer parking hours? Providing parking spaces costs money. For any given parking facility, the occupation of any space precludes others from parking at the same spot at the same time, i.e., the opportunity costs. If the supply of parking facilities is at the optimal level, the marginal costs of increasing space should equal the marginal opportunity costs. If someone wishes to park on a particular spot and pay the full cost of doing so, there is no good reason that she should be denied that opportunity. Thus, parking fines for metered parking should only be reserved for parking without paying the fees, which is similar to shoplifting.

---

[1] As noted by Migotti (2015, p. 373), to 'investigate the promise and pitfalls of the economic approach to the study of law as a whole, [is] an undertaking that would require a large book, not a medium-sized article', and our brief discussion of a few paragraphs cannot cover all relevant aspects.

This is not just limited to the issue of parking, we may also increase the use of fees/prices for many other areas instead of fines. We should only use fines if fees are inadequate or too costly. Where legal penalties are needed, we should use fines as far as possible, with additional penalties like whipping and imprisonment only when necessary, as discussed in Chapter 16.

Within limits, market expansion should be regarded as a sign of progress rather than as retrogression (Chapter 8). Sandel himself notes a specific instance of this progress with approval. Discussing the fines imposed by commercial video stores for late returns, he writes, 'a video store is a business. Its purpose is to make money by renting videos. So if I keep the movie longer and pay for the extra days, I should be regarded as a better customer, not a worse one. Or so I thought. Gradually, this norm has shifted. Video stores now seem to treat overdue charges as fees rather than fines' (Sandel 2012a, p. 68). My suggestion is that we may extend this business (mutually beneficial activities more generally) view to many other areas, changing many fines into fees/prices with higher benefits.

Then, why do I still morally disapprove of that hypothetical can tosser in the Grand Canyon? Partly, despite my pro-market arguments made in this book largely dictated by my head, I still have anti-market and anti-inequality sentiments at heart. Partly, motivating people to do the right things only through prices and fees may not be enough or may be very costly. Thus, we rely also partly on the morality of people. In this age where environmental crisis threatens our long-term survival, the need to be environmentally conscious is one of the most important moral imperatives. Tossing a beer can into the Grand Canyon is very much against this imperative. These imperatives are ultimately justified on their utilitarian or welfarist grounds, and, hence, does not contradict my welfarist stand.

Despite the environmental protection imperative, I am still in favour of the use of emission trading where emitters may exchange their emission quotas at a price. 'Legal environmentalists, on the other hand, have raised the concern that emissions trading will function as a price, and lead to a greater degradation of the environment' (Feldman & Teichman 2008, p. 234). This may be true. However, as long as the fees for emission are at sufficiently high levels, it is efficient for emitters to emit. We want to avoid excessive emission, not to minimize emission at excessive costs. Nevertheless, instead of setting emission quotas and allowing emitters the freedom to trade them, it would be much better to tax emission (i.e., setting emission fees or prices). If quotas are used instead, they should not be allocated free, especially not in accordance to the previous or existing levels of emission, as this would encourage future undesirable activities, not only in environmental areas, but also more generally.[2]

In a liberal society, we do not want to fine people unless it is important to discourage certain activities. Consider again the issue of lateness in picking up children, as discussed in Chapter 2. Most people have to be late occasionally. Instead of using fines or moral obligations to force parents to be always punctual, thus imposing high costs, including the possible causing of accidents, it would be much better for day care centres to charge extra fees for late pick-ups, as practiced in Singapore. We then extend the use of the market to this area. However, as most people concerned will be made better off, we should not deplore the expansion. The day care centres have extra business to do; the parents have extra services to use; some innocent third parties are saved from injury in accidents.

It is true that, 'In deciding whether to commodify a good, we must consider more than efficiency and fairness. We must also ask whether market norms will crowd out nonmarket norms, and if so, whether this represents a loss worth caring about' (Sandel 2013, p. 130). Where the crowding out is significant, it should be taken into account. As a welfarist and an economist, I naturally wish to examine both the costs and benefits involved, with these based ultimately on social welfare or the happiness of people. Not only the costs of crowding out, but also the possible benefits of crowding in, the direct benefits in being able to trade to the parties concerned, and not to mention the possible external effects on third parties. Additional studies of these various effects both analytically and empirically may be quite useful. Even before these studies, our tentative discussion already suggests that legalizing kidney sales and prostitution is likely most desirable, while blood donation may be kept without financial compensation, especially if the lesson that donation is good for the donors is taught at schools. We have also discussed a number of areas where the market has been under-utilized, including the excessive use of conscription (Chapter 13), the under-pricing of water (Chapter 15), and the underusing of fines instead of imprisonment (Chapter 16). Here, let us consider the

---

[2] One relevant consideration is the following argument on the use of prices versus fines/sanctions: 'If obtaining accurate information about external costs is cheaper for officials than obtaining accurate information about socially optimal behavior, then they should control the activity by pricing it; if the converse is true, then they should control the activity by sanctioning it' (Cooter 1984, p. 1533). As the socially optimal behaviour depends on the amount of the external costs, the latter option is really only relevant if there exists reliable community standards on roughly socially optimal behaviour. In the case of the can tosser in the Grand Canyon, the violation of standards is obvious.

general conceptual issues involved in deciding the desirability or otherwise of letting the market expand.

When two persons or parties enter into a mutually agreeable exchange without the use of force, false pretence, and without serious misinformation and irrationality, the presumption must be that both persons will benefit, or at least not lose, from the exchange. Then, under our welfarist philosophy (the non-welfarist like the Kantian ones are demolished in Appendix B), any objection must be based on some possible external costs imposed on third parties. These third parties may include animals, but must be sentients (otherwise, they have no welfare to speak of). The external costs may be the ones emphasized in traditional economic analysis like pollution. These are not the focus of the commodification discussion, as pollution occurs mainly in the production and consumption of traditional goods, rather than in the scope of operation for these controversial new goods such as organ sales, prostitution, blood donation, line standing/sitting, etc. Thus, the external costs concerned are the generalized ones, including the possible crowding out of intrinsic motivation and morality. In Chapter 3 and Appendix C, I formally extend economic analysis to allow for such generalized external costs. Thus, I am not against the communitarians in focusing on these possible costs. In Chapters 6 and 7, I discuss these costs, including the possible feeling of repugnance against organ sales and the crowding out of intrinsic motivation and morality in using the markets in certain controversial areas. My review of the relevant literature in these areas is that both crowding out and crowding in exist with the relative magnitudes largely uncertain and subject to variation depending on context.

If the external effects of allowing an expansion of the market are of opposing signs, with the net effects being of ambiguous sign, it seems clear that whether we should allow the expansion should depend on the direct effects, i.e., the benefits of the two parties to the exchange. These must be positive, but the absolute magnitudes may be either large or small. For the case of organ (kidney in particular) sales, the benefits involved are clearly overwhelming, as life saving is involved. For prostitution, the benefits are also clearly huge. Sexual desire is a very basic and important need. There are various factors making commercial sex necessary (including millions of men in China destined to be unable to get a wife, and millions of temporary migrants from rural to urban areas). Denying them their rights of buying sex is disgraceful and immoral. We may also see the point by comparing countries with legal (e.g., Australia, the Netherlands, Germany, and Nevada) and illegal prostitution (e.g., China). The incidence of prostitution is very high with or without legality. That people are willing to violate the law and social sanction to buy illegal sex shows how important it is. The legalization of prostitution must bring enormous benefits, not to mention the benefits of generating higher government revenues, reducing crimes and corruption, and a general higher standard of law observation. Thus, the cases for legalizing kidney (and many other organ) sales and prostitution are more than strongly justified, as argued in Chapters 9 and 12, and by many other authors.

The fact that kidney sales remain illegal in most countries is partly due to the mistaken feeling of repugnance by the public. They should sympathize with those who have to buy a kidney to save their life or that of a loved one, and with those who are desperate enough to sell one of their kidneys. The feeling of repugnance is partly due to our biological nature (Chapter 6) and partly due to our largely mistaken anti-market sentiments (Chapter 4). The bias against market expansion is further promoted by the largely mistaken views regarding inequality and exploitation or fairness. Exploitation normally does not take place in the absence of force, and/or serious misinformation and irrationality; inequality should mainly be addressed through general equality promotion policies, and not by restricting the functioning of the market (Chapter 5). These mistaken views are partly based on an inadequate understanding of economics.

In addition, if Beard et al. (2013) are correct, the failure to legalize kidney sales is a serious government failure, caused partly by the collusion to erect barriers to entry in order to protect a global cartel of transplant surgeons and allied specialized personnel that benefit greatly from the right to allocate organs for transplantation, as mentioned in Chapter 9. If this is true, the misuse of such power is highly shameful.

I am not an extreme 'big society, small government' free-market believer. Markets fail in many important aspects, environmental protection is the most important example. In addition, as most, if not all, individuals are not perfectly informed and rational, we need government intervention in areas like food safety regulation. Where problems of misinformation and irrationality are serious, the operation and expansion of the market may be counter-productive. However, for most of such cases, the default policy option should be information provision and regulation, rather than outright bans. Thus, we should have food safety regulation, and not ban the market transaction of food. Similarly, for the case of imperfect knowledge about the net overall effects of crowding out and crowding in, the burden of proof should fall upon those in favour of banning than those in favour of legalization of the relevant exchange. This is based partly on the clear positive effects of the direct parties involved (the two parties to a trade both benefit from it), and partly on the useful principle of liberalism. In the absence of overwhelming evidence to the contrary, we should not limit the freedom of individuals, including their right to trade.

People with an egalitarian inclination (which applies to most people, myself included) are instinctively and culturally educated to be pro-poor, anti-rich, anti-market, and, hence, tend to prefer some egalitarian allocation, even at some high costs of efficiency. Thus, many people find queuing, lotteries, first-come-first-served, etc. more acceptable or desirable, instead of using the market methods of pricing and willingness to pay. Thus, 'the willingness to stand in line ... may be a better indicator of who really wants to attend than the willingness to pay' (Sandel 2012a, p. 32). This naïve and shallow thinking largely ignores the point that the costs of standing in line are purely wasted, benefitting no one, while the higher prices paid by those willing to pay could be used to provide for a larger and better supply. Moreover, by using the more efficient method of willingness to pay, fairness and equality need not be sacrificed if overall equality is promoted, such that all income groups could be made better off, as explained in Chapter 5. This is a point ignored not only by the anti-commodification theorists, but also by the defenders of markets.

In addition, as argued in Chapter 8, the use of the market contributes to efficiency, economic growth, and the associated increases in income, education, liberal attitudes, and a better understanding of economics. This, in turn, promotes a broader acceptance of the use of markets across a larger scope, creating a self-reinforcing cycle that is increasingly beneficial to society in the long run. Thus, unless the expansion really causes serious negative effects that overwhelm the positive ones (yet to be shown in any substantial scope), we should in general view the expansion of markets as a laudable progress, rather than something to be deplored.

Welfare versus Preference[*]

Across many instances in this text, for the sake of simplicity, we take (individual) utility (which represents the preference of the individual concerned) as the same as welfare. There are, however, three reasons why this may not always be so.

First, preference may differ from welfare due to ignorance and imperfect foresight. While an individual may prefer X to Y believing he will be better off in X than in Y, it may turn out to be the converse the other way round. This is the question of *ex ante* estimate versus *ex post* welfare and is widely recognized as obviously true.[1] While the *ex ante* concept is relevant for explaining behaviour, it is the *ex post* one which is his actual welfare that is of value.

Second, the preference of an individual may not only be affected by his own welfare, but may also be affected by his consideration for the welfare of other individuals (including animals). Thus, it is possible for a person to personally have a higher happiness level in Y than in X, yet prefer and choose X over Y because she believes that other people are happier in X than in Y. While it is true that the belief that other people are happy may make her happy, these positive feelings may not be strong enough to outweigh the loss that she has to suffer for changing from Y to X. However, for her to continue to choose X on the basis of her moral concern is indicative of what we term non-affective altruism, a true and highest form of altruism.

For example, a person may vote for party X, knowing that she will be better off with party Y in government. The reason she votes for X is that she believes that the majority of the people will be much better off with X. This may make

---

[*] This appendix is partly based on Ng (1979/1983, 1999, 2004b).

[1] The distinction by Kahneman et al. 19979781107194946rfa_Revised.docx - rfa_188 Harsanyi (1997) also emphasized that informed preferences should be used for normative purposes instead of actual preferences. I went further by using welfare or happiness (Ng 1999).

her *feel* better (affective altruism) and is a form of external effect. However, this external benefit may not be important enough to overbalance, in terms of her subjective happiness, her personal loss, say, in income, under X. She may yet vote for X due to her moral concern (non-affective altruism) for the majority. To give an even more dramatic example, consider an individual who expects to lead a very happy life. When her country is being invaded, she may volunteer for a mission which will bring her the certainty of death. The prospect of being a citizen of a conquered nation, especially with a guilty conscience of failing to volunteer for a mission, may not be too bright. But overall she may still expect to be fairly happy leading such a life. Yet, she chooses death for the sake of her fellow countrymen. She is not maximizing her own welfare. (This source of divergence between welfare and preference due to a consideration for others is discussed in Ng 1969, p. 43, 1999, and Sen 1973.)

Some economists have difficulty in seeing this distinction between preference and welfare, saying that whenever an individual prefers X to Y, he must be, or at least believe himself to be happier in X than in Y. This difficulty completely baffles me. Clearly, a father (or mother) may sacrifice his (her) happiness for the welfare of his (her) children. I cannot see why similar sacrifices cannot be made for a friend or a relative, and further for a countryman or any human being, and, finally, any sentient. For some interviews with real-life altruists see Monroe 1996, Part I. For a survey of evidence for true altruism, see Hoffman 1981. One type of evidence is that a person is more likely to help others when he/she is the only person around, contrary to the egoistic explanation of helping on the ground of approval gaining (cf. Charness & Rabin 2002).

It may be doubted that the existence of true non-affective altruism is inconsistent with Darwinian natural selection. However, as preferences are the result of both cultural and genetic inheritance, one can demonstrate that pro-social traits could have evolved under the joint influence of cultural and genetic transmission, as shown by Boyd & Richerson 1985, Sober & Wilson 1998, and Bowles 2000.[2]

If some readers still doubt the existence of truly non-affective altruism, they are likely to be convinced that in fact they themselves possess some degree of non-affective altruism by considering the following hypothetical

---

[2] Moreover, 'highly developed human capacities for insider-outsider distinctions and cultural uniformity within communities greatly increase the likely importance of group selection of genetically transmitted traits and hence the evolutionary viability of group-beneficial traits' (Bowles & Gintis 2000, p. 1419). On the evolutionary basis of altruism towards one's relatives, see Hamilton (1964) and Bergstrom (1996).

choice. Like Einstein's thought experiments, such choices cannot be criticized for being unrealistic. Suppose that you are asked by the Devil to press either button A or B within two seconds. You know with certainty that one of the following will happen depending on which button you press. Within the two seconds, you will be so preoccupied with pressing the right button such that your welfare will be zero despite the button that you press. After pressing, you will lose your memory of the present world and, hence, will not have feelings of guilt, a warm glow or the like related to which button you press.

- A: You will go to Bliss with a welfare level of 1,000 trillion units. Everyone else will go to Hell with a welfare level of minus 1,000 trillion units each.
- B: You will go to Bliss Minus with a welfare level of 999 trillion units. Everyone else will go Nice-land with a welfare level of 99 trillion units each.
- C: If you do not press either button within the two seconds, you and everyone else will go to Hell.

By construction, choosing A will maximize your welfare but most people will choose B out of non-affective altruism. If you still think that you would choose A, change Bliss Minus into a welfare level of 999.999 trillion units. If you still opt for A, I have to concede that you are not altruistic non-affectively. But how could you have the heart to condemn all others to Hell for a fractional increase in your own welfare? (In my view, the existence and degree of non-affective altruism marks true morality.)

Third, an individual may have irrational preferences. The preference of an individual is here defined irrational if he prefers X over Y despite the fact that his welfare is higher in Y than in X, and his preference is unaffected by considerations of the welfare of other individuals (any sentient can be an individual here), or by ignorance or imperfect foresight. The definition of irrationality here is such so as to make the three factors discussed here exhaustive causes of divergence between preference and welfare.

While few, if any, individuals are perfectly ignorant and irrational, some degree of ignorance (or imperfect information) and imperfect rationality clearly apply to most individuals[3]. However, some alleged irrationalities could be simply due to errors, computational limitations, and incorrect

---

[3] See Cohen (1983), Evans & Over (1996), Kahneman & Tversky (1996), and Stein (1996) for reviews of the relevant literature in philosophy and psychology.

norm by the experimenters (Stanovich & West 2000). There are a number of causes that may make preferences differ from happiness other than ignorance and a concern for the welfare of others, and, hence, irrational according to the definition here. On some factors accounting for irrational preferences, see Ng 2004b, Section 1.3.

Happiness as the Only Ultimate Value: A Moral Philosophical Perspective[*]

Since the normative foundation of this book is based exclusively on welfare or happiness (defined to be synonyms), this appendix provides a case in favour of happiness as the only thing that is ultimately of intrinsic value. The meaning of happiness is first discussed in Section B.1. The remaining sections are concerned with the main point that all queries to our basic principle can be explained by the effects on our happiness in the future or of others (hence really no qualification) and that their apparent acceptability is due to our imperfect rationality or the like.

B.1 WHAT IS HAPPINESS?

I use happiness in its subjective, affective, or feeling sense. Anyone must be capable of feeling to have happiness. Stone, water, and, almost certainly, all plants do not have happiness. You may perceive that the colour of the cover of this book is green. However, if you feel neither positively nor negatively for this colour, your feeling is neutral to you. Your happiness in this feeling is zero. Thus, one needs to have affective feelings (such as pleasure or pain) to have happiness. Your feeling of happiness or unhappiness may also differ in intensity at any point in time. For a given period, say from the time you wake up this morning until now, you may draw a diagram depicting the situation of your affective feeling. Let the horizontal axis be time and the vertical axis be the intensity of your affective feeling. Then the horizontal axis represents zero or no affective feeling. The higher up from this line of neutrality, the higher is the intensity of your positive affective feeling; the

[*] This appendix is partly based on Ng (1990).

lower down from this line, the higher is the intensity of your negative affective feeling. Draw a curve representing the intensity of your affective feeling over different points in time over this period. Your net happiness over this period is then the areas above neutrality minus the areas below neutrality.

This affective or subjective definition of happiness is called 'hedonic' in philosophy. However, for the general public, the term hedonism has a tendency to be interpreted as being exclusively or excessively concerned with current pleasure, and to disregard the future and the happiness of others. Thus, I try to avoid using 'hedonic'. If properly interpreted in its philosophical sense, there is nothing wrong with hedonism. What is wrong is harming others, not enjoying yourself.

Our definition of happiness here is purely subjective. Many scholars do not subscribe to this concept, based on a variety of grounds; all unacceptable in my view. Here, let us discuss just three main (somewhat interrelated) grounds for diverging from or qualifying the purely subjective definition.

First, from Aristotle to Adler et al. (2017a), many knowledgeable scholars require, on top of the component of subjective affective feelings, some consistency with morality to qualify for happiness or eudemonia. In my view, this unnecessarily confuses two different concepts. Being happy and being moral are two quite different concepts. One may be happy without being moral and one may be moral without being happy. Lumping the two together leads to confusion. It may be socially very desirable for us to encourage people to be moral, and/or convince them that one important way to be happy is to be moral, etc. But the two are conceptually very distinct. Essentially, to be immoral is to cause unnecessary unhappiness or a reduction in happiness to others. We should use happiness to define morality, not use morality to define happiness. The latter is standing things on their head, and will likely lead to unclear thinking.[1]

If we view Aristotle's eudemon as 'an ethical doctrine that would provide guidelines for how to live' (Ryff & Singer 2008, p. 15), then it may be a very good guide, especially from a social perspective. However, viewed as what is ultimately of value, it is debatable. Whether it is eudemon, self-actualization, self-autonomy, etc., if the resulting outcomes involve much more misery than happiness, such that net happiness is a large negative sum, it is ultimately not a desirable world in the intrinsic sense.

---

[1] Thus, I find the contrast between utility and morality, as discussed in the discussion forum on Amitai Etzioni (Amitai Etzioni – Twenty years of 'The Moral Dimension: Toward a New Economics'. *Socio-Economic Review*, 6: 135–173) that fails to recognize points made in this Appendix as rather shallow.

To avoid misunderstanding, but at the risk of repetition, let us clarify one important point. The need to take into account the effects on others and future effects does not mean that the happiness of any individual for any period has to be adjusted to take into account these indirect effects on others and in the future. If we required such adjustment, it would become something similar to Aristotle's eudemon. Rather, we take the happiness of any individual in any period as such, unadjusted, and as of intrinsic value. Thus, if Mr A enjoyed his binge drinking one evening, that happy feeling then was of intrinsic value. However, if his binge drinking led to his drunk driving that killed/wounded Ms B, the great suffering imposed on Ms B or her big loss of future happiness should be taken into account. Such accounting may thus lead us to agree that binge drinking should be discouraged or even banned. This is justified based on the negative effects on others and in the future, not on having to adjust the happy feelings of Mr A that evening. In other words, no distinction is made between personal happiness and moral happiness (or eudemon). Happiness is happiness. But the morality of a certain act does not depend only on the effects on the happiness of the person concerned, but also on the effects on others and in the future.

Second, many scholars want to add some objective component to the definition of happiness. For example, as described by Adler et al. (2017a, pp. 24–25), 'The most salient objective approach among psychologists is the "eudaimonic", or self-realization, paradigm, where well-being is construed as an on-going, dynamic process of effortful living by means of engagement in *activities* perceived as meaningful (e.g., Ryan & Deci, 2001). Advocates of this approach maintain that living a life of virtue, understood as developing the valuable parts of one's human nature, or actualizing one's inherent potentials in the service of something greater, constitutes the good life for an individual (Boniwell & Henry, 2007; Delle Fave, Massimini & Bassi, 2011). From this perspective, positive experiences are not in themselves important for a good life, and are relevant only insofar as they are involving appreciating objectively worthwhile ways of being or functioning.' Similarly, Adler et al. (2017a, p. 22) defines happiness or well-being as '*everything that makes a person's life . . . goes well*' (italics original).

Some happiness researchers (e.g., Kahneman 1999, Di Tella et al. 2003, Köszegi & Rabin 2008, Layard 2005, 2010) are in favour of the hedonic concept while others (e.g., Ryff 1989, Waterman 1993) are in favour of the eudemonic concept. The majority seem to regard both as relevant. The problem with the 'eudemonic', 'prudential', and/or 'objective' approach to the definition of happiness is that it confuses happiness with (objective) factors that are usually conducive to happiness, and elements that are usually important for happiness in the future and of others. To reduce the disturbance to the common meaning of the concept of happiness, and to be consistent with the universally accepted point (again from Aristotle to Adler et al. 2017a) that happiness is intrinsically valuable (the controversial part is that it is ultimately the only thing that is intrinsically valuable, a point to be discussed in Section B.2), happiness must be subjective. However, our subjective happiness is affected by a host of objective factors. The different ways or methods we lead our lives may also have very different effects on our own health and, hence, happiness in the future, and may also have different effects on the happiness of others. For example, a person may be happy getting drunk, but may do harm to his health (hence reducing happiness in the future) or cause harm to others by drink driving.

Perhaps, Aristotle was largely right that a life of contemplation and virtue, and actualizing one's inherent nature (Delle Fave et al. 2011), is the right way to well-being or happiness (Norton 1976), and that usually the result of eudemonic action is hedonic happiness (Kashdan et al. 2008). 'At the opposite end, a selfish individual who has little regard for another's welfare and is primarily, or even exclusively, concerned with the pursuit of his personal interest ... will usually fail to achieve both his own happiness and that of others' (Ricard 2017, pp. 160–161). Lasting happiness is associated more with selflessness rather than self-centredness (Dambrun & Ricard 2011). Disinterested kindness to others provides profound satisfaction (Seligman 2002). All these wise observations and research results are very important for individuals and societies in terms of promoting a good life. However, as requirements for the definition of happiness, they serve to confuse. For example, they lead to such assertions as 'psychological wellbeing cannot exist just in your own head: it is a combination of feeling good as well as actually having meaning, engagement, good relationships, and accomplishment' (Adler et al. 2017b, p. 122). It is simpler and clearer to regard your happiness or psychological well-being as just existing in your own head, but your engagement, relationships, accomplishment, etc. may affect your own happiness in the future and that of others.

Adler et al. (2017b, p. 123) allege that the purely hedonic concept of happiness ('just in your head') 'stumbles fatally on the fact that human beings persist in having children: couples without children are likely happier, subjectively, than childless couples, and so if all humans pursued ... [such] subjective happiness, the species would have died out long ago'. Clearly, this is due to the lack of consideration for the happiness of people/children in the future. A life with children may be less happy, but may be a better life as it gives rise to future people with additional happiness.

Thus, if happiness in the future is not ignored, the hedonic concept of happiness does not 'stumble'.[2]

True, 'Objective and subjective indicators of well-being are both important' (Stiglitz et al. 2010, p. 15). However, the objective indicators are important only because: 1. they are indirect indicators of subjective well-being (SWB); 2. they are important for SWB in the future; or 3. they are important for the SWB of others. One of the reasons the second factor may be important may be because they contribute to the prevention of government's manipulation of 'people's preferences and/or knowledge' (Unanue 2017, p. 75). Similar to this possible usefulness of objective indicators of happiness, the 'operational definition' of happiness (Thin et al. 2017, p. 40) may also be useful. However, properly understood, it should be 'operational *indicators*', not *definition* of happiness.[3]

Third, many scholars (including Sumner 1996, Feldman 2004, and Chekola 2007) want to include some cognitive element into happiness or SWB. Some define SWB as being inclusive of both the affective happiness and the cognitive satisfaction with life. I find this confusing, if not misleading. I find the definition of happiness, welfare, and SWB as synonymous in the affective sense, most consistent with common usage and most useful analytically. Then, usually one's life satisfaction (defined cognitively) may largely be affected by one's own happiness, but also by one's belief in contribution to society (ultimately and rationally, should be to happiness). Then, it is at least conceptually possible for most, or even all, individuals in a society to be unhappy (net happiness being negative) and yet to have high life satisfaction. This may be due to each believing that he or she has made a huge contribution to the happiness of others. Yet, due to imperfect knowledge or misfortunes, the believed (perhaps mistakenly) contributions did not really materialize into happiness of most individuals. At least in outcome, such a society of unhappy individuals is miserable, despite high life satisfaction. Life satisfaction is not meaningless and may be useful for certain purposes,

---

[2] On the relevance of future people, especially potential future people, see Ng (1989). On the other 'stumbling' allegations such as those based on *Brave New World*, see Ng (1990, 1999, 2000, chapter 2).

[3] For discussions of the various concepts of happiness, see, e.g., Veenhoven (1984, 2000), Kim-Prieto et al. (2005), Brülde (2007), and Haybron (2007). The subjective concept I use is what philosophers call the hedonistic theory, or what Haybron (2000) calls 'psychological happiness'. This is distinct from 'prudential happiness' (or 'eudemonic') and differs from the concept of happiness as life satisfaction itself or something similar, e.g., 'happiness as involving the realizing of global desires, a life plan, requires a level of rationality to develop' (Chekola 2007, p. 67). My concept is a purely affective view, a mental-state concept, and internalist (in your head/mind). For a recent anthology on the various concepts of happiness, see Mulnix & Mulnix (2015).

including the potential to affect happiness in the future. Happiness and life satisfaction also tend to be mutually reinforcing. However, ultimately, it is happiness that is of intrinsic value. Thus, I prefer to focus mainly on happiness, especially when the two differ, as discussed further in the next section.

B.2   HAPPINESS AS THE ONLY INTRINSIC VALUE

A number of reasons may make life satisfaction diverge from happiness. In particular, person A may have low or even negative (net) happiness, but yet have high life satisfaction as she believes that she has made significant contributions towards increasing the happiness of others. Whether this belief is correct or not, it can be argued that only her happiness, not her life satisfaction, should be counted as the ultimate social objective. For simplicity, consider only the extreme cases where her belief is either entirely correct or entirely wrong. The intermediate cases are also taken care of by the combination of the arguments for each of the two pure cases.

If A's belief is incorrect, she did not actually contribute to raising the happiness of other individuals. Her belief that she did so may increase her own happiness. If so, that increased happiness is already counted in the social objective that takes account of her happiness. If A's belief is correct, she did contribute to raising the happiness of other individuals. The higher happiness levels of other individuals from her contribution are already accounted for in a social objective function[4] that takes account of the welfare or happiness levels of all individuals. ('Welfare' and 'happiness' are used interchangeably as a happiness definition of welfare is adopted.)[5] Knowing or believing that her contribution has made other individuals happier probably makes A happier. However, A's happiness level may remain low, although her life satisfaction level may be fairly high. It should be the low happiness level rather than the high life satisfaction level that should count towards social welfare. Why? Suppose person B does voluntary social work that contributes to the happiness of some elderly people. Obviously, the higher happiness levels of these elderly

---

[4]   Any Paretian social welfare (or objective) function is increasing when it comes to individual welfare levels. A utilitarian social welfare function sums all individual welfare levels with equal weights. For an argument in favour of a utilitarian social welfare function, see Ng (1975, 1990, 2000, chapter 5). The case for welfarism is in appendix B.

[5]   Welfare has been used in a variety of senses. Here, only the happiness concept of welfare is used. Even for those who regard welfare as happiness, usually welfare is used to denote longer-term happiness. However, either holding the time period concerned the same, or taking account of relevant effects in the future, we may use welfare and happiness interchangeably, as already remarked in the text earlier.

people count towards social welfare. Moreover, if B himself gets happiness from the social work and/or from knowing/believing that he contributed to the happiness of these elderly people, his higher happiness level should also be accounted for in social welfare. Thus, it is not because the increased happiness of the individuals that A has helped have already been accounted for in social welfare, which precludes the accounting of higher life satisfaction for A; rather, it is simply that happiness should be accounted for, but life satisfaction should not; why?

Happiness, either in the form of pleasure of the flesh, like eating delicious food or having sex, or in the form of spiritual fulfilment is what the individual directly enjoys and, hence, is inherently valuable to the individual. Each and every individual wants to have a high level of happiness for his or her own sake. Happiness is valuable in itself. This is self-evident to anyone. In fact, this trait of being able to enjoy and suffer is so important for our survival that individuals completely without this capability are extremely rare, if they have ever existed. Thus, we do not need any philosophical arguments to justify this (that happiness is valuable in itself). However, we do have to justify the point that, ultimately speaking, only happiness is valuable and that all other valuable things derive their values from their contributions to happiness.

First, it may be pointed out that arguments on what is good, valuable, or ought to be done, etc. belong to the normative sphere.[6] In contrast to the positive sphere where statements/judgements may be either true or false in some objective sense, value judgements can only be persuasive or not. Thus, it is not logically possible for one to *prove* that only happiness is ultimately or intrinsically valuable, or to prove the truth of any other value judgement. One could only try to make the arguments persuasive. Moreover, noting that different people have different views on such normative issues, one does not expect complete agreement.

Let us try to see the persuasiveness or even the compellingness of the main point in a number of steps.

Step 1: In an Isolated World of No Affective Sentients, Nothing Is of Any Normative Significance

Here, an isolated world means a world/universe that is completely isolated from any other existence in the sense that there exists no informational or other flows between it and others, but also with no causal connections (such as

---

[6] I use the term 'normative' in its wider sense, being in contrast to 'positive' and inclusive of elements of 'evaluative' and 'prescriptive'.

through gravity) with any other existence. We may conduct our analysis along the lines of Einstein's thought experiments; the question of realism is not relevant. One way to imagine this isolated world is to assume that the real world does not exist. That isolated world is the only existence and, hence, has no informational or any other causal connections with others. If the whole world has no affective sentients from beginning to end (if there was a beginning and an end), it seems clear that nothing is of any normative significance. Here, affective sentients are beings that are capable of enjoying happiness and/or suffering pain/unhappiness. Whether that world is getting warmer or colder, more chaotic or more orderly, etc., nothing will be made better or worse off. It is of no normative significance.

Step 2: Other Things Being Equal, It Is Undesirable to Inflict Pain/ Unhappiness; It Is Desirable/Valuable to Have Happiness

If pain/unhappiness is inflicted upon some affective sentient beings without anything desirable, either directly or indirectly, it is clearly undesirable. Similarly, if happiness can be enjoyed without causing anything negative directly or indirectly, it is desirable, as affective sentient beings (like us humans) can testify to that, at least in principle. This does not rule out the possible desirability of pain/unhappiness that leads to more happiness in the future and/or for others and the possible undesirability of happiness that leads to more unhappiness in the future and/or for others.

Step 3: If Something Is of Normative Significance, It Must Be, Ultimately Speaking, Due to Some Effects on the Enjoyment of Happiness or the Suffering of Pain/Unhappiness

Comparing Steps 1 and 2, it can be seen that, if nothing is of any normative significance in a world of no affective sentients, then in a world with normative significance, the normative significance must be due, directly or indirectly, to the affective feelings (happiness and/or unhappiness) of the affective sentients, since this is the only difference between the two cases.

Consider the situation illustrated in Figure 1 where a host of factors may directly or indirectly affect the affective feelings (happiness and pain) of sentients. These factors and doing things that may affect these factors may thus be important or being of normative significance from Step 2. However, if the top box (affective feelings) does not exist right from the beginning and to eternity, then we are in the world of Step 1 and nothing is of any normative significance. Thus, in the world where affective feelings exist and something

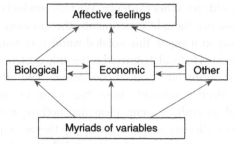

FIGURE 1 Affective Feelings of Sentience

may be of normative significance, the normative significance must be based on, or due to, ultimately speaking, the effects on the normatively important affective feelings (top box in Figure 1).

Consider an analogy illustrated in Figure 2 where the final profits of a firm is shown in the top box. The analogy is not perfect because things other than the final profits may be significant, even just to the firm (or its owners). Thus, to make the analogy hold, we have to either assume that things other than profits are insignificant, or hold all other things that may be significant unchanged in the comparison, as indicated in the top right box. For example, if the firm is concerned with the welfare of its employees over and above the effects on its final profits, the welfare of its employees must be among those factors that are held unchanged in our comparison. Apart from these factors that are held unchanged, many variables may affect the final profits of the firm directly or indirectly. Assume that, apart from those factors held constant, the firm is only concerned with its final profits and not, say, with its cash flow and sales except for their effects on profits. These effects are usually on the future period. However, to abstract away from the complication of dynamic illustration, we take all the effects as occurring simultaneously or in the a-temporal framework of Figure 2. Then, any combined changes (e.g. some decrease in cash holdings plus some increase in stock holdings) that leave the final profits unchanged must be deemed as equally desirable and, hence, of no evaluative consequences to the firm. Changes that are of consequence must be those that do affect the final profits.

An exogenous change that increases the sales of the firm is usually of positive consequence to the final profits. Thus, some middle managers, especially those in charge of sales, may think it is highly desirable to advertise to increase sales. However, this endogenous increase has

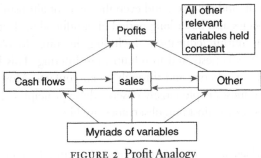

FIGURE 2 Profit Analogy

significant costs in the form of advertising outlays. The top management should know that even highly effective advertising may not be desirable if it is too costly. What is desirable or not has to be judged by the net effects on the final profits. Similarly, for the case of Figure 1, what is normatively desirable or not has to be judged by the final effects on affective feelings, ultimately speaking.

Step 4: Something that Is Not in Itself Happiness or Unhappiness but that May Affect Happiness or Unhappiness either Directly or Indirectly May Also Be of Normative Significance

If I surreptitiously put a tasteless poison in your coffee, it may have no effect on your enjoyment of that cup of coffee. However, if it makes you seriously sick the next day, it is obviously a bad thing for me to do that, at least if you deserve no punishment and no other benefits comes from this. More indirectly, telling a certain lie may in itself cause no or little unhappiness or may even save some embarrassment, but it may have the indirect undesirable effects of reducing the degree of trust between people and even the degree of observance of other basic moral principles in general. Hence, this may eventually have more negative effects on happiness and is undesirable as a result.

Step 5: Normative (Including Moral) Principles May Be Fostered to Promote Happiness and/or Reduce Suffering or to Promote Things that May Be Indirectly Conducive to Happiness

Due to the reliance of the human species on sociability (including cooperation in hunting) for survival, we have inborn (naturally selected or God-made) abilities like the capability to learn languages, the instinct for moral sentiments and outrages, and even the gene for altruism[7]. However, as the human species also has a long period of childhood for learning, we also rely much on nurture/education, including learning to observe certain principles such as honesty and to refrain from littering. This learning takes place at home, in schools, and through social contacts. Most of us benefit greatly because most people largely observe these principles. Thus, the peer and social pressures against non-observance are big.

Step 6: The Adherence of Certain Outdated Normative Principles May Cause Great Suffering

As circumstances change, certain previously sensible normative principles may no longer be conducive to happiness and may even cause great suffering. Just a single example suffices to convince. At least in ancient China (for a millennium from the Southern Song Dynasty to the recent Qing Dynasty), it was regarded as immoral for a woman to marry twice, even after the early death of her husband (while a man must remarry to have offspring and could even have more than one wife simultaneously). The long tradition to continue adhering to this moral principle caused great suffering and was the theme of many realistic novels. Very slowly, but eventually, this principle was given up over the early decades of the 1900s.

Step 7: Just Like People May Adhere to Inappropriate Normative Principles, People, Including Moral Philosophers, May Inappropriately Believe that Certain Things Are Valuable Independent of, and Over and Above, their Contributions to Happiness

Influenced both by our inborn inclinations (including moral intuitions for equality and justice) and our upbringings, many people (including learned moral philosophers) may mistakenly believe in the normative significance of things other than happiness, and independent of their contributions to happiness. This is a mistake (in the normative sense, being inappropriate, unpersuasive, or even wrong, rather than being false) since it violates Step 3. This may need some elaboration.

---

[7] Evolutionary biology suggests that we are probably programmed to be sociable, increasing our fitness for survival and reproduction. In fact, even the gene that gives those who possess it a high in helping others has been found; see Bachner-Melman et al. 2005. This, however, does not negate the importance of upbringing and social influences.

Step 3 says that if something is of normative significance, it must ultimately be due to some effects on the enjoyment of happiness or the suffering of pain/unhappiness. These include the effects on future happiness/unhappiness and the effects on the happiness/unhappiness of others, including other individuals and possibly other affective sentients. When we examine closely normative principles/arguments supposedly based on considerations independent of happiness, we can always find that either they are really related, directly or indirectly, to effects on future happiness or effects on the happiness of others, or that the principles are not acceptable.[8] To consider all such principles/arguments would require a monograph in itself. Here, let us just consider some examples that can be discussed and answered together in Section B.3.[9]

B.3 ANSWERING SOME OBJECTIONS

One is the multi-century-old argument that it is better to be the unhappy Socrates than a happy pig. A more modern version of this or a similar argument is the so-called pleasure- or experience-machine argument (Nozick 1974); most people prefer their less happy current situations than to be hooked-up to pleasure machines that will give them much more machine-induced pleasurable feelings. Another argument is on the common dis-preference for happiness based on falsehood. An example is a happy woman whose husband is disloyal to her. These and similar arguments are apparently very persuasive, making modern welfarists and utilitarians to be largely preference (or attitudinal) utilitarians rather than the classical hedonistic ones. Welfarism maximizes social welfare as a function only of individual welfare; utilitarianism goes for a social welfare function (SWF) that is just the unweighted, or equally weighted, sum of individual happiness. Classical utilitarianism maximizes the unweighted sum of individual happiness; preference utilitarianism maximizes the unweighted sum of individual preferences or utilities. The principle of happiness as the only appropriate ultimate objective is defended against these arguments in the rest of this appendix.[10]

---

8 Thus, Mill's (1848) distinction of happiness of higher and lower quality is either reducible to quantities of happiness when the indirect effects on others and in the future are taken into account or not really acceptable.

9 For these and similar arguments, see, e.g., Elster (1983), Sen (1987), Sumner (1996), Jost & Shiner (2002), Brülde (2007), and Chekola (2007). In contrast, see, e.g., Silverstein (2000), Feldman (2004), Crisp (2006), Tännsjö (2007), and Haines (2010).

10 For hedonistic utilitarianism, one needs the additional unweighted sum of utility/happiness not discussed in this appendix. It is argued for in Ng (2000, chapter 5).

Consider Mr C. He believes that, in the presence of uncertainty, the appropriate thing to do is to maximize the expected welfare. Welfare is used interchangeably with net happiness. For simplicity, consider only choices that do not affect the welfare of others. Suppose you put C in the privacy of a hotel room with an attractive, young, and willing lady. C can choose to go to bed with her or not to. C knows that the former choice involves a small, but not negligible, risk of contracting AIDS. He also calculates that the expected welfare of this choice is negative. Nevertheless, he agrees that, provided the lady is beautiful enough and the risk not too high (although high enough to reduce his expected welfare), he will choose to go to bed with her. This choice of C, although irrational (at least from the welfare point of view), is far from atypical. Rather, I am confident that it applies to at least 70% of adult males, the present writer included. Men are genetically programmed to want to make love to attractive (usually implying healthy) women in their reproductive ages who have not yet conceived (simultaneously explaining why slimness in waist and young girls are attractive), since this helps them to pass on their genes.

After the evolution of consciousness to help in our making of on-the-spot choices (like fight or flight), evolution (or God) ensures that consciousness-guided choices are consistent with fitness (for survival and reproduction), by also endowing conscious species with affective feelings. So, activities consistent with fitness (like eating nutritious food when hungry and having sex with reproductive members of the opposite sex) are rewarded with pleasures and fitness-reducing activities (like injuries to the body) or are penalized with pain. Thus, fitness-consistent choices are usually also welfare-maximizing choices. However, since the ultimate decisive factor is fitness, the coincidence is not 100% (Ng 1995). In particular, programming the organism to be excessively (from the viewpoint of welfare maximization) in fear of death or to be excessively inclined to mate may be fitness-maximizing. This explains why a man like Mr C will likely choose to have sex with the attractive girl even if he knows that this reduces his expected welfare. This example suggests that the choice or preference of a person may not be a perfect guide to what should ultimately be valuable to her/him.

Should our ultimate objective be happiness or should it be our preference? Preference may diverge from happiness or welfare for three reasons: a concern for the welfare of others (possibly including animals), ignorance, and irrationality (or imperfect rationality), as discussed in Appendix A. These three factors are exhaustive as 'irrational preference' is defined to be the preference against one's own welfare due neither to ignorance nor a concern for the welfare of others. Obviously, if the divergence is due to ignorance, happiness should prevail over preference. If due to a concern for the welfare of others, a distinction should be made between the individual and the society. It is admirable for an individual to sacrifice her own happiness for the welfare of others. However, for society, the social objective should take into account the welfare of all individuals. For simplicity, we ignore animal welfare here. If the divergence is due to irrational preference, it is also clear that happiness should prevail, since preferences based on irrationality are similar to those based on ignorance. For the case of this divergence due to the genetically programmed tendency to mate, it may be pointed out that our (i.e. persons like you and me) welfare is the affective feelings that we enjoy over our life time, not that of our genes that 'aim' at fitness. We should aim at happiness, not fitness (although, the maximization of long-term welfare requires sufficiently high fitness.) We are the feeling persons, not the unfeeling genes. Thus, Mr C, in his calm and reflective moment, may agree that it is in his interest to resist going to bed with the attractive lady to avoid contracting AIDS. However, due to biology, few men can successfully resist in that hotel room. However, for the ultimate social objective, we should go with his reflective moment rather than the moment that he was tempted by the attractive lady in the hotel room; we should go with our feeling persons, not with the unfeeling genes. Although the possible feeling of great pleasure for Mr C in that hotel bed should be counted, it is likely more than offset by the expected decrease in welfare in contracting AIDS.

Just as we are born with the excessive inclination to mate, we are also genetically programmed with certain traits that tend to increase our fitness even if our happiness may be compromised somewhat, perhaps at the margin. One such trait is our inclination to do things rather than to just enjoy existing accomplishments or to just enjoy the stimulation of a pleasure machine. The drive to achieve helps us to increase our fitness. This drive is also much reinforced by education and social influences. We find such drives so natural and so important that we do not know that, when such drives conflict with our happiness, they (usually only at the margin, as too low a drive level is bad both for fitness and for welfare) are really bad for our true interest, just like the excessive drive to mate in the case of Mr C in his hotel room. Thus, while it may be true that most persons will reject the pleasure machine option that offers many times the amount of happy feelings, the choice of this option (assuming no external costs on others) is the more rational one, just like the choice of not sleeping with the lady.

Will I choose the pleasure machine option? Still not, because I believe that I can contribute to the welfare of others through my work. If I cannot and if hooking-up to the machine will not put anyone in misery, I will in fact gladly choose to hook-up![11] Similarly, I prefer to be a happy pig rather than be a learned philosopher if my philosophy cannot help others, directly or indirectly, to increase happiness by a lot more. My choice may be the exception. However, as already explained, most people (the present author included) are not perfectly rational due to our genetic programmes and our upbringings.

We are similarly programmed and influenced socially to be curious about the truth. Thus, our preference for 'authentic happiness' or dis-preference for a happy but deluded life may again be explained by either the effects on the happiness in the future or of others, or by our imperfectly rational preferences. For the ultimate social objective, we should go with the rational objective of happiness rather than the imperfectly rational preferences. In fact, it may be argued that it is a mistake for failing to see that happiness is the only rational and ultimate objective. All supposed qualifications to this can be explained by the effects on happiness in the future or of others (hence really no qualification) or that their apparent acceptability is fundamentally due to our imperfect rational preferences, which are inherent in our genes and further shaped by our upbringings and social interactions. If moral philosophers can see this fundamental point in ethics, they would probably have no difficulties in accepting happiness as the only right and ultimate moral principle.

This does not deny the value of secondary virtues like truth, autonomy, accomplishment, justice, etc. However, it is important to keep in mind that all these virtues are ultimately based on the effects on happiness. Failure to do so may end up causing great suffering, such as the case of blindly adhering to the moral principle of not permitting a woman to marry twice in ancient China. Injustice is the denial of due happiness or the undue imposition of unhappiness. Why certain denial is or is not due denial or undue imposition is ultimately also based on the effects on happiness. However, once secondary virtues/principles are accepted, their violation may be detrimental to happiness not only due to the direct effects, but also due to indirect effects, including reducing the general adherence to good moral principles. Viewing happiness as ultimately the only thing of value does not preclude taking all of these direct and indirect effects into account.

---

[11] The amount of happiness from the pleasure machine has to be very, very large for it to be worthwhile for all individuals to hook-up if that means no further advance in knowledge, science, and technology which may help to increase the happiness of our grandchildren very spectacularly.

Griffin (2007, p. 147) asks, 'What could be the bridging notion that would allow us to compare a short life of supreme moral achievement with a long ordinary life?' A short life of supreme moral achievement (safeguarding the country in Griffin's example) may be more valuable, but only because it helps others to achieve more happiness, both directly in safeguarding the country and in setting a good example for virtuous and courageous acts. Accepting happiness as the only ultimately valuable thing allows us (subject to practical difficulties of estimating the quantitative effects) to compare different secondary values and to make the logical choice when different secondary principles are in conflict.[12]

Most, if not all, objections to happiness as the only ultimate value ignore the effects on others and in the future. For example, consider Hausman's (2010, p. 336) objection: 'A crucial problem with the proposal to diminish the time people spend doing things they find unpleasant is that a myopic policy of maximizing current net pleasure is no more likely to maximize net pleasure over a lifetime than is a policy of maximizing weekly profits likely to maximize profits over a decade.' Obviously, if adequate effects on the future and on others are taken into account, maximizing (net) happiness is not open to such objections.

This argues in favour of happiness mainly against preference (as the ultimate objective). However, the difference between happiness and life satisfaction and that between happiness and preference are very similar. Thus, our argument in favour of happiness against preference can also be used to argue in favour of happiness against life satisfaction where the two differ.

B.4 REJECTING KANT'S CATEGORICAL IMPERATIVES

Our welfarist position that only welfare or happiness is of intrinsic value ultimately is different, or even inconsistent with some other moral

---

[12]   Our pure happiness theory also avoids many asymmetrical positions difficult to sustain. For example, among others, Brülde (2007) argues against the pure happiness theory based, in my view, either on effects on others, the future, or on unacceptable grounds. However, he concludes, 'The pure (unmodified) happiness theory is not a plausible theory of the good life, but it may well be a plausible theory of the bad life' (p. 47). Such asymmetries are difficult to justify. If a happy life may not be good due either to the detrimental effects on others and the future (which I accept as a valid reason, but not inconsistent with the pure happiness theory) or to the violation of some principles/virtues not based on happiness (which I reject), then it seems that we should also symmetrically have the result that a miserable life may not be bad due to the favourable effects on the happiness of others, and/or the future, or due to the observance of some principles/virtues not based on happiness.

philosophical positions, especially that of the Kantians. While this is not a place to provide a full refutation of these alternative positions, I will just briefly explain that welfarism/utilitarianism is not inconsistent with the valid parts in Kant (e.g. universalizability; treating humanity not as mere means); and that parts in Kant not consistent with welfarism/utilitarianism are unacceptable (e.g. disclosing the hiding place of potential victims to a murderer). For simplicity, we ignore the difference between utility and welfare discussed in Appendix A.

If you want to quench your thirst, you have to drink something. Drinking something is then a conditional imperative, being conditional on wanting to quench your thirst. A categorical imperative is not conditional on anything; it is something you must do (morally speaking) unconditionally. Accepting some imperatives or moral principles categorically, irrespective of their welfare consequences may certainly be inconsistent with welfarism, as discussed later with reference to Kant.

I have no qualms with Kant's first formulation of universalizability: 'Act only according to that maxim whereby you can at the same time will that it should become a universal law' (Kant 1785/1993, p. 30, 4:421). Obviously, it is also consistent with welfarism and utilitarianism. Each individual utility or welfare value has the same significance with any anonymous SWF. Since welfarism/ utilitarianism does not rule out or even require anonymity, there is no inconsistency with universalizability.

Now consider Kant's second formulation of humanity: 'Act in such a way that you treat humanity, whether in your own person or in the person of any other, never merely as a means to an end, but always at the same time as an end' (Kant 1785/1993, p. 36, 4:429). The consistency of this with welfarism is ambiguous, depending on interpretation.

Kant's imperative of 'no mere means for humanity' may be interpreted in a morally compelling way and as being consistent with welfarism. The central part of treating any person 'never merely as a means to an end, but always at the same time as an end' is certainly consistent with welfarism. Welfarism requires that the utility of each and every individual should enter into the SWF (i.e. taken into account of) positively. This is inconsistent with treating a person as a mere means, not also as an end. If person is a mere means, his utility does not enter the SWF directly but may only affect social welfare by contributing (as a means) to the utility levels of some other individuals that enter the SWF. Welfarism requires the consideration of the utility of each and every person. We may use a pencil as a mere means. We may also use a person as a means to achieve something, but, in doing so, we must also consider her feelings. If we use her as a mere means, not also as an end, then we do not need to consider her feelings, just like we do not have to consider the feelings of a pencil.

In fact, for this compelling part of 'never merely as a means to an end, but always at the same time as an end', I would go beyond humanity and include all sentients capable of welfare (enjoyment and suffering). Animal welfare should be a part of human morality. Readers interested in my views about animal welfare may consult Ng (1995, 2016).

Both Kant and many interpreters of Kant go beyond the compelling part of 'not merely a means'. Without entering into a full discussion, I will just mention two points quickly.

First, from his categorical imperative, Kant derived some moral principles too absolutely, to the disregard of possible huge welfare losses. One clearly unacceptable example is Kant's insistence that 'To be truthful (honest) in all declarations is therefore a sacred unconditional command of reason, and not to be limited by any expediency' (Kant 1799/2012, last page), even to an intended murderer about the hiding place of the potential victim. Kant clearly insisted on this absolute imperative in his reply to Benjamin Constant's criticism. Most people, myself clearly included, find this unacceptable.

One reason that led Kant astray is his mistaken all-or-nothing reasoning. This happened in many of his arguments. Just one other simple example is in his argument against stealing, Kant considered the moral proposition that it is permissible to steal. He argued that this proposition would result in a contradiction upon universalization. The concept of stealing itself presupposes the existence of private property rights. However, the universalization of stealing would lead to no property rights, leading to a logical contradiction. This reasoning is based on contrasting only the two opposite extremes of free stealing for all and absolutely no stealing in any circumstances. In the real world, we are always in-between these two non-existent extremes. Most morally upright persons would avoid stealing as far as possible, but may be compelled to steal if that is the only way, say, to avoid his children starving to death. Such a morality that allows stealing in some extreme circumstances does not end up with the complete absence of property rights. For a similar mistake of an all-or-nothing comparison by a Nobel laureate, which ends up with the grave mistake where he opposed the sensible taxation of pollution, see Ng 2007, 2011.

Second, considering some real-world examples where the observance of some categorical imperatives has ended up in dismal situations may illustrate the unacceptability of sticking to some imperatives without regard for their welfare consequences. As already discussed, in ancient China, for nearly a thousand years since the Southern Song dynasty in the twelfth century, people universally believed in the categorical imperative that 'one woman should not serve two men/husbands'. This does not just mean that a woman should not marry two husbands at the same time. Rather, it means that, once a woman is married to a man, she should not marry again, even after the death of her husband, and even if the death occurs on the wedding night, after the ceremony, but before real consummation of the marriage. This imperative or principle was dictated by the sacred unconditional command of chastity, irrespective of its welfare consequences. For many centuries, this imperative led to enormous misery. It was only after many decades of severe criticisms, including by many novelists, that the imperative was gradually given up over the early decades of the twentieth century. The change was partly assisted by the Western thinking of gender equality and women emancipation.

It may be thought that such backward moral principles as 'one woman should not serve two men/husbands' were only observed by ignorant people in a backward country in the past; modern people do not commit such a silly mistake. Actually, even today, throughout the whole world, with the exception of one or two countries, we have a similar sacrosanct moral principle of categorical imperative that has contributed to the unnecessary, intense, and prolonged suffering of many people. Those trying to help reduce this suffering have been persecuted and jailed. What is this principle? The sanctity of (human) life.

At least in some important aspects, the belief in the sanctity of life serves some very useful purposes. When a person dies, she can no longer enjoy life. Thus, ending a life prematurely is a grave matter. In addition, living persons are also threatened by the possibility of premature death. The costs of causing deaths are enormous. Emphasizing the sanctity of life helps to prevent or at least reduce wanton disregard to lives and serves some useful purpose. The mistake consists in making it absolute and divorcing it from welfare. This absolute sanctity leads to the imprisonment of doctors helping desperate patients to end their miserable lives earlier. This has led to much unnecessary suffering.

In conclusion, Kant and other deontic arguments have not refuted welfarism. Welfarism is consistent with the parts of their argument that are acceptable; those parts inconsistent with welfarism are not really acceptable.

B.5 A CRITIQUE OF RAWLS

If all welfare-independent rights are unacceptable as fundamental moral principles, Rawls' (1971) second principle of justice (maximin), despite its widespread influence, is absurd.

Rawls' first principle requires that each person is to have an equal right to the most extensive total system of equal basic liberties compatible with a similar system of liberty for all. I am prepared to accept this first principle on the following understanding:

(1) that it is adopted *because* it promotes general welfare;
(2) in circumstances where it is disastrous to the general welfare, it may have to be suspended;
(3) in deciding what is the "most extensive total system" and "what is compatible ... for all", the ultimate criterion is general welfare.

A sex maniac may be in favour of freedom to rape and claim that this is compatible with everyone's freedom to rape.[13] It may also happen that the sex maniac is the person of the lowest welfare level such that freedom to rape for all will maximize the welfare of the worst-off, which is hence consistent with the spirit of Rawls' second principle to be discussed. However, if freedom to rape results in the reduction of the welfare of those raped and those afraid of being raped by more than (in aggregate) the welfare gain of the rapists (even though the former still have higher welfare levels than the latter group despite the freedom to rape), then freedom to rape should be regarded as incompatible with the freedom to not be raped. The 'most extensive total system of basic liberties' should then reject the freedom to rape. However, thus interpreted, the first principle is really a device to promote the general welfare. It is not ultimate.

Despite its obvious absurdity, Rawls' second principle is very popular. For example, Temkin believes that, in 'one form or another, many philosophers have come to advocate a maximin principle of justice, and one can see why. There is strong appeal to the view that just as it would be right for a mother to devote most of her effort and resources to her neediest child, so it would be right for society to devote most of its effort and resources to its neediest members' (Temkin 1986, p. 109). In my view, the ethical appeal of this argument as well as that of the maximin principle of justice itself is not difficult to question.

I agree that, in most cases, a mother should devote more, and, in many cases, most, of her effort and resources to her neediest child, but only because this maximizes the welfare of the whole family. The most disadvantaged child

---

[13]   It is true that Rawls would argue that freedom to rape is not a basic liberty while the right to non-violation of the body is. However, how do we determine what are basic liberties? Either it is based on the welfarist principle or it is open to the objection of Section B4, on the unacceptability of rights-based ethics.

is usually the neediest one because he/she will suffer most in the absence of extra help. Thus, the extra care for the most disadvantaged need not be inconsistent with overall welfare maximization. However, the maximin principle requires the mother to go much further.

For simplicity, suppose that the mother is faced with only two alternatives. One is to go away with the most disadvantaged child to live in a mountain resort for certain marginal benefit to the health of the sick child. The other is to stay at home looking after all five children, but still with the possibility of caring more for the most disadvantaged child. Suppose the two welfare profiles for the children are

$$WP_A = (10, \ 10, \ 10, \ 10, \ 9)$$

$$WP_H = (9000, \ 9000, \ 9000, \ 9000, \ 8)$$

and that the mother is indifferent herself and no one else is affected by the choice. The maximin principle requires choosing WP_A. This, in comparison to the alternative of staying at home, increases the welfare of the worst-off child from 8 to 9 at the costs of a huge reduction in welfare (from 9000 to 10) for every other child. No sane mother in the world would make such an absurd choice.

Note that the welfare profiles WP_A and WP_H are ultimate outcomes, as must be the case for all discussion of the ultimate ethical principles. Thus, the more equal welfare profile of WP_A would not promote further gain in welfare through, say, a more harmonious family relationship. Such effects, if any, should already have been incorporated into WP_A and WP_H.

Consider the much-cherished principle, 'From each according to his ability; to each according to his needs' (which I personally approve, assuming no disincentive effect). Why doesn't it read, 'An equal amount of work from each; an equal amount of income to each'? If a weak man is tired by four hours of work, it is better for a stronger man to work longer to relieve him. Similarly, if the worst-off child will not gain much more happiness by extra effort and resources, it is better that these resources be spent on other children.

In the original position, behind the veil of ignorance as to which child I would be born as, I would not have the slightest hesitation in wishing that my mother would maximize the welfare of all the children, i.e., the unweighted sum of all children's welfare (the welfare of the mother and those of all other persons are being held constant in this comparison). This maximizes my, as well as the other children's, expected welfare.

It is sometimes argued that a risk-averse person may not want to maximize expected welfare. I think it is quite rational to be risk averse with respect to income or any other objective rewards since one may have, with good reasons, diminishing marginal utility/welfare of income. But since utility/welfare is the ultimate objective one is presumably maximizing, it is irrational to not maximize expected utility/welfare, if the relevant utility/welfare profiles have already included all relevant effects, such as anxiety, excitement, etc. which explain most paradoxes of choices involving risk such as the Allais paradox (Allais and Hagen 1979; see Harsanyi 1976, Part A, and Ng 1984b). Second, if one chooses to be risk averse with respect to welfare, it is still impossible to reasonably justify an *absolute* degree of risk-averseness as implied by the maximin principle.

After the lifting of the veil of ignorance, I would still think that it is right for my mother or anyone's mother to maximize the welfare of all children together whether I were the worst-off child or not. Again, my bias in favour of my own welfare may mean that I would hope that my mother would spend more effort and resources on *me* somewhat beyond the level justified by unweighted sum maximization. But I think it is unjust for my mother to follow the partial wish of any child. However, even then, I would definitely not *want* my mother to maximin in my favour, implying a zero trade-off with the welfares of my brothers and sisters as long as their welfares remain higher than mine. Thus, given the welfare profiles WP_A and WP_H, even if I were the worst-off child, I would want my mother to choose WP_H. It may be thought that since my welfare is higher in WP_A, I could not have wanted my mother to choose WP_H. This ignores the differences between welfare and preference due to a concern for the welfares of others as discussed in Appendix A.

From this, it may be concluded that the maximin principle of justice is not only utterly unacceptable, but an ethical principle similar to the one in favour of its adoption interestingly suggests that the *worst-off group* should reject the said maximin principle. Why then is the principle so popular? One possible explanation is that it appeals to the guilty feelings of the better-off. They have admirable sympathy for the worst-off, but yet are unprepared and/or find it ineffective to alleviate this by substantial personal contribution to the worst-off (by charity or the like). Paying lip service by advocating the maximin principle of justice is a much more cost-effective way of alleviating their sense of guilt. Of course, this explanation need not apply to all advocates of the maximin principle.

B.6 FURTHER OPPOSING ARGUMENTS CONSIDERED

In commenting on happiness economics, in general, and on Layard (2005), in particular, Barrotta (2008, p. 151) gives the example of the refusal of Freud to take drugs to reduce his painful conditions because of his desire to retain his clear thinking. If the reason to prefer clear thinking is to directly or indirectly contribute to his own and/or others' happiness in the future (perhaps through contribution to knowledge), there is no problem (no inconsistency with welfarism). If the clear thinking or autonomy does not contribute to happiness of anyone at any time, the rationality of preferring it at the cost of much pain is questionable.

For another example, Benjamin et al. (2010, p. 3) find that 'predicted SWB and choice coincide in our data 83 percent of the time' (in choices between income and leisure). Even for the rest beyond the 83%, no conflict needs to be indicated, as people could choose more income and less happiness now, for the benefits of higher future happiness. In other words, the option with shorter leisure hours (believed to involve less happiness now) may actually give more happiness overall, because the higher income could (or at least believed to) contribute to future happiness by more. The framing of their main question on p. 6 does not rule out this likely possibility. Similarly, apparently non-utilitarian factors beyond happiness such as justice, rights, freedom, and priority may all be justified based on the important effects on others and the future.

Consider this conclusion: 'The evaluation of current mood is furthermore proposed to be situation-dependent such that in congruent situations (e.g., a celebration party) a positive mood leads to a positive evaluation of the positive mood and increased happiness, in incongruent situations (e.g., a funeral) a positive mood is evaluated negatively (Västfjäll & Gärling 2006) and thus paradoxically would lead to decreased happiness' (Gamble & Gärling 2012, p. 33). Obviously, when one laughs at something funny at a funeral, it is not that one does not enjoy the humour; rather, one is embarrassed by laughing during an inappropriate occasion. The reason for this is again considering the effects on others and in the future. One then refrains from laughing loudly in a funeral. This may reduce the positive enjoyment, and the embarrassment further reduces the net evaluation. However, the positive mood, to the extent it is felt, is still positive.

The point that negative feelings should count negatively in (net) happiness does not mean that pain or suffering are useless. In fact, the sensation of pain when, for example, our fingers are burned, triggers the withdrawal of our hand to avoid further damage and to teach us to avoid being burned in the future.

However, the sensation of pain as such is of negative value. It is also questionable to say that 'happiness and unhappiness are not ends, but means, and quite possibly "aspects of mechanisms that influence to act in the interests of our genes" (Nesse 2004, p. 1337)' (Nes 2010, p. 375). The problem of such statements is that they are based on confusing the (as-if) ends/means of our genes with our own ends/means. We are the feeling selves, not the unfeeling genes. It is quite true that our affective feelings were evolved/created to make us do things that help to spread our genes. However, the spreading of the unfeeling genes as such has no value. If the organisms that do have affective feelings have a lot more pain/unhappiness than happiness/pleasure and this miserable situation has no hope of being changed, the spreading of such genes is highly undesirable. Even for the reverse cases of more happiness, the valuable thing is the happy feelings, not the spreading of genes as such.

Consider the view 'that well-being is not so much an outcome or end state as it is a process of fulfilling or realizing one's daimon or true nature' (Deci & Ryan 2008, p. 2, describing the eudemonic view of well-being in *Journal of Happiness Studies*). If our true nature is interpreted as the biological one of survival and reproduction, a similar confusion of the (as-if) ends of our genes with our own ends may be involved. On the other hand, if our 'true nature' or eudemonia are interpreted to require some elements of virtue (as required from Aristotle to Waterman), then the confusion is between happiness (that individuals and hence society values ultimately) and morality, as discussed earlier. A morally virtuous person may be very unhappy due to, say, sickness; a very happy person may be morally vicious by intentionally causing harm to others. While his happiness is valuable in itself, his causing of unhappiness on others may more than negate this. Again, once we take adequate account of the effects on others and the future, there is no need to go beyond the hedonic concept of happiness.

While many diverse desiderata (e.g. self-acceptance, self-determination, self-realization, relatedness, relationship, capability and functioning, environmental mastery, and purpose) have been advanced by believers in eudemonia, let us consider here the need for autonomy as emphasized by a number of authors. We may well have a natured and nurtured need for autonomy, as normally we will survive and thrive better with autonomy. Rationally, one may value autonomy only for its instrumental value in contributing directly (through fulfilling our desire to be autonomous) and indirectly (through its beneficial effects on other important things) towards our happiness. Thus, if I were mad and allowing me to be autonomous would cause great unhappiness upon myself and others, and this outweighs the good feeling of being autonomous, I would not want to be autonomous.

For self-development, there is clearly the possibility that it be valuable now, because of its instrumental effects in contributing to the future happiness of oneself and possibly also of others. The fact that self-development is regarded as more important by younger people tends to support this interpretation. For the last dimension of contribution to others, it is also clear that if people find that happiness is the one that is valuable ultimately, then contribution to others must also be contributing to their happiness ultimately for it to be a real contribution. Thus, provided happiness is taken to be net happiness and encapsulates the positives and negatives of affective feelings, and provided the effects on others and in the future are not excluded, happiness needs only to be of one dimension. Ultimately, it is the only thing that is really valuable.

Viewing happiness as the only ultimately valuable thing also does not conflict with the so-called 'hedonic paradox' where the intentional pursuit of happiness, especially if narrowly and excessively focused on the pleasures of the flesh, usually leads to unhappiness or less happiness (Veenhoven 2003, Martin 2008). To the extent that this is true, it means that a good way to achieve happiness is not to have myopic focus on the pleasures of the flesh in the short run, especially not excessively, but to do things more meaningful in contributing to one's own development and to the goodness (which has to be defined in terms of the effects on happiness ultimately) of the society in general. This does not negate the proposition that, ultimately speaking, only happiness is valuable.

Accepting happiness as the only ultimately valuable thing does not rule out the possibility that things other than happiness may be of interest due to their instrumental values to happiness or for other purposes. For example, Waterman et al. (2008) and Huta & Ryan (2010) examine both 'hedonia' (similar to our concept of happiness here) and 'eudamonia' (which goes beyond happiness to require some elements of virtue) in affecting 'intrinsic motivation' or 'motives for acting'. Obviously, as both these factors do affect people's motives for acting, it is useful in studying the effects of both, even if one views virtue (like the present author) as ultimately being based on the contribution to happiness, especially to the happiness of others.

A specific implication of using the enjoyment/suffering sense of happiness (especially in contrast to using life satisfaction) may be briefly mentioned. It supports the Easterlin paradox (increases in incomes failing to increase happiness after a relatively low income level; Easterlin 1974, 2002) the validity of which has been questioned (Stevenson & Wolfers 2008, Angeles 2011). As reported in Graham (2011), Kahneman & Deaton (2010), in a study of

450,000 respondents in a Gallup daily survey of US respondents from 2008 to 2009, found that hedonic well-being correlated less closely with income than did life satisfaction. Both 'correlated closely with income (in a log-linear manner) at the bottom end of the income ladder, but the correlation between hedonic well-being and income tapered off at about $75,000 per year'. Since hedonic well-being is the one of intrinsic value, its lower correlation with income makes the Easterlin paradox more important.

Regarding things other than welfare as intrinsically valuable is of questionable acceptability. For example, 'Non-economic modes of valuing typically result in intrinsic motivation. If one values an environmental good in itself or because of esthetic, historical or ecological reasons (valuation), one is likely to protect it regardless of whether doing so helps to achieve some other goal (motivation)' (Neuteleers & Engelen 2015, p. 259). In my view, aesthetic, historical, and ecological values are valuable because they contribute to our welfare, not in themselves. If there is no sentient to appreciate them, they have no value.

On the other hand, it is also incorrect to say: 'If something has a price then it is not intrinsically valued' (Walsh 2015, p. 406). A pet animal has a price, but also has an intrinsic value as it has affective feelings. I have intrinsic value, at least to myself and my family members; however, I also have a price. I am willing to sell myself, even for slavery if possible, for say $100 billion or higher. The extra money has no value to me, as my marginal utility/happiness of consumption is virtually zero. However, if I have a large sum of money like $100 billion, I think I could use it to do a lot of good, and this could increase the welfare of other people and animals, such that, even if I value the welfare of others and animals only at 1% of that of mine, it may still be worth it for me to slave for the rest of my life, provided that I have at least six months to spend the money first. Arguably, I should be prepared to sell myself for something less than $100 billion; that is just a price I am willing to accept, not the minimum one.

In conclusion, despite the variety of objections to our central argument, I have never come across one that truly negates it. Most arguments ignore some relevant effects on others and in the future.

APPENDIX C

Extending Economic Analysis to Analyze Policy Issues More Broadly

ABSTRACT*

By extending traditional economic policy analysis to include factors emphasized by other social scientists and philosophers, more social and public policy issues may be analyzed more adequately. For example, should the market expand beyond its traditional confines of goods and services? Should more immigration be allowed? Wider effects like social harmony, repugnance, and morality should also be considered. Although the extended analysis does not provide a definite general answer, in combination with the first theorem of welfare economics and the principle of treating a dollar as a dollar in specific issues, it provides some general propositions that guide the analysis of relevant costs and benefits of specific policy changes beyond narrow economic efficiency.

Largely following Mäki (2009), we may distinguish between economic imperialism and economics imperialism. The former describes the expansion of the economic way of doing things (monetary transaction, exchange, prices, and markets) beyond its traditional confines of material goods and services to other spheres of the society. The manifestation of this expansion includes diverse activities like paying your child to study or to mow the lawn, paying someone to line up for you, paying for blood donation, organ donation, surrogate motherhood, prostitution, etc. The communitarians (e.g.

---

* This appendix is based on a keynote address presented at the Western Economic Association International conference, 2016; see: www.weai.org/PR2016.

This appendix involves some technical economic analysis which may not be easily understandable by those not trained in economics. Readers who find it too difficult to comprehend may be contented with the non-technical summary presented in Chapter 3 in the text.

Anderson 1993, Sandel 2012a, 2013) deplore this expansion as threatening to turn a market economy into a market society.[1]

On the other hand, economics imperialism describes the expansion of economic analysis into other areas of social sciences like marriage, family, having children, racial discrimination, laws, politics, etc., as pioneered by Gary Becker (1957/1971 on discrimination, 1978 on behaviour, 1981 on family), Anthony Downs (1957 on democracy), Buchanan & Tullock (1962 on political decisions), Olson (1965 on collective action), etc. While these forerunners typically assumed perfect markets, and just applied core economic analysis of rational constrained maximization to other areas, newer versions (e.g., Fine & Milonakis 2009) recognize and tackle market imperfections. 'Economic imperialism' may also be taken as the conquest of other nations by economic means or for economic purposes. However, this national conquest is not the concern here. Instead, this appendix attempts to make a generalization along the line of economics imperialism and apply the generalized method to analyze some issues of economic imperialism, in particular, on whether the expansion of the market is desirable.

In the words of Stigler (1984, p. 311), economists have been 'aggressive in addressing central problems in ... neighboring social disciplines ... without any invitations'. This economics imperialism has made very significant impact. It has been supported (e.g. Hirshleifer 1985, Lazear 2000), opposed (e.g. Coase 1978, Fine 2002), and analyzed (e.g. Mäki 2009). 'What gives economics its imperialist invasive power is that our analytic categories – scarcity, cost, preferences, opportunities, etc. – are truly universal in applicability. Even more important is our structured organization of these concepts into the distinct yet intertwined processes of optimization on the individual decision level and equilibrium on the social level of analysis' (Hirshleifer 1985, p. 53).

To this important observation, it may be added that, in all social sciences, especially where public policy is concerned, a crucially important issue is how decisions are made at the individual and collective levels and how these act and interact to ultimately affect the welfare of people which is of ultimate value. Economics is particularly suitable for such analysis, but some extensions may be desirable. While the expansion of economic analysis to more social issues may be regarded as economics imperialism, the extension to incorporate factors such as altruism, fairness, and morality may also be regarded as reverse imperialism, which is the conquest of traditionally non-

---

[1] This explicit concern can be traced back to, at least, Polanyi (1944), but has intensified in the recent decade or so; e.g., see Satz (2010) and McPherson & Satz (2017).

economic concepts from other social sciences and philosophy into the hard-core of economic analysis. Thus, instead of speaking of imperialism, perhaps unification and pluralism may be better descriptions.[2]

Since most, if not all, public policy issues, whether economic, political, sociological, and beyond, are, directly or indirectly, concerned with the well-being of individuals in the society, the economists' concepts of individual utility, social welfare and their methods of analyzing them may be usefully applied to analyze issues beyond the traditional concern of economics to cover many, if not largely all, social issues, whether within the traditional confines of economics or not. It is true that much of social sciences are concerned with the more objective/positive issues of things like social processes and changes without necessarily investigating their effects on individual welfare. However, even fundamental knowledge in either maths/logics, natural sciences, or social sciences may be useful, perhaps after many steps of application. Thus, the construction of bridges requires engineering knowledge which is based on physics and so on. The pursuit of fundamental research and pure science should certainly be encouraged. However, ultimately speaking, bearing fruits is more important than shedding lights, as Pigou (1922) put it, although light shedding will most certainly lead to fruit bearing at some stage. This is particularly true for social sciences.

Fruit bearing may include literal fruits like apples and pears, but also other economic products and beyond, including social harmony, peace, freedom, love, etc. What may be included in this wider sense of fruits depends on the ultimate objective of individuals. (For simplicity, I focus on human individuals and ignore issues like animal welfare, on which see Ng 1995, 2016.) Rationally, ignoring the effects on others (accounting for that may involve double counting if not careful), the ultimate objective of an individual is her welfare, well-being, or happiness, as discussed in Appendix B. Given the time period and ignoring the degree of formality, these three terms are just different descriptions of the same thing, at least in accordance to the definitions adopted here. Thus, provided effects on others and in the future are not ignored, welfare may be used as the ultimate fruit.

For the level of individuals, economists usually use the concept of utility instead of welfare. In modern economics, the utility of an

---

[2] Davis' (forthcoming) case against economics imperialism and for multidisciplinarity has some validity, but some of the claims seem excessive, e.g., 'agents were interdependent ... standard optimization analysis was thus meaningless' (p. 10). The interdependency may make standard optimization analysis not fully recognizing the interdependency inadequate (and may need supplementation with analysis of such additional complicating factors as external effects, social interaction, institutions, networks, dynamic, etc.), but certainly not meaningless.

individual just represents her preference such that (1) individual i prefers X to Y; and (2) the utility level of individual i at X is higher than at Y, are taken to be the same thing. With preference referring only to ordinal ranking, then the relevant utility function is said to be ordinal and subject to any increasing transformation. As long as a higher indifference curve carries a higher utility number, how much higher is not relevant. Whatever the cardinal utility numbers (with ordering unchanged), the same set of indifference curves will yield the same demand functions for goods (subsumed services). Economists concerned only with positive theories of production and consumption may thus ignore the cardinal intensities of preferences. However, for policy choices beyond what may be judged by the Pareto principle or for changes that make some individuals better off and some worse off, interpersonal comparisons of cardinal utilities are needed to make reasonable decisions (Mueller 2003, chapter 23). Since this book is not just concerned with the positive theories of production and consumption, but with public policy, intensities of preferences are not abstracted away.

The preference of an individual may differ from her welfare due to ignorance or imperfect knowledge/foresight, or to a concern for the welfare of others over-and-above the effects on one's own welfare (non-affective altruism), or to irrational preferences, as discussed in Appendix A. For simplicity, these divergences between individual preference (utility) and welfare will be ignored here as raising different sorts of issues. Thus, to be more distinct from social welfare, 'utility' instead of 'welfare' will be used. This leads us to the question: How should individual utilities be aggregated into social welfare? Although I have argued for a utilitarian social welfare function (SWF) that maximizes the sum of equally weighted individual utilities (Ng 1975), for most purposes here, a welfarist SWF (in Equation 1) observing the Pareto principle (social welfare, W, being an increasing function of all individual utilities), as accepted by most economists and consequentialist philosophers and social scientists, will be sufficient.

$$(1)\ W = W(U^1, U^2, \ldots, U^I);\ \partial W / \partial U^i > 0 \text{ for all i.}$$

A welfarist SWF as in Equation 1 may violate some deontological rules like the categorical imperatives of Kant or the constitutional constraints of a country. First, it may be argued that, provided effects on others and in the future are adequately taken into account, there is no need to take account of non-welfare factors/rules (Ng 1990). Rules (including moral principles, legal laws, and constitutions) are taken as useful, precisely for the promotion of long-term overall welfare.[3] Why do we have some rules but not others? The choice must be based on some considerations; for society as a whole, long-term social welfare is the most acceptable one, as discussed in Appendix B. Second, for the strict Kantians, they may regard our analysis as only valid within the scope where the compelling deontic rules are not violated. Since individual utilities may still differ due to changes in economic and social factors without affecting any deontic rules or constitutional constraints, our analysis is still of some relevance, although somewhat limited, being subject to the non-violation of these rules. Alternatively, the Kantians may take our framework of analysis, but regard the violation of certain categorical imperatives as meaning a huge reduction in general morality, M, that will certainly be unacceptable (or will hugely reduce social welfare).

In either case, we may proceed on the understanding that, at least for the important part of fruit bearing, all social sciences are interested in effects on social welfare through individual utilities. Then, the basic framework of economics, its welfare analysis in particular, is applicable (applicability does not imply completeness) to all social sciences, except that what enters individual utility functions should be much broader, and not confined to the traditional economic factors of goods and services only. At least to some extent, this has been accepted or used in the imperialistic conquests of economics. For example, the most important figure in economic imperialism, Gary Becker (1992, p. 38) said at the beginning of his Nobel lecture: 'I have tried to pry economists away from narrow assumptions about self-interest. Behavior is driven by a much richer set of values and preferences.' However, instead of applying economics imperialism on specific issues (as done with great successes by Becker and his followers), this appendix attempts to obtain some general results (generality does not imply exhaustiveness). In particular, it is shown that some useful propositions may be derived from some compelling axioms.

Axiom 1: The utility level of an individual may be affected by the activities of other individuals.

An individual may seclude herself from society and lives perhaps in the mountain. Even such a secluded individual may be affected by the activities of others through, say, climate change. This axiom is thus compelling. Obviously, an individual is affected by the activities of others, which may include those generating pollution and outright illegal ones.

---

[3]   See Kaplow & Shavell (2007) for a theoretical analysis of the use (with costs) of moral sanctions (feelings of guilt) and rewards (feelings of virtue) for social welfare maximization.

Axiom 2: The prevailing morality in a society may affect the utility levels of individuals in the society.

This axiom is not only compelling, it also represents a concession by an economist to the communitarians on the importance of morality. It is clearly acceptable, especially to the communitarians. That it is compelling even to economists can be seen by noting that no economists deny the existence of social interaction in a wide sense beyond market exchange. Even on your way to the supermarket, you may be affected by the behaviour of people you encounter, including whether they are polite and friendly, whether they rob you, etc. At least to some extent, their behaviour is affected by their morality. Hence, morality affects utilities. In a deeper sense for professional economists, note that the relevance of this point is related to the fact that not all interpersonal effects/relationships are negotiated/effected only through market exchange; there are some direct and subtle effects beyond monetary transaction. In addition, morality (or social capital like trust more generally) may also contribute to individual utilities through its contribution to cooperation and economic growth (Tabellini 2008, 2010, James 2015). Similarly, other possible indirect effects may be allowed for.

It may, however, be argued that morality may affect utilities only through affecting activities, especially if the latter term is defined widely. For simplicity, an a-temporal model typical of most economic (especially welfare-related) analysis is used. However, the real world is on-going. Thus, the morality in this period may affect activities and, hence, utilities in future periods. Allowing morality to possibly affect utilities independently of its effects on activities this period may thus be a simple way of allowing for its time-delayed effects. Moreover, allowing for its effects only through activities does not affect the validity of our later propositions, as will become clearer later.

Axiom 3: The prevailing morality may be affected by the activities of individuals in the society.

The compellingness of this axiom is also obvious, especially since 'activities' may include writing/doing media articles/interviews, engaging in political persuasion, teaching students/children including by doing, etc. Some influences must be possible. As the direction of influence is not specified, the axiom is uncontroversial.

Axiom 4: Each individual in the society maximizes utility subject to a budget and a time constraint.

Although psychologists and behavioural economists have shown that individuals may deviate from perfect rationality of utility maximization, such deviations are not the focus of this book. We thus simplify matters by using the simplification of traditional analysis here. Also, since we allow for factors beyond the narrow economic ones in the utility functions, this simplification is much less restrictive.

Axiom 5: Each individual is small enough in comparison to the whole society that she takes the aggregate/average variables in the whole society as beyond her control or ignores her negligible effects on the aggregate/average variables.

Admittedly, some monopolistic power for firms may exist and similarly some influences of some individuals on selected others (e.g. family members and friends) must exist. However, these are not the focus of this book and are abstracted away for simplicity and to concentrate on the overall picture.

Under the axioms above, the utility/welfare of individual i may be written as

$$(2)\ U^i = U^i(x^i_1, \ldots, x^i_n, X_1, \ldots, X_n, M)\ \text{for}\ i = 1, \ldots, I$$

Where x^i_j is the activity levels (i.e., in excess of the original endowed amount if viewed as the amount of excess demand) for all relevant activities (subsuming economic and non-economic) j by individual i, X_j is the total/average amount/degree of activity j in the society/economy. Under our simplification of a given set of I individuals, there is no need to distinguish the total from the average amount. Axiom 1 actually allows for the possible differential effects of activities of different individuals. In (Equation 2), we simplify by just allowing for the aggregate values of activities. Similarly, only the general level of morality, M, is taken into account for simplicity. From Axiom 3, M may be a function of $X_1, \ldots, X_n$ plus some exogenous factors which are held constant and thus ignored.

$$(3)\ M = M(X_1, \ldots, X_n)$$

From Axioms 4 and 5, each individual i chooses $(x^i_1, \ldots, x^i_n)$ to maximize U^i subject to both a budget and a time constraint, taking aggregate variables $X_1, \ldots, X_n$, M as beyond her control. The budget constraint is

$$(4)\ \sum_j p_j x^i_j = 0$$

where p_j is the price of the economic component of the activity j, and x^i_j is the excess demand of individual i for the relevant economic components j. Note that some of the x's may be negative, signifying negative excess demand or positive excess supply, such as for labour services. Also note that some of the p's may be zero (economically free goods/activities) and some may be effectively infinite (illegal or physically impossible activities).

The time constraint for each individual is stated implicitly as

$$(5)\ F^i(x^i_1, \ldots, x^i_n) = 0;\ i = 1, \ldots, I.$$

The first-order conditions for maximization are:

$$(6)\ U^i_j = \lambda^i p_j + \mu^i F^i_j;\ j = 1, \ldots, n;\ i = 1, \ldots, I.$$

where $U^i_j \equiv \partial U^i / \partial x^i_j$, $F^i_j \equiv \partial F^i / \partial x^i_j$ and λ^i and μ^i are the respective Lagrangian multipliers.

On the other hand, the condition for Pareto optimality or social optimality may be obtained by the maximization of a Paretian SWF (Equation 1). The individual time constraints in Equation 5 still apply for the society's maximization problem. However, instead of individual budget constraints, the society faces a production possibility constraint

$$(7)\ G(X_1, \ldots, X_n) = 0$$

where $X_j \equiv \sum_i x^i_j$ is the total amount of activity, j, of the whole society.

The first-order conditions are

$$(8)\ W_i U^i_j + \sum_{i=1}^{I} W_i (U^i_{Xj} + U^i_M M_j) = \lambda G_j + \mu^i F_j;\ j = 1, \ldots n;\ i = 1, \ldots, I.$$

where $W_i \equiv \partial W / \partial U^i$, $U^i_{Xj} \equiv \partial U^i / \partial X_j$, $U^i_M \equiv \partial U^i / \partial M$, $M_j \equiv \partial M / \partial X_j$.

In a market economy with perfect competition and no external effects, the price of each good faced by the individual equals its marginal cost of production, and the price ratio for any pair of goods equals the marginal rate of substitution for any consuming individuals, which also equals the marginal rate of transformation. Comparing Equation 8 with Equation 6, note that, for any particular activity j, if $U^i_{Xj} = 0$ for all i (i.e. no aggregate or external effects) and either $U^i_M = 0$ for all i, and/or $M_j = 0$, it may be regarded as a private activity affecting only the utility of the individual taking it. If all activities are private in this sense, then Equation 8 may be collapsed into Equation 6 by making $p_j / p_k = G_j / G_k$ for all j and k and rewriting in proportionate terms of ratios. This is so under perfect competition for a market economy without distortions. This is consistent with the first theorem of welfare economics (which says that a perfectly competitive equilibrium is Pareto optimal under certain conditions including the absence of external effects like pollution).

However, when $U^i_{Xj} + U^i_M M_j$ is significantly different from zero for some good j and some individuals i, there may be divergence between the conditions for private optimality and those for social optimality. In terms familiar to economists, this is due to external effects through U^i_{Xj} and to generalized external effects through $U^i_M M_j$. In fact, even just under U^i_{Xj}, we may include the more traditional external effects like pollution and the generalized external effects like the feeling of repugnance of some individuals against the prevalence of certain goods or activities X_j.[4] Thus, if for a particular good j, X_j enters some individual utility functions negatively and that this negative effects are sufficiently large and widespread, it is possible that the prohibition of the market transaction of this good, even if it may decrease consumer and producer surpluses for some participants, may yet be consistent with Pareto and overall social optimality, as well known by economists.

Note that in Equation 8, as a change in X_j may potentially affect the utility levels of many individuals both directly (through $U^i_{X_j} \equiv \partial U^i / \partial X_j$) and indirectly through affecting M, but these external effects do not appear in Equation 6, so the potential divergences between private and social values of some goods could be large. The estimation of the actual values of such external effects awaits much future research. However, it may be noted that such analysis like the amounts of efficiency (such as in increasing the number of kidneys for transplant) that individuals are willing to trade with morality (including repugnance), as done in Elías et al. (2016), may be helpful in such estimation.

To facilitate the statement of propositions that I will set out, some clarification of the terms used must be given here. Familiar terms like perfect competition and market power are used in the same way as their common usage in economics. However, a 'social equilibrium' is defined in a sense that is broader than the traditional 'general equilibrium' used in economics, as the variables involved include not only goods and services produced and consumed, but a wider concept of 'activities'. Otherwise, 'equilibrium' is in the same traditional sense: 'the absence of departure from the position'. From this note and the axioms and earlier discussion, we have, somewhat trivially, Proposition 1 whose content is well known from basic economics.

Proposition 1: A social equilibrium may be Pareto inefficient even in the absence of any monopolistic power (i.e. Axiom 5 holds and the equilibrium is perfectly competitive) if there exist uncorrected real external effects like untaxed pollution.[5]

---

[4] What we call real vs generalized external effects corresponds roughly to physical vs psychological external effects of Mueller (2009, pp. 241-243). See also the emotional externalities discussed by Sgroi et al. (2016).

[5] The word 'real' is added to qualify 'external effects', because pecuniary external effects through the price system do not cause inefficiency under classical conditions. 'Real' also indicates a distinction from 'generalized' or 'psychological' external effects discussed in the text.

Proof: The validity of the proposition is trivial as is well known from basic economic analysis. The existence of uncorrected real external effects like pollution may make a perfectly competitive equilibrium Pareto inefficient. The validity of this proposition is also intuitively obvious to non-economists. If some serious pollutants/emissions may be reduced at small costs to the polluters, but if this is not done due to some reason, the resulting situation may be inefficient in the sense of having too much pollution. The additional consideration of some 'non-economic' factors like morality does not change the validity of this obvious result, except in the trivial knife-edge case of perfect offsetting of different opposite effects from sheer chance.

Proposition 2: A social equilibrium may be Pareto inefficient even in the absence of any monopolistic power (i.e. Axiom 5 holds and the equilibrium is perfectly competitive) and uncorrected real external effects like untaxed pollution, if uncorrected generalized external effects exist.

Proof: Given the validity of Proposition 1, Proposition 2 is established by analogy to Proposition 1. Even in the absence of monopoly power, a social equilibrium may be inefficient if some external-cost generating activities like pollution exist and are not offset by some measures like taxes and regulations, as stated in Proposition 1. Analogously, even in the absence of these uncorrected real external effects like untaxed pollution, a social equilibrium may be inefficient if uncorrected generalized external effects exist. From Axioms 1 and 2, the utility level of a non-secluded individual may be affected by the activities of other individuals and the prevailing morality. Thus, just like excessive/unchecked pollution may cause inefficiency under Proposition 1, the existence of activities that decrease the utility levels of others and through the prevailing morality may also adversely affect others. In maximizing their own utility levels, individuals may thus carry out such activities to excessive levels if unchecked by some counter measures like taxes, regulations, or morality. Thus, Proposition 2 must also be true.

Remark 1: The validity of Proposition 1 does not mean that all activities generating some real external costs like pollution must be taxed or regulated. For those with trivial effects, the administrative costs of taxation or regulation may be more than the efficiency gains achieved. In addition, there may also be indirect costs of having too much government intervention. Similarly, the validity of Proposition 2 does not mean that the government has to be the saviour of morality and police all activities that may adversely affect others and the general morality. The direct and indirect costs of excessive paternalism may far outweigh its positive effects, if any. Nevertheless, both Propositions 1 and 2 remain valid. In considering measures that may address the inefficiencies stated in these propositions, we have to consider both the positive and side effects of the measures which are beyond the scope of Propositions 1 and 2 themselves.

Proposition 3: In general, a conceptual/theoretical analysis without empirical evidence is insufficient to establish whether a certain expansion of the market (or some other policy or social change) is desirable or undesirable according to a Paretian SWF, even in the absence of ignorance, imperfect information, and irrationality and in the absence of traditional real external effects like pollution.

Proof: Consider a certain market expansion A to some area/scope not available for market transaction before. (For something more concrete, one may think of the lifting of a ban on the import of some good or the legalization of kidney sales.) In the absence of ignorance, imperfect information, and irrationality, and in the absence of traditional real external effects like pollution, simple economic analysis shows that parties to the newly created market benefit from the additional exchanges. This is amply shown in the literature on the efficiency of free international trade. However, in our expanded model, the increase in economic surpluses through the added exchanges may be more than offset by the non-traditional external effects including repugnance effects ($U^i_{x_j}$ may be sufficiently negative for some i and j) and intrinsic motivation- and/or morality-reduction effects (M_j) may be sufficiently negative for some j.

Remark 2: For the case of free international trade in traditional goods and services, it is generally assumed by economists and accepted by most communitarians that the relevant repugnant effects and crowding-out (of intrinsic motivation and morality) effects are negligible if not non-existent. Given this additional empirical assumption/condition/evidence, then a case for free trade may be made and regarded as acceptable. But, evidently, some empirical support in the form of either formal evidence, explicit or implicit assumption, or tacit agreement, is needed. To see this more clearly, consider the case of the legalization of kidney sales. With the exception of Iran, all countries ban kidney sales. One of the reasons for this ban is that many people feel repugnance (e.g., Roth 2007, Elías 2014) at the legal transaction of human organs. One may argue that, despite this repugnance, kidney sales should be legalized as the enormous benefits of saving lives should more than offset such feelings of repugnance, even if by a large number of individuals (as in fact argued in Chapter 9 in the text). However, this is again a form of empirical support, either with solid evidence or by intelligent guess. The absence of a general result regarding, for example, the desirability of market expansion or some other social change, does not mean that no analysis is possible; it is just that some support from the empirical side regarding the likely signs and sizes of the different effects involved are, in general, needed.

Proposition 4: In general, in judging the likely sign and magnitude of the different effects involved in the desirability of a policy or social change, long-term effects as well as current effects should be taken into account.

Illustration: The proposition is stated in general terms and is obviously true; an illustration will suffice. Consider the case of the legalization of kidney sales. Despite the enormous benefits of saving lives, it is possible (need not be likely) that legalization may lead to significant feelings of repugnance by so many people that the current benefits are overwhelmed by current costs. (For simplicity, ignore possible other benefits and costs.) However, it may also be possible (if not likely) that, as people get used to legal transactions of kidneys, the feeling of repugnance fades into insignificance over time, making the long-term effects dominated by the benefits of saving lives. That this fading is highly likely is further supported by the next proposition.

Proposition 5: The objection (including feelings of repugnance) to the expansion of the market is likely to decrease over time as people become accustomed to the transaction and as society becomes more advanced in the degree of division of labour (and specialization), education (especially with more understanding of basic economics), and liberal thinking.

Demonstration: Since this proposition is moderately stated as only being 'likely', its validity may be demonstrated by looking at some historical and current evidence. At the time of Adam Smith (undisputed father of economics), people viewed selling one's service of singing in public as a 'discredit' and Smith cited this to explain the higher pay needed (Smith 1776/1982, p. 209). We now not only regard singing in public as acceptable, but as honourable. Other examples regarding life insurance and others are discussed in Chapter 8.

In terms of Equation 3, the content of this proposition may be reflected in possible changes in the effects of the various X_j on individual utilities and on M. This is especially so if the model is extended into a dynamic one that involves multi-periods, as the persistence of some X_j over time may affect how these effects change over time.

Our analysis does not provide a definite conclusion regarding the desirability of a certain policy or social change such as the expansion of the market beyond its traditional confines. However, it indicates certain pathways that should be taken into account and it reaches some general conclusions that may provide some guides in the specific analysis of particular changes.

Our proposed extended analysis, although focusing on morality M, need not be so confined. For example, we may interpret M to cover more than just morality, or add another variable A to stand for say atmosphere. We may then have the atmosphere of a place, say the city centre, being affected by the various buildings (housing or commercial) around it. Then, an individual or a firm may build its building which enters its own production/utility function, but also affects the overall atmosphere A. If collecting individual revenues from the enjoying of the valued atmosphere is impossible or too costly, the atmosphere contributions of the various private buildings then have external benefits or costs, depending on the sign of the contribution. The private decision makers do not take into account these external effects in their building renovation or rebuilding decisions. Such external benefits may then delay the speed of renovation to a sub-optimal (socially) level for a growing city, and such external costs may hasten the decay of a declining city. Then, it may be possible that an external event like a big city fire, like the big Boston fire of 1872, may provide some gains by hastening the upgrading in a growing city, as analyzed by Hornbeck & Keniston (2017). They allow the nearby or overall quality of buildings (our atmosphere) to affect rentals positively; our formulation has the advantage of tracing the external effects to the more fundamental level of utility functions.

Similarly, if we interpret M to include something like fellowship or social harmony or have another variable B for this, we may include effects some communitarians find important. For example, in arguing against the Sky-boxification of life, where the rich and the poor or the average work, shop, and play in different places, and their children go to different schools, Sandel (2012a, p. 203) argues thus: 'Democracy does not require perfect equality, but it does require that citizens share in a common life. What matters is that people of different backgrounds and social positions encounter one another, and bump up against one another, in the course of everyday life. For this is how we learn to negotiate and abide our differences, and how we come to care for the common good.' If this is true and important, then some ways of catering to the preferences of the rich such as Sky boxes for watching sports may generate some generalized external costs. Not only that such expenses should not be tax-deductible, they should perhaps be taxed much more to discourage the Sky-boxification of life.

CONCLUDING REMARKS

Public policy issues are very complicated and typically involve many factors that extend beyond the domain of economics, including fairness, harmony, relationships, networks, altruism, morality, etc. Nevertheless, as it is ultimately individuals in society that feel the effects of social events or changes, the traditional economic analysis focusing on individual utilities and social welfare may be extended to incorporate these wider effects. This appendix provides a modest attempt at such an extension, with some general propositions that may provide some guides to the analysis of wider costs and benefits of specific social changes and/or public policies. While this extended framework certainly does not capture all complications involved, it may provide some useful extensions in some respects. For example, applying the general results to examine the desirability of extending the market, we reach the tentative conclusion that keeping blood donation voluntary without financial payment is likely desirable, especially with adequate education on the usefulness of donation to the donors (Chapter 11); on the other hand, legalizing kidney sales is clearly desirable, although certain regulations and more studies may be desirable (Chapter 9). In Appendix D, the complicated issues involved on the desirability of immigration are discussed. Further extension and applications await future research.

Immigration Typically Makes Existing Residents Better Off*

This appendix considers the desirability of allowing immigration into a country/city from the viewpoint of the existing residents/people and also from a wider perspective. In particular, some common mistakes are dispelled. Contrary to popular beliefs, immigration typically makes existing residents better off, provided social harmony is maintained. We focus on immigration here. A larger population through natural increases (more births) has some similarities and some differences (family aspects). For a more specific treatment of this case of natural increases, please consult my *Common Mistakes in Economics: By the Public, Students, Economists and Nobel Laureates* (Ng 2011, section 1.3 and chapters 10 and 11) which is available open access online.

The concern about congestion and pollution (itself correct) is particularly likely to lead to incorrect anti-immigration thinking. For example, when people encounter serious congestion, they would likely think: 'If the number of cars on the road (or passengers in the carriages) were halved, how nice it would be!'. Thus, people tend to blame congestion and pollution on population size. A more complete analysis should consider the following. Given the amount of per capita investment and taxes, if the population size and number of cars were halved, the width of the roads would also roughly be halved. Congestion would likely increase as a result. With fewer people, public transportation would have fewer routes, and the frequency of trains and buses would be lower.

For example, I live inside the Nanyang Technological University campus and have had occasions to catch the 179 bus. Once, just before reaching the bus stop, I saw two 179s passing. I thought I had to wait at least 20 minutes, but the next 179 came in less than 2 minutes. In contrast, five decades ago (I was

---

* Some points in this appendix are from Quah & Ng (2018).

a student on the same campus) when Singapore had a population of less than a third of its current size, if one missed a bus going out of the campus, one had to wait a full half an hour. This is a concrete example of an advantage of a larger population that most people overlook. It is odd that few people take into account the fact that transportation is much more convenient in densely populated cities like London, Shanghai, Singapore, and Tokyo, than in the countryside or even in smaller towns.

Although a larger population leads to larger requirements and challenges, it also provides much more resources. With adequate catching up in the provision of relevant infrastructure, a larger population typically provides net benefits, especially to the original people. For the same job, at the same salary, most people prefer to work in a bigger city, despite having to pay more for housing. As often reported, medical practices in small towns have difficulties attracting medical doctors to work there, despite offering double the amount of salary. The advantages of a larger population typically more than offset the costs, contrary to popular belief.

For any country, do people in the sparsely populated countryside or do people in the densely populated cities have higher per capita incomes? On earth, do people in a densely populated continent (Europe) or do people in the least densely populated Africa (ignoring the example of the island continent of Australia) have higher incomes? Did the spectacular scientific/technological flowering and the Industrial Revolution take place in sparsely populated or densely populated areas?

"Proximity increases teamwork possibilities. It enables larger, more complete organizations. For most of history, organizations have needed people to live nearby, and before cities there were no large organizations. At the same time, proximity increases the brainpower of society, enabling people to learn from others with different skills, knowledge, and background. So a city of 50,000 people can solve problems that would baffle the same 50,000 scattered in farms over the countryside. Innovations have always come from the city" (Friedman & McNeill 2013, p. 41).

With a narrow economic perspective, one may be prone to argue that, unless the immigrant takes with her an enormous amount of capital or skill, allowing an additional person/family to share the given limited natural resources of the country, will reduce per capita resources and per capita incomes and is hence undesirable for the current local/domestic people. Even on its own ground of a narrowly economic perspective and even if all external effects (traditional and generalized), ignorance, and morality issues are ignored, this simple or even naïve case against immigration is invalid, even ignoring complications such as increasing returns (to scale, to scope, to specialization at different levels of the firm, the industry, and the economy).

To see this, consider the simple textbook case of constant returns to scale, perfect competition, no external effects, no government, and payment to factors of production in accordance to marginal productivity. For simplicity, consider the immigration of unskilled labour without capital or any other economic ability like entrepreneurship, a case probably regarded as least favourable. For simplicity and concreteness, but without real loss of generality for this simplified case, suppose that the production function of this relevant economy is $Y = L^{1/2} K^{1/2}$, where L is unskilled labour and K is the composite of all other factors, including land and capital which is held constant at K = 100. Before immigration, L = 100, Y = 100, and with the normalization of one person being one unit of labour supply, the per capita income is 1, with, on average, each person earning half of her unit of income from L and another half from K, and with the price/wage rate for L and K (being equal to $\partial Y/\partial L$ and $\partial Y/\partial K$, respectively), both at ½. Now introduce the immigration of 10 persons each with one unit of L, but no K. The total output after immigration increases from 100 to approximately 104.9, but the per capita income decreases from 1 to approximately 0.9535. Have the original 100 local residents been made worse off economically?

No. The marginal product of L (MPL) decreases from 0.5 to 0.47673, but the marginal product of K increases from 0.5 to 0.5244. For an average local who own 1 L and 1 K, her income increases from 1 to 1.0011344. She actually gains from the immigration. This gain is due to the fact that, even ignoring other possible positive factors like increasing returns and more ideas, the immigration of a particular factor decreases the marginal product of this factor, but increases the marginal products of complementary factors by more. Thus, the original residents, as a whole group, actually gain economically from immigration. This is so despite of the possible decrease in per capita income. The decrease in per capita income applies to all people including the new immigrants. Focusing on the per capita income hides the fact that local residents may gain despite a fall in per capita income calculated to include the new immigrants.

This gain may also be seen by the point that the 10 immigrants earns the MPL when L = 110, but their total contribution to production equals the integration of MPL from L = 100 to L = 110. With diminishing marginal productivity of L (as K is held constant and constant returns to scale is assumed), MPL is higher at L = 100 than at L = 110. Thus, the total contribution to production of these 10 immigrants is higher than their total earnings. They contribute more than their incomes. The original 100 residents must benefit as a group. If these 100 residents do not own the same amount of L and K, those that mainly or exclusively own L may lose, but those that mainly own K will gain, and this gain more than offsets the loss by L, leading to a net overall benefit. Local residents benefit from immigration even in this simple model with no increasing returns and public goods. The recognition of these latter factors makes the gain much larger, and may lead to an increase in per capita income (even calculated to include the new immigrants).

In terms of magnitude, it is likely that the cost sharing in the provision of public goods like defence, research, and broadcasting is probably much more important than the gain identified earlier. However, our simple model also does not allow for such negative factors like congestion and pollution. Does the introduction of these negative factors make local residents worse off with immigration? As shown by Clarke & Ng (1993), if external costs like congestion and pollution are taxed according to their marginal damages, even if immigration worsens the situation of congestion and pollution, local residents still benefit from the larger population size. However, this positive result does not apply to immigrants who rely on government subsidies that cannot be offset by their future tax payment. We also ignore intertemporal cohort effects, on which see, e.g., Lacomba & Lagos 2010.

There is a possible distributional consideration as yet not covered. Thus, in this simple model, while local residents as a group gain, owners of L may lose. If they belong to the lower-income groups, inequality may increase. The loss of the poor of $X may more than offset the gain of the rich of $2X in welfare terms. However, as discussed in Chapter 5, it is more efficient to focus on efficiency on each specific issue, and try to promote equality as a general policy. Moreover, although the immigration of unskilled workers into country A may make the distribution of income within country A less equal, it actually makes distribution more equal globally.

Two further economic arguments against immigration may be considered: unemployment and international terms of trade. The argument that immigration increases unemployment has been thoroughly demolished. Economists, including Neville Norman and Julian Simon, have shown convincingly that immigration and higher population growth, at least within limits, does not increase unemployment and slow the rate of growth in income per head. If anything, the reverse is true.

People who see that some job vacancies are filled by migrants, and hence conclude that immigration reduces employment opportunities to existing residents, are displaying a very narrow-minded view. While some migrants take away jobs that would otherwise be available to existing residents, they also help to create jobs in various ways. First, with what the capital migrants bring in and the incomes they generate here, migrants add to the demand for goods and services. Second, some migrants are entrepreneurial and set up their own enterprises which provide employment, both for new migrants and existing residents. Third, some migrants provide skills not available among existing residents and, hence, help to make certain business ventures possible. This helps to create employment opportunities that can be filled by existing residents.

A more sophisticated argument that immigration makes existing residents worse off relies on the worsening terms of trade with other countries. However, this result is largely based on the assumption that while immigration increases demand for imports, it does not increase our opportunities for exports and, hence, decreases our international terms of trade. This is quite untrue. Migrants increase domestic demand for imports but also increase domestic export opportunities by: increasing network connections to their countries of origin, and by increasing the output levels and variety of the domestic economy. International terms of trade fluctuate over time due to the balance of many different factors. However, the terms of trade of a country of large immigration over centuries does not see its terms of trade collapsing towards zero.

Our discussion of the economic effects of immigration, although shedding some light, is inadequate to answer the general question on the desirability of immigration, even just from the viewpoint of local residents only. This is so because there may be negative non-economic effects that could more than offset the positive economic effects. Obviously, if immigration leads to serious social disharmony or even outright conflict, all people involved may be made seriously worse off overall, even if the per capita income increases significantly. In addition to this well-known issue of social harmony, our analysis in the previous appendix (and Chapter 3) also suggests that more subtle effects through generalized external effects including the effects on morality may also have to be taken into account. This is particularly so for immigration, as immigrants may bring in new cultures, possibly giving rise to both the benefits of multiculturalism and variety, as well as potential conflicts. As these wider effects of immigration may either be positive or negative, again a definitive conclusion is not possible before examining the particular cases in detail, echoing our general point discussed in Appendix C and Chapter 3.[1] All these suggest that an adequate analysis of a public policy or social change is likely to involve a host of relevant factors and calls for a multidisciplinary study.

---

[1] An analysis focusing on the effects of immigration on institutions 'find no evidence of negative and some evidence of positive impacts in institutional quality as a result of immigration' (Clark et al. 2015).

A Democratic Decision on COEs: Striking a Balance between Elitism and Populism[*]

I attended a wrap-up session to public consultation on COEs (certificates of entitlement for owning cars) and car-ownership issues on 26 August 2013 at the LTA (Land Transport Authority, Singapore). During the discussion, I realized that even professional car dealers who routinely bid for COEs do not know that the existing bidding system is very efficient. Even after I used simple examples (see later) to explain why the popular pay-as-you-bid system is inefficient, most people seem to have difficulties seeing the simple point. At the end of the session, I was discussing with two fellow economists, one from Nanyang Technological University (NTU) and one from the National University of Singapore (NUS). The NTU economist predicted that the government will soon (before the next general election, subsequently held in 2015) be forced by popular public opinion to use the inefficient pay-as-you-bid system; he believes that the public will not be able to see its inefficiency against the current Vickrey auction (named after a Nobel laureate). The NUS economist and I took up a bet of $10 each to counteract his claim. Here, I explain why the current Vickrey auction is efficient. I also trust that the Singapore government is wise enough not to give in completely to incorrect but popular demand. The general election in Singapore was held on 11 September 2015, and the government has held its ground until now, Dec 2018. The NUS economist and I won our bet, but we have yet to collect our $10 each.

The Vickrey auction is also called a second-price auction, because, for the simple case of a single item, the winner pays only the second-highest price bid. To see why this is most efficient, suppose that there are only two items of the

---

[*] This appendix is rewritten from Ng (2013b).

same type to be auctioned. There are four bidders each willing to pay a maximum price of $4000, $3000, $2000, and $1000, respectively. But each bidder only knows her own willingness to pay, not those of others. Under the Vickrey auction, each bidder has the right incentive to bid her true maximum willingness to pay. After the bids are collected, the two items are allocated to bidders 1 and 2. However, instead of paying their respective bids of $4000 and $3000 (as are required under the pay-as-you-bid system), they pay only the highest losing bid of $2000 + $1. The items are allocated to those who value the items highest. Those missing out are not willing to pay for the price actually paid ($2001).

In contrast, if the pay-as-you-bid method is used, if bidders 1 and 2 still bid their true maximum willingness to pay, they will have to pay $4000 and $3000, respectively, making them not gain anything from 'winning' the bids, as they have to pay the maximum amounts over which they do not want to get the items. This will motivate them not to bid their true willingness to pay. As all bidders try to underbid in different proportions, the final outcome may involve allocating the items to bidders with lower willingness to pay.

Also, using pay-as-you-bid need not result in lower COE prices as its proponents hope. While the marginal winning prices may fall, the average prices may in fact increase. We should also not worry too much about high COE prices since car ownership is not a necessity in Singapore; the revenues from COE may also be used to improve public transportation or to provide other public goods. In addition, the rich–poor question should be tackled by the general distribution policies (Chapter 5).

Thus, if one really understands the inefficiency of the pay-as-you-bid system, one should not blame the existing efficient system. On the other hand, if my NTU colleague is correct that the public will not understand, should we not regard the issue as a technical one that should be left to the experts? We leave the details of bridge construction to the engineers and the choice of different medicines to the doctors; should we not leave the choice of different auctioning systems to the economists or auction theorists? Leaving difficult decisions to the experts is especially sensible where the public does not understand the technicalities and where there is a virtual consensus among the experts. I bet my professional reputation on the consensus among experts regarding the efficiency of the Vickrey auction.

The government has moved towards being more liberal and more responsive to public opinions. This is a healthy trend. However, where it is really in the long-term interest of the people, it should dare to persist in good policies despite temporary unpopularity. On COEs, it has already given significant concession to populism by creating the category for small cars, although it should further eliminate expensive cars from this category, to lower its COE prices. It should also impose high taxes on luxurious cars and on petrol on the grounds of efficiency for diamond goods (goods valued for their values, discussed in my paper in *American Economic Review*, 1987) and external costs. Insistence on the excellent Vickrey auction will mark a right balance between elitism and populism, a desirable property of true democracy.

References

ABEL, Gillian. (2010). Decriminalisation: A harm minimisation and human rights approach to regulating sex work. PhD Thesis. Christchurch: University of Otago.

ADLER, Alejandro, BONIWELL, Ilona, GIBSON, Evelyn, et al. (2017a). Chapter 2: Definitions of Terms. *Happiness: Transforming the Development Landscape.* Thimphu, Bhutan: The Centre for Bhutan Studies and GNH. 21–38.

ADLER, Alejandro, UNANUE, Wenceslao, OSIN, Evgeny, RICARD, Matthieu, ALKIRE, Sabina, & SELIGMAN, Martin. (2017b). Chapter 7: Psychological Wellbeing. *Happiness: Transforming the Development Landscape.* Thimphu, Bhutan: The Centre for Bhutan Studies and GNH. 118–159.

ALESINA, Alberto. (2016). Review of *Political Order and Inequality: Their Foundations and Their Consequences* by Carles Boix. *Journal of Economic Literature,* 54(3): 935–941.

ALESINA, Albeto & GIULIANO, Paola. (2015). Culture and institutions. *Journal of Economic Literature,* 53(4): 898–944.

ALI, Ayaan Hirsi. (2008). Does the free market corrode moral character? American Enterprise Institute, 1 October. Retrieved from: www.aei.org/publication/does-the-free-market-corrode-moral-character-2/.

ALLAIS, Maurice & HAGEN, Ole. (1979). *Expected Utility Hypotheses and the Allais Paradox.* Dordrecht: Reidel Publishing Company.

ALTMAN, Stuart & BARRO, Robert. (1971). Officer supply-the impact of pay, the draft, and the Vietnam War. *American Economic Review,* 61(4): 649–64

ANDERSON, Elizabeth. (1993). *Value in Ethics and Economics.* Cambridge, MA: Harvard University Press.

ANDREONI, James. (1990). Impure altruism and donations to public goods: A theory of warm-glow giving. *Economic Journal,* 100(401): 464–477.

ANGELES, Luis. (2011). A closer look at the Easterlin paradox. *Journal of Socio-Economics,* 40: 67–73.

ARIELY, Dan, BRACHA, Anat, & MEIER, Stephan. (2009). Doing good or doing well? Image motivation and monetary incentives in behaving prosocially. *American Economic Review,* 99(1): 544–555.

ARROW, Kenneth J. (1972). Gifts and exchanges. *Philosophy and Public Affairs*, 1(4): 343–362.

BACHNER-MELMAN, R., GRITSENKO, I., NEMANOV, L., ZOHAR, A. H., DINA, C., & EBSTEIN, R. P. (2005). Dopaminergic polymorphisms associated with self-report measures of human altruism: A fresh phenotype for the dopamine D4 receptor. *Molecular Psychiatry*, 10, 333–335.

BANDOW, Doug. (2012). A new military draft would revive a very bad old idea. *Forbes*, 16 July.

BARBER, R. N. (1969). Prostitution and the increasing number of convictions for rape in Queensland. *Australian & New Zealand Journal of Criminology*, 2(3): 169–174.

BARKER, G. & GOUCHER, C., eds. (2015). *The Cambridge World History: Volume 2: A World with Agriculture, 12,000 BCE–500 CE*. Cambridge: Cambridge University Press.

BARROTTA, Pierluigi. (2008). Why economists should be unhappy with the economics of happiness. *Economics and Philosophy*, 24: 145–165.

BARTLING, Björn, WEBER, Roberto A., & YAO, Lan. (2015). Do markets erode social responsibility? Quarterly Journal of Economics, 130(1): 219–266.

BASU, Kaushik. (2007). Coercion, contract and the limits of the market. *Social Choice and Welfare*, 29(4): 559–579.

BEARD, T. Randolph, KASERMAN, David L., & OSTERKAMP, Rigmar. (2013). *The Global Organ Shortage: Economic Causes, Human Consequences, Policy Responses*. Stanford, CA: Stanford University Press.

BEARD, T. Randolph & OSTERKAMP, Rigmar. (2014). The organ crisis: A disaster of our own making. *European Journal of Health Economics*, 15: 1–5.

BECKER, Gary S. (1957/1971). *The Economics of Discrimination*. Chicago: University of Chicago Press.

BECKER, Gary S. (1978). *The Economic Approach to Human Behaviour*. Chicago: University of Chicago Press.

BECKER, Gary S. (1981). *A Treatise on the Family*. Cambridge, MA: Harvard University Press.

BECKER, Gary S. (1992). The economic way of looking at life, Nobel Lecture.

BECKER, Gary S. (2012). What limits to using money prices to buy and sell? The Becker-Posner Blog, 21 October.

BECKER, Gary S. & ELÍAS, Julio Jorge. (2007). Introducing incentives in the market for live and cadaveric organ donations. *Journal of Economic Perspectives*, 21(3): 3–24.

BEHAN, Paul. (2013). Prostitution: Legal vs. Illegal. *The University Times*, 25 October. Retrieved from: www.universitytimes.ie/2013/10/prostitution-legal-vs-illegal/.

BÉNABOU, Roland & TIROLE, Jean. (2006). Incentives and prosocial behavior. *American Economic Review*, 96(5): 1652–1678.

BÉNABOU, Roland &TIROLE, Jean. (2016). Mindful economics: The production, consumption, and value of beliefs. *Journal of Economic Perspectives*, 30(3): 141–164.

BENJAMIN, Daniel J., HEFFETZ, Ori, KIMBALL, Miles S., & REES-JONES, Alex. (2010). Do people seek to maximize happiness? Evidence from new surveys. Working Paper 16489, National Bureau of Economic Research. Retrieved from: www.nber.org/papers/w16489.

BENOIT, C., JANSSON, S. M., SMITH, M., & FLAGG, J. (2018). Prostitution stigma and its effect on the working conditions, personal lives, and health of sex workers. *Journal of Sex Research*, 55(4–5): 457–471.

BERETTI, Antoine, FIGUIERES, Charles, & GROLLEAU, Gilles. (2017) An instrument that could turn crowding-out into crowding-in. Working Paper, https://dumas.ccsd.cnrs.fr/INRA/hal-01487107v1.

BERGGREN, Niclas & NILSSON, Therese. (2013). Does economic freedom foster tolerance? *Kyklos*, 66(2): 177–207.

BERGSTROM, Theodore C. (1996). Economics in a family way. *Journal of Economic Literature*, 34: 1903–1934.

BHAGWATI, Jagdish. (2004). In Defense of Globalization: With a New Afterword. Oxford: Oxford University Press.

BISIN, Alberto. (2017). The evolution of value systems: A review essay on Ian Morris's *Foragers, Farmers, and Fossil Fuels*. *Journal of Economic Literature*, 55(3): 1122–1135.

BISWAS, Siddhartha, CHAKRABORTY, Indraneel, & HAI, Rong. (2017). Income inequality, tax policy, and economic growth. *Economic Journal*, 127(601): 688–727.

BLANCHFLOWER, David G. & OSWALD, Andrew J. (2004). Well-being over time in Britain and the USA. *Journal of Public Economics*, 88(7–8): 1359–1386.

BONIWELL, Ilona & HENRY, Jane. (2007). Developing conceptions of well-being: Advancing subjective, hedonic and eudamonic theories. *Social Psychology Review*, 9: 3–18.

BOWLES, Samuel. (2000). Group Conflicts, Individual Interactions, and the Evolution of Preferences. *Social Dynamics* (eds, DURLOUF, S. & YOUNG, P.). Cambridge, MA: MIT Press.

BOWLES, Samuel. (2008). Policies designed for self-interested citizens may undermine 'the moral sentiments', *Science*, 320: 1605–1609.

BOWLES, Samuel & GINTIS, Herbert. (2000). Walrasian economics in retrospect. *The Quarterly Journal of Economics*, 115(4): 1411–1439.

BOWLES, Samuel & POLANIA-REYES, Sandra. (2012). Economic incentives and social preferences: Substitutes or complements? *Journal of Economic Literature*, 50(2): 368–425.

BOYD, Robert & RICHERSON, Peter J. (1985). *Culture and the Evolutionary Process*. Chicago: University of Chicago Press.

BRENNAN, Geoffrey & BUCHANAN, James. (1984). Voter choice: Evaluating political alternatives. *American Behavioral Scientist*, 28(2): 185–201.

BRENNAN, Jason & JAWORSKI, Peter M. (2016). Markets without Limits: Moral Virtues and Commercial Interests. New York: Routledge.

BREYER, Friedrich & WEIMANN, Joachim. (2015). Of morals, markets and mice: Be careful drawing policy conclusions from experimental findings! *European Journal of Political Economy*, 40: 387–390.

BRÜLDE, Bengt. (2007). Happiness theories of the good life. *Journal of Happiness Studies*, 8: 15–49.

BUCHANAN, James M. & TULLOCK, Gordon. (1962). *The Calculus of Consent*. Ann Arbor: University of Michigan Press.

BUCHHOLZ, Todd G. (2007). *New Ideas from Dead Economists: An Introduction to Modern Economic Thought*. New York: Penguin.

BUGGIANO, L. (2015). When does the sex market need new legislation? *The Zephyr*.

CAMERON, J. S. & HOFFENBERG, R. (1999). The ethics of organ transplantation reconsidered: Paid organ donation and the use of executed prisoners as donors. *Kidney international,* 55(2): 724–732.

CAMPANA, P. & VARESE, F. (2016). Exploitation in human trafficking and smuggling. *European Journal on Criminal Policy and Research,* 22(1): 89–105.

CAMPOS, N. F., DIMOVA, R., & SALEH, A. (2016). Corruption and economic growth: An econometric survey of the evidence. *Journal of Institutional and Theoretical Economics,* 172(3): 521–543.

CHANG, Chun-Ping & HAO, Yu. (2017). Environmental performance, corruption and economic growth: Global evidence using a new data set, *Applied Economics,* 49(5): 498–514.

Charities Aid Foundation (2016). Gross domestic philanthropy: An international analysis of GDP, tax and giving. Retrieved from: https://futureworldgiving.org/2016/02/02/gross-domestic-philanthropy-an-international-analysis-of-gdp-tax-and-giving/.

CHARNESS, Gary & RABIN, Matthew. (2002). Understanding social preferences with simple tests. *The Quarterly Journal of Economics,* 117(3): 817–869.

CHASE, Michael S. (2008). *Taiwan's Security Policy: External Threats and Domestic Politics.* Boulder, CO: Lynne Rienner Publishers.

CHEKOLA, M. (2007) Happiness, rationality, autonomy and the good life. *Journal of Happiness Studies,* 8: 51–78.

CHEN, Daniel L. & YEH, Susan. (2014). The construction of morals. *Journal of Economic Behavior & Organization,* 104: 84–105.

CHERRY, Mark J. (2017). Organ vouchers and barter markets: Saving lives, reducing suffering, and trading in human organs. *Journal of Medicine and Philosophy: A Forum for Bioethics and Philosophy of Medicine,* 42(5): 503–517.

CHETTY, Raj, SAEZ, Emmanuel, & SÁNDOR, Laszlo. (2014). What policies increase prosocial behavior? An experiment with referees at the *Journal of Public Economics. Journal of Economic Perspectives,* 28(3): 169–188.

CHO, Seo-Young. (2016). Liberal coercion? Prostitution, human trafficking and policy. *European Journal of Law and Economics,* 41(2): 321–348.

CHOTIKAPANICH, Duangkamon, GRIFFITHS, William E., RAO, D. S. Prasada, & VALENCIA, Vicar. (2012). Global income distributions and inequality, 1993 and 2000: Incorporating country-level inequality modeled with beta distributions. *Review of Economics and Statistics,* 94(1): 52–73.

CHRISTIAN, David. (2015). *The Cambridge World History: Volume I: Introducing World History, to 10,000 BCE.* Cambridge: Cambridge University Press.

CLARK, J. R., LAWSON, Robert, NOWRASTEH, Alex, POWELL, Benjamin, & MURPHY, Ryan. (2015). Does immigration impact institutions? *Public Choice,* 163(3–4): 321–335.

CLARKE, Harry & NG, Yew-Kwang. (1993). Immigration and economic welfare: Resource and environmental aspects. *Economic Record,* 69(206): 259–273.

COASE, Ronal H. (1978). Economics and contiguous disciplines. *Journal of Legal Studies,* 7(2): 201–211.

COHEN, Lloyd. (1989). Increasing the supply of transplant organs: The virtues of a futures market. *George Washington Law Review,* 58: 1–51.

COHEN, I. Glenn. (2014). A fuller picture of organ markets. *The American Journal of Bioethics'* 14: 19–21.

COHEN, L. Jonathan. (1983). The controversy about irrationality. *Behavioral and Brain Sciences, 6*: 510–517.

COOTER, Robert. (1984). Prices and sanctions. *Columbia Law Review, 84*(6): 1523–1560.

COSTA-FONT, Joan, JOFRE-BONET, Mireia, & YEN, Steven T. (2013). Not all incentives wash out the warm glow: The case of blood donation revisited. *Kyklos, 66*(4): 529–551.

COWEN, Tyler. (1998). *In Praise of Commercial Culture.* Cambridge, MA: Harvard University Press.

COWEN, Tyler. (2008). No, on balance. *Does the Free Market Corrode Moral Character?* Conshohocken, PA: John Templeton Foundation. Retrieved from: www.templeton.org/market.

CRISP, Roger. (2006) Hedonism reconsidered. *Philosophy and Phenomenological Research, 73*(3): 619–645.

CUNDIFF, Kirby. (2004). Prostitution and sex crimes. *ProCon.org.* http://citeseerx.ist.psu.edu/viewdoc/summary?doi=10.1.1.566.1479.

DALAL, Aparna R. (2015). Philosophy of organ donation: Review of ethical facets. *World Journal of Transplantation, 5*(2): 44.

DAMBRUN, Michaël & RICARD, Matthieu. (2011). Self-centeredness and selflessness: A theory of self-based psychological functioning and its consequences for happiness. *Review of General Psychology, 15*: 138–157.

DAVIS, John B. (forthcoming). Economics imperialism versus multidisciplinarity. *History of Economic Ideas.* Available at SSRN.

DE GRAUWE, Paul. (2016). *The Limits of the Market: The Pendulum between Government and Market.* Oxford: Oxford University Press.

DE HAAN, Jakob & STURM, Jan-Egbert. (2000). On the relationship between economic freedom and economic growth. *European Journal of Political Economy, 16*(2): 215–241.

DEARDEN, Lizzie. (2016). Brexit research suggests 1.2 million Leave voters regret their choice in reversal that could change result. *The Independent,* 1 July.

DECI, Edward L. (1971). Effects of externally mediated rewards on intrinsic motivation. *Journal of Personality and Social Psychology, 18*: 105–115.

DECI, Edward L., KOESTNER, Richard, & RYAN, Richard M. (1999). A meta-analytic review of experiments examining the effects of extrinsic rewards on intrinsic motivation. *Psychological Bulletin, 125*(6): 627–668.

DECI, Edward L. & RYAN, Richard M. (2008). Hedonia, eudaimonia, and well-being: An introduction. *Journal of Happiness Studies, 9*: 1–11.

DEERING, Kathleen N., AMIN, Avni, SHOVELLER, Jean, et al. (2014). A systematic review of the correlates of violence against sex workers. *American Journal of Public Health, 104*(5): e42–e54.

DELLE FAVE, A., MASSIMINI, F., & BASSI, M. (2011). *Psychological Selection and Optimal Experience across Cultures.* Heidelberg: Springer.

DI TELLA, Rafael, MACCULLOCH, Robert, & OSWALD, Andrew. (2003). The macroeconomics of happiness. *Review of Economics and Statistics, 85*: 809–827.

DOWNS, Anthony. (1957). *An Economic Theory of Democracy.* New York: Harper.

DWORKIN, Andrea. (1997). Prostitution and Male Supremacy. Life and Death (ed., DWORKIN, A.). New York: Free Press, 138–216.

EASTERLIN, Richard A. (1974). Does Economic Growth Improve the Human Lot? Some Empirical Evidence. *Nations and Households in Economic Growth, Essays in Honor of Moses Abramovitz*. New York: Academic Press.

EASTERLIN, Richard A., ed. (2002). *Happiness in Economics*. Cheltenham: Edward Elgar.

EASTERLY, William. (2001). *The Elusive Quest for Growth: Economists' Adventures and Misadventures in the Tropics*. Cambridge, MA: MIT Press.

EDGREN, G., TRAN, T. N., HJALGRIM, H., et al. (2007). Improving health profile of blood donors as a consequence of transfusion safety efforts. *Transfusion*, 47(11): 2017–2024.

EGHTESAD, B., JAIN, A. B., & FUNG, J. J. (2003). Living donor liver transplantation: Ethics and safety. *Transplantation proceedings*, 35(1): 51–52.

EISENBERGER, Robert & CAMERON, Judy. (1996). Detrimental effects of reward: Reality or myth? *American Psychologist*, 51: 1154–1166.

ELÍAS, Julio J. (2014). The role of repugnance in the development of markets: The case of the market for kidneys for transplants. *CESifo Conference on Social Economics, Munich, 21–22 March*.

ELÍAS, Julio J., LACETERA, Nicola, & MACIS, Mario. (2015). Sacred values? The effect of information on attitudes toward payments for human organs. *American Economic Review*, 105(5): 361–365. http://dx.doi.org/10.1257/aer.p20151035.

ELÍAS, Julio J., LACETERA, Nicola, & MACIS, Mario. (2016). Efficiency-morality trade-offs in repugnant transactions: A choice experiment. Working Paper 22632, National Bureau of Economic Research.

ELÍAS, Julio J., LACETERA, Nicola, MACIS, Mario, & SALARDI, Paola. (2017). Economic development and the regulation of morally contentious activities. *American Economic Review*, 107(5): 76–80.

ELSTER, Jon. (1983). Sour Grapes. New York: Cambridge University Press.

EPSTEIN, Richard A. (2008). Altruism and valuable consideration in organ transplantation. When Altruism Isn't Enough: The Case for Compensating Kidney Donors (ed, SATEL, S.). Washington, DC: AEI Press.

ETZIONI, Amitai. (2008). 'The Moral Dimension' revisited. *Socio-Economic Review*, 6(1): 168–173.

EVANS, Jonathan St. B. T. & OVER, David E. (1996). *Rationality and Reasoning*. Hove: Psychology Press.

EVREN, Özgür & MINARDI, Stefania. (2017). Warm-glow giving and freedom to be selfish. *Economic Journal*, 127(603): 1381–1409.

FACCHINI, Francois & COUVREUR, Stéphane. (2015). Inequality: The original economic sin of capitalism? An evaluation of Thomas Piketty's 'Capital in the twenty-first century'. *European Journal of Political Economy*, 39: 281–287.

FALK, Armin & SZECH, Nora. (2013). Morals and markets. *Science*, 340: 707–711.

FARAVELLI, M. & STANCA, L. (2014). Economic incentives and social preferences: Causal evidence of non-separability. *Journal of Economic Behavior & Organization*, 108: 273–289.

FEHR, Ernst & FALK, Armin. (2002). Psychological foundations of incentives. *European Economic Review*, 46: 687–724.

FELDMAN, Fred. (2004). *Pleasure and the Good Life*. New York: Oxford University Press.

FELDMAN, Yuval & TEICHMAN, Doron. (2008). Are all 'legal dollars' created equal? *Northwestern University Law Review*, 102: 223.

FERNÁNDEZ-REAL, José Manuel, LÓPEZ-BERMEJO, Abel, & RICART, Wifredo. (2002). Cross-talk between iron metabolism and diabetes. *Diabetes*, 51(8): 2348–2354.

FESTRÉ, Agnès & GARROUSTE, Pierre. (2015). Theory and evidence in psychology and economics about motivation crowding out: A possible convergence? *Journal of Economic Surveys*, 29(2): 339–356.

FINE, Ben. (2002). Economic imperialism: A view from the periphery. *Review of Radical Political Economics*, 34: 187–201.

FINE, Ben & MILONAKIS, Dimitris. (2009). *From Economics Imperialism to Freakonomics: The Shifting Boundaries between Economics and Other Social Sciences*. London: Routledge.

FRANK, Robert H. (1987). If *Homo Economicus* could choose his own utility function, would he want one with a conscience? American Economic Review, 77: 593–604; also 1989, 89: 588–596.

FRASER, Nancy. (2014). Can society be commodities all the way down? Post-Polanyian reflections on capitalist crisis. *Economy and Society*, 43(4): 541–558.

FREIMAN, Christopher. (2015). Cost-benefit analysis and the value of environmental goods. *Georgetown Journal of Law & Public Policy*, 13: 337–347.

FREY, Bruno S. (1997) *Not Just for the Money: An Economic Theory of Personal Motivation*. Cheltenham: Edward Elgar.

FREY, Bruno S. & JEGEN, Reto. (2001). Motivation crowding out theory. Journal of Economic Surveys, 15(5): 589–611.

FREY, Bruno S. & OBERHOLZER-GEE, Felix. (1997). The cost of price incentives: An empirical analysis of motivation crowding-out. *The American Economic Review*, 87(4): 746–755.

FREY, Bruno S., OBERHOLZER-GEE, Felix, & EICHENBERGER, Reiner. (1996). The old lady visits your backyard: A tale of morals and markets. *Journal of Political Economy*, 104(6): 1297–1313.

FREY, Bruno S. & STUTZER, Alois. (2000). Happiness, economy and institutions. *Economic Journal*, 110(466): 918–938.

FREY, Bruno S. & STUTZER, Alois. (2002). *Happiness and Economics: How the Economy and Institutions Affect Human Well-Being*. Princeton, NJ: Princeton University Press.

FRIEDMAN, Daniel & McNEILL, Daniel. (2013). *Morals and Markets: The Dangerous Balance*, 2nd edition. Basingstoke: Palgrave/Macmillan.

FRIEDMAN, Milton. (1967). Why Not a Volunteer Army? *The Draft: A Handbook of Facts and Alternatives* (ed, TAX, Sol). Chicago: University of Chicago Press, 200–207.

GAGNON, Julien & GOYAL, Sanjeev. (2017). Networks, markets, and inequality. *American Economic Review*, 107(1): 1–30.

GAMBLE, Amelie & GÄRLING, Tommy. (2012). The relationships between life satisfaction, happiness, and current mood. *Journal of Happiness Studies*, 13(1): 31–45.

GHODS, Ahad J. & SAVAJ, Shekoufeh. (2006). Iranian model of paid and regulated living unrelated kidney donation. *Clinical Journal of the American Society of Nephrology*, 1: 1136–1145.

GILLESPIE, Ryan. (2017). What money cannot buy and what money ought not buy: dignity, motives, and markets in human organ procurement debates. *Journal of Medical Humanities*, 1–16. https://doi.org/10.1007/s10912-016-9427-z.

GLAESER, Edward L. (2017). A review essay on Alvin Roth's Who Gets What – and Why. *Journal of Economic Literature*, 55(4): 1602–1614.

GLAZIER, Alexandra K. (2011). The principles of gift law and the regulation of organ donation. *Transplant International*, 24(4): 368–372.

GNEEZY, Uri, MEIER, Stephan, & REY-BIEL, Pedro (2011). When and why incentives (don't) work to modify behavior. *Journal of Economic Perspectives*, 25(4): 191–209.

GNEEZY, Uri & RUSTICHINI, Aldo. (2000). A fine is a price. *The Journal of Legal Studies*, 29(1): 1–17.

GOETTE, Lorenz, STUTZER, Alois, & FREY, Beat M. (2010). Prosocial motivation and blood donations: A survey of the empirical literature. *Transfusion Medicine and Hemotherapy*, 37(3): 149–154.

GRAHAM, Carol. (2011) Happiness measures as a guide to development policy? Promise and potential pitfalls. Paper presented at the Annual Meetings of the American Economic Association, Denver, CO, 7 January.

GREIF, Avner & IYIGUN, Murat. (2013). What did the old poor law really accomplish? A redux. Discussion Paper 7398, Institute for the Study of Labor.

GRIFFIN, James. (2007). What do happiness studies study? *Journal of Happiness Studies*, 8: 139–148.

GROSSMAN, Gene M., HELPMAN, Elhanan, OBERFIELD, Ezra, & SAMPSON, Thomas. (2017). Balanced growth despite Uzawa. *American Economic Review*, 107(4): 1293–1312.

GRUBER, Jonathan & MULLAINATHAN, Sendhil. (2005). Do cigarette taxes make smokers happier? *Advances in Economic Analysis & Policy*, 5: 1–43.

GUDEMAN, S. (2008). *Economy's Tension: The Dialectics of Community and Market*. Berghahn, Oxford.

GUNDERSON, Anne. (2018). The effect of decriminalizing prostitution on public health and safety. Chicago Policy Review (online), http://chicagopolicyreview.org/.

HAINES, William A. (2010). Hedonism and the variety of goodness. *Utilitas*, 22(2): 148–170.

HAMBURGER, J. & CROSNIER, J. (1968). Moral and Ethical Problems in Transplantation. Human Transplantation (eds, RAPPORT, F. T. & DAUSSET, J.). New York, London: Grune & Stratton, Inc.

HAMILTON, William D. (1964). The genetical evolution of social behavior, I and II. *Journal of Theoretical Biology*, 7(1): 1–52.

HANSEN, W. Lee & WEISBROD, Burton A. (1967). Economics of the military draft. *The Quarterly Journal of Economics*, 81: 395–421.

HANSMANN, Henry. (1989). The economics and ethics of markets for human organs. *Journal of Health Politics, Policy and Law*, 14(1): 57–85.

HARSANYI, John C. (1953). Cardinal utility in welfare economics and in the theory of risk-taking. *Journal of Political Economy*, 61: 434–435.

HARSANYI, John C. (1955). Cardinal welfare, individualistic ethics, and interpersonal comparisons of utility. *Journal of Political Economy*, 63: 309–321.

HARSANYI, John C. (1976). Essays on Ethics, Social Behaviour, and Scientific Explanation. Heidelberg: Springer.

HARSANYI, John C. (1997). Utilities, preferences, and substantive goods. SCW, 14: 129–145.

HAUSMAN, Daniel M. (2010). Hedonism and welfare economics. Economics and Philosophy, 26: 321–344.

HAYBRON, Daniel M. (2000). Two philosophical problems in the study of happiness. Journal of Happiness Studies, 1: 207–225.

HAYBRON, Daniel M. (2007). Life satisfaction, ethical reflection, and the science of happiness. Journal of Happiness Studies, 8: 99–138.

HAYEK, Friedrich A. (1960). The Constitution of Liberty. Chicago: University of Chicago Press.

HE, Qinglian. (2008). No. Does the Free Market Corrode Moral Character? Conshohocken, PA: John Templeton Foundation. Retrieved from: www .templeton.org/market, 8–9.

HEALY, Kieran. (2006). Do presumed consent laws raise organ procurement rates? DePaul Law Review, 55: 1017–1043.

HEATH, Joseph. (2012). Letting the world in: Empirical approaches to ethics. Ethics Forum, 7(3): 93–107.

HEIDT-FORSYTHE, Erin. (2017). Morals or markets? Regulating assisted reproductive technologies as morality or economic policies in the states. AJOB Empirical Bioethics, 8(1): 58–67.

HELD, P. J., MCCORMICK, F., OJO, A., & ROBERTS, J. P. (2016). A cost-benefit analysis of government compensation of kidney donors. American Journal of Transplantation, 16: 877–885.

HIPPEN, Benjamin E. (2005). In defense of a regulated market in kidneys from living vendors. Journal of Medicine and Philosophy, 30: 593–626.

HIPPEN, Benjamin E. & SATEL, Sally. (2008). Crowding out, crowding in, and financial incentives for organ procurement. When Altruism Isn't Enough: The Case for Compensating Kidney Donors (ed, Satel, Sally). Washington, DC: The American Enterprise Institute Press. 96–110.

HIRSCH, Fred. (1976). Social Limits to Growth. Cambridge, MA: Harvard University Press.

HIRSCHMAN, Albert O. (1982). Rival interpretations of market society: Civilizing, destructive, or feeble? Journal of Economic Literature, 20(4): 1463–1484.

HIRSCHMAN, Albert O. (1992). Rival Views of Market Society and Other Recent Essays. Cambridge, MA: Harvard University Press.

HIRSCHMAN, Albert O. (2013). The Passions and the Interests: Political Arguments for Capitalism before Its Triumph. Princeton, NJ: Princeton University Press.

HIRSHLEIFER, Jack. (1985). The expanding domain of economics. American Economic Review, 75(6): 53–68.

HOFFMAN, Martin L. (1981). Is altruism part of human nature? Journal of Personality and Social Psychology, 40: 121–137.

HOLMSTRÖM, Bengt. (2017). Pay for performance and beyond. American Economic Review, 107(7): 1753–1777.

HORNBECK, Richard & KENISTON, Daniel. (2017).Creative destruction: Barriers to urban growth and the Great Boston fire of 1872. American Economic Review, 107(6): 1365–1398.

HUTA, Veronika & RYAN, Richard M. (2010). Pursuing pleasure or virtue: The differential and overlapping well-being benefits of hedonic and eudaimonic motives. *Journal of Happiness Studies*, 11: 735–762.

IMAS, Alex. (2014). Working for the 'warm glow': On the benefits and limits of prosocial incentives. *Journal of Public Economics*, 114: 14–18.

IMMORDINO, Giovanni & RUSSO, Francesco Flaviano. (2015a). Laws and stigma: The case of prostitution. European Journal of Law and Economics, 40(2): 209–223. http://dx.doi.org/10.1007/s10657-015-9491-2.

IMMORDINO, Giovanni & RUSSO, Francesco Flaviano. (2015b). Regulating prostitution: A health risk approach. Journal of Public Economics, 121: 14–31. http://dx.doi.org/10.1016/j.jpubeco.2014.11.001.

JAHNSEN, Synnøve Økland & Hendrik WAGENAAR, eds. (2017). *Assessing Prostitution Policies in Europe*. Abingdon: Routledge.

JAMES, Harvey S., Jr. (2015). Generalized morality, institutions and economic growth, and the intermediating role of generalized trust. *Kyklos*, 68(2): 165–196.

JANSSEN, Maarten C. W. & MENDYS-KAMPHORST, Ewa. (2004). The price of a price: On the crowding out and in of social norms. *Journal of Economic Behavior and Organization*, 55(3): 377–395.

JARL, J., GERDTHAM, U. G., DESATNIK, P., & PRÜTZ, K. G. (2018). Effects of kidney transplantation on labour market outcomes in Sweden. *Transplantation*, 102(8): 1375–1381. http://dx.doi.org/10.1097/TP.0000000000002228.

John Templeton Foundation (2008). *Does the Free Market Corrode Moral Character?* Retrieved from: www.templeton.org.

JONSSON, Sofia & JAKOBSSON, Niklas. (2017). Is buying sex morally wrong? Comparing attitudes toward prostitution using individual-level data across eight Western European countries. *Women's Studies International Forum*, 61: 58–69.

JOST, Lawrence J. & SHINER, Roger A., eds. (2002). *Eudaimonia and Well-Being: Ancient and Modern Conceptions*. Edmonton: Academic Printing and Publishing.

KAHNEMAN, Daniel. (1999). Objective happiness. *Well-Being: The Foundations of Hedonic Psychology* (eds, KAHNEMAN, D., DIENER, E., & SCHWARTZ, N.). New York: Russell Sage, 3–25.

KAHNEMAN, Daniel & DEATON, Angus. (2010). Does Money Buy Happiness . . . or Just a Better Life. Mimeo: Princeton University.

KAHNEMAN, Daniel & TVERSKY, Amos. (1996). On the reality of cognitive illusions. *Psychological Review*, 103(3): 582–591.

KAHNEMAN, Daniel, WAKKER, Peter P., & SARIN, Rakesh. (1997). Back to Bentham? Explorations of experienced utility. *The Quarterly Journal of Economics*, 112(2): 375–405.

KANE, Tim. (2006). No justification for a military draft. *The Heritage Foundation*, 28 November. Retrieved from: http://s3.amazonaws.com/thf_me dia/2006/pdf/wm1263.pdf.

KANT, Immanuel. (1785/1993). Grounding for the Metaphysics of Morals, 3rd edition. Translated by Ellington, James W. Indianapolis, IN: Hackett.

KANT, Immanuel. (1799/2012). *On the Supposed Right to Lie from Benevolent Motives*. Long Island: Sophia Omni.

KAPLOW, Louis. (1996). The optimal supply of public goods and the distortionary cost of taxation. *National Tax Journal*, 49(4): 513–533.

KAPLOW, Louis & SHAVELL, Steven. (2007). Moral rules, the moral sentiments, and behavior: Toward a theory of an optimal moral system. *Journal of Political Economy*, 115(3): 494–514.

KASHDAN, Todd B., BISWAS-DIENER, Robert, & KING, Laura A. (2008). Reconsidering happiness: The costs of distinguishing between hedonics and eudaimonia. *Journal of Positive Psychology*, 3: 219–233.

KESSLER, Judd B. & ROTH, Alvin E. (2014). Getting more organs for transplantation. *American Economic Review*, 104(5): 425–430. http://dx.doi.org/10.1257/aer.104.5.425.

KIM-PRIETO, Chu, DIENER, Ed, TAMIR, Maya, SCOLLON, Christie N., & DIENER, Marrisa. (2005). Integrating the diverse definitions of happiness: A time-sequential framework of subjective well-being. *Journal of Happiness Studies*, 6: 261–300.

KOHN, Alfie. (1999). *Punished by Rewards: The Trouble with Gold Stars, Incentive Plans, A's, Praise, and Other Bribes*. Boston: Houghton Mifflin Co.

KOHN, Alfie. (2005). *Unconditional Parenting: Moving from Rewards and Punishments to Love and Reason*. New York: Atria Books.

KOOP, C. Everett. (1984). Promoting organs for transplantation. *Journal of the American Medical Association*, 251(12): 1591–1592.

KOPLIN, Julian. (2017). Beyond fair benefits: Reconsidering exploitation arguments against organ markets. Health Care Analysis, 26(1): 1–15.

KŐSZEGI, Botond & RABIN, Matthew. (2008). Choices, situations, and happiness. *Journal of Public Economics*, 92(8): 1821–1832.

KOTSADAM, Andreas & JAKOBSSON, Niklas. (2011). Do laws affect attitudes? An assessment of the Norwegian prostitution law using longitudinal data. *International Review of Law and Economics*, 31: 103–115.

KRUSELL, Per & SMITH Jr, Anthony A. (2015). Is Piketty's 'Second law of capitalism' fundamental? *Journal of Political Economy*, 123(4): 725–748.

LACETERA, Nicholas, MACIS, Mario, & SLONIM, Robert. (2012). Will there be blood? Incentives and displacement effects in pro-social behavior. *American Economic Journal: Economic Policy*, 4(1): 186–223.

LACETERA, Nicholas, MACIS, Mario, & SLONIM, Robert. (2013). Public health. Economic rewards to motivate blood donations. *Science*, 340(6135): 927–928.

LACOMBA, Juan A. & LAGOS, Francisco. (2010). Immigration and pension benefits in the host country. *Economica*, 77(306): 283–295.

LANNOYE, Vincent. (2015). *The History of Money for Understanding Economics*, 2nd edition. Scotts Valley, CA: CreateSpace.

LARDY, Nicholas R. (2014). *Markets over Mao: The Rise of Private Business in China*. New York: Columbia University Press.

LAYARD, Richard. (2005). *Happiness: Lessons from a New Science*. New York: Penguin.

LAYARD, Richard. (2010). Measuring subjective well-being. *Science*, 327: 534–535.

LAZEAR, Edward. (2000). Economic imperialism. *Quarterly Journal of Economics*, 115(1): 99–146.

LEE, Dwight R. & MCKENZIE, Richard. (1992). Reexamination of the relative efficiency of the draft and the all-volunteer army. *Southern Economic Journal*, 58(3): 644–654.

LEIDER, Stephen & ROTH, Alvin E. (2010). Kidneys for sale: Who disapproves, and why? *American Journal of Transplantation*, 10(5): 1221–1227.

LEÓN, Gianmarco & MIGUEL, Edward. (2017). Risky transportation choices and the value of a statistical life. *American Economic Journal: Applied Economics*, 9(1): 202–228.

LEUN, van der J. & SCHIJNDEL, van A. (2016). Emerging from the shadows or pushed into the dark? The relation between the combat against trafficking in human beings and migration control. *International Journal of Law, Crime and Justice*, 44: 26–42.

LEVITT, Steven D. & LIST, John A. (2016). The behavioralist goes to school: Leveraging behavioral economics to improve educational performance. *American Economic Journal: Economic Policy*, 8(4): 183–219.

LI, Weisen. (2017). Self preface to *The True Logic of China's Economic Growth*. China-Review Weekly [《中评周刊》], 29: 7–11.

LINDERT, Peter H. (2004). *Growing Public: Volume 1, The Story: Social Spending and Economic Growth since the Eighteenth Century*. Cambridge, New York: Cambridge University Press.

LINDERT, Peter H. (2009) *Growing Public: Volume 2, Further Evidence: Social Spending and Economic Growth since the Eighteenth Century*. Cambridge, New York: Cambridge University Press.

LIM, Meng Kin. (2008). *Legalization of Organ Trade*. Singapore: National University of Singapore.

LOWNIK, E., RILEY, E., KONSTENIUS, T., RILEY, W., & MCCULLOUGH, J. (2012). Knowledge, attitudes and practices surveys of blood donation in developing countries. *Vox sanguinis*, 103: 64–74.

MACKLIN, Ruth. (2003). Human dignity is a useless concept. *British Medical Journal*, 327(7429; 20 December): 1419–1420.

MAHDAVI-MAZDEH, M. (2012). The Iranian model of living renal transplantation. *Kidney International*, 82: 627–634.

MÄKI, Uskali. (2009). Economics imperialism concept and constraints. *Philosophy of the Social Sciences*, 39(3): 351–380.

MARTIN, Mike W. (2008). Paradoxes of happiness. *Journal of Happiness Studies*, 9: 171–184.

MASZAK, Serena. (2018). *Violence in Prostitution*. New York: City University of New York Academic Works. https://academicworks.cuny.edu/jj_etds/66/.

MATAS, Arthur J. & SCHNITZLER, Mark. (2004). Payment for living donor (vendor) kidneys: A cost-effectiveness analysis. *American Journal of Transplantation*, 4(2): 216–221.

McCLOSKEY, Deirdre N. (2006). *The Bourgeois Virtues: Ethics for an Age of Commerce*. Chicago: University of Chicago Press.

McCLOSKEY, Deirdre N. (2014). Measured, unmeasured, mismeasured, and unjustified pessimism: A review essay of Thomas Piketty's Capital in the twenty-first century. *Erasmus Journal for Philosophy and Economics*, 7(2): 73–115.

McCLOSKEY, Deirdre N. (2016). *Bourgeois Equality: How Ideas, Not Capital or Institutions, Enriched the World*. Chicago, London: University of Chicago Press, xlii, 787.

McGRAW, A. Peter & TETLOCK, Philip E. (2005). Taboo trade-offs, relational framing, and the acceptability of exchanges. *Journal of Consumer Psychology*, 15(1): 2–15.

McINERNEY, Laura, NOBLE, Toni, & BONIWELL, Ilona. (2017). Chapter 10: Education. *Happiness: Transforming the Development Landscape*. Thimphu, Bhutan: The Centre for Bhutan Studies and GNH. 202–225.

McPHERSON, Michael S. & SATZ, Debra. (2017). *Economic Analysis, Moral Philosophy, and Public Policy*. Cambridge: Cambridge University Press.

MELLSTRÖM, Carl & JOHANNESSON, Magnus. (2008). Crowding out in blood donation: Was Titmuss right? *Journal of the European Economic Association, 6*(4): 845–863.

MEYERS, David G., JENSEN, Kelly C., & MENITOVE, Jay E. (2002). A historical cohort study of the effect of lowering body iron through blood donation on incident cardiac events. *Transfusion, 42*: 1135–1139.

MIGOTTI, M. (2015). Paying a price, facing a fine, counting the cost: The differences that make the difference. *Ratio Juris, 28*(3): 372–391.

MILANOVIC, Branko. (2011). More or less. *Finance & Development, 48*(3): 6–11.

MILL, John S. (1848). *Principles of Political Economy with some of their Applications to Social Philosophy* (ed, Ashley, William J.). London: Longmans, Green and Co.

MIRRLEES, James A. (1971). An exploration in the theory of optimum income taxation. *Review of Economic Studies, 38*: 175–208.

MISHAN, Ezra J. (1967/1993). *The Costs of Economic Growth*. London: Weidenfeld & Nicholson.

MOEN, Ole Martin. (2014). Is prostitution harmful? *Journal of Medical Ethics, 40*(2): 73–81.

MOKYR, J. (2014). A flourishing economist. *Journal of Economic Literature, 52*(1): 189–196.

MONAST, Jonas J., MURRAY, Brian C., & WIENER, Jonathan B. (2017). On morals, markets, and climate change: Exploring Pope Francis' challenge. *Law & Contemporary Problems, 80*: 135.

MONROE, Kristen R. (1996). *The Heart of Altruism*. Princeton, NJ: Princeton University Press.

MOVSESIAN, Mark. (2018). Markets and morals: The limits of doux commerce. *William and Mary Business Law Review, 9*(2): 449–475. Retrieved from: SSRN: https://ssrn.com/abstract=3099712.

MUELLER, Dennis. (2003). *Public Choice III*. New York: Cambridge University Press.

MUELLER, Dennis. (2009). *Reason, Religion, and Democracy*. Cambridge: Cambridge University Press.

MULLER, Laurent, LACROIX, Anne, LUSK, Jayson L., & RUFFIEUX, Bernard. (2017). Distributional impacts of fat taxes and thin subsidies. Economic Journal, 127(604): 2066–2092.

MULNIX, J. W. & MULNIX, M. J. (2015). *Theories of Happiness: An Anthology*. Peterborough, ON: Broadview Press.

MURDOCK, George P. (1967). 1962–1967 Ethnographic Atlas. *Ethnology 1*: 1–4.

MUZAALE, A. D., MASSIE, A. B., WANG, M. C., et al. (2014). Risk of end-stage renal disease following live kidney donation. *Journal of the American Medical Association, 311*(6): 579–586.

NAUGHTON, Barry. (2017). Is China socialist? *Journal of Economic Perspectives, 31*(1): 3–24.

NES, Ragnhild Bang. (2010). Happiness in behaviour genetics: Findings and implications. *Journal of Happiness Studies*, 11: 369–381.

NESSE, Randolph. (2004). Natural selection and the elusiveness of happiness. *Philosophical Transactions of the Royal Society of London*, series B, 359: 1333–1347.

NEUTELEERS, Stijn & ENGELEN, Bart. (2015). Talking money: How market-based valuation can undermine environmental protection. *Ecological Economics*, 117: 253–260.

NG, Yew-Kwang. (1969). A study of the interrelationships between efficient resource allocation, economic growth, and welfare and the solution of these problems in market socialism. PhD thesis. Sydney: University of Sydney.

NG, Yew-Kwang. (1975). Bentham or Bergson? Finite sensibility, utility functions and social welfare functions. *Review of Economic Studies*, 42(4): 545–569.

NG, Yew-Kwang. (1979/1983). *Welfare Economics: Introduction and Development of Basic Concepts*, London: Macmillan.

NG, Yew-Kwang. (1984a). Quasi-Pareto social improvements. *American Economic Review*, 74(5): 1033–1050.

NG, Yew-Kwang. (1984b). Expected subjective utility: Is the Neumann-Morgenstern utility index the same as the Neoclassical's? *Social Choice and Welfare*, 1: 177–186.

NG, Yew-Kwang. (1987). Diamonds are a government's best friend: Burden-free taxes on goods valued for their values. *American Economic Review*, 77: 186–191.

NG, Yew-Kwang. (1988). Economic efficiency versus egalitarian rights. *Kyklos*, 41, 215–237.

NG, Yew-Kwang. (1989). 'What should we do about future generations? the impossibility of Parfit's Theory X', *Economics and Philosophy*, 5: 135–253.

NG, Yew-Kwang. (1990). Welfarism and utilitarianism: A rehabilitation. *Utilitas*, 2(2): 171–193.

NG, Yew-Kwang. (1995). Towards welfare biology: Evolutionary economics of animal consciousness and suffering. *Biology and Philosophy*, 10: 255–285.

NG, Yew-Kwang. (1996a). Happiness surveys: Some comparability issues and an exploratory survey based on just perceivable increments, *Social Indicators Research*, 38(1): 1–29.

NG, Yew-Kwang. (1996b). The enrichment of a sector (individual/region/country) benefits others: The third welfare theorem? *Pacific Economic Review*, 1(2): 93–115.

NG, Yew-Kwang. (1997). A case for happiness, cardinalism, and interpersonal comparison. *Economic Journal*, 107(445): 1848–1858.

NG, Yew-Kwang. (1998). Quality adjusted life years (Qalys) versus willingness to pay in matters of life and death. *International Journal of Social Economics*, 25: 1178–1188.

NG, Yew-Kwang. (1999). Utility, informed preference, or happiness? *Social Choice and Welfare*, 16(2): 197–216.

NG, Yew-Kwang. (2000). *Efficiency, Equality, and Public Policy: With a Case for Higher Public Spending*. Basingstoke: Macmillan.

NG, Yew-Kwang. (2003). From preference to happiness: Towards a more complete welfare economics. *Social Choice and Welfare*, 20: 307–350.

NG, Yew-Kwang. (2004a). Optimal environmental charges/taxes: Easy to estimate and surplus-yielding. *Environmental and Resource Economics*, 28(4): 395–408.

NG, Yew-Kwang. (2004b). *Welfare Economics: Towards a More Complete Analysis*. Houndmills: Macmillan/Palgrave.

NG, Yew-Kwang. (2007). Eternal Coase and external costs: A case for bilateral taxation and amenity rights. *European Journal of Political Economy*, 23: 641–659.

NG, Yew-Kwang. (2008). Happiness studies: Ways to improve comparability and some public policy implications. *Economic Record*, 84: 253–266.

NG, Yew-Kwang. (2009). *Increasing Returns and Economic Efficiency*. Houndsmill: Palgrave/Macmillan, xiii, 200.

NG, Yew-Kwang. (2011). *Common Mistakes in Economics by the Public, Students, Economists and Nobel Laureates*. Hauppauge, NY: Nova. Available online on open access.

NG, Yew-Kwang. (2013a). *The Road to Happiness*. Shanghai Shi: Fudan University Press; in Chinese.

NG, Yew-Kwang. (2013b). Leave auctioning choice to economists. *Business Times*, 13 September, p. 19.

NG, Yew-Kwang. (2015a). Some conceptual and methodological issues on happiness: Lessons from evolutionary biology. *Singapore Economic Review*, 60(4): 1–17.

NG, Yew-Kwang. (2015b). Is an increasing capital share under capitalism inevitable? *European Journal of Political Economy*, 38: 82–86.

NG, Yew-Kwang. (2016). How welfare biology and commonsense may help to reduce animal suffering. *Animal Sentience*, 7(1): 1–10.

NG, Yew-Kwang. (forthcoming, a). Ten rules for public economic policy. Economic Analysis and Policy.

NG, Yew-Kwang. (forthcoming, b). Happiness: Facts and Fallacies.

NG, Yew-Kwang & HO, Lok Sang. (2006). *Happiness and Public Policy: Theory, Case Studies, and Implications*. London: Palgrave/Macmillan.

NG, Yew-Kwang & LIU, Po-Ting. (2003). Global environmental protection – solving the international public-good problem by empowering the United Nations through cooperation with WTO. *International Journal of Global Environmental Issues*, 3(4): 409–417.

NG, Yew-Kwang & SANG, Benqian. (2016). Should human organs be legally bought and sold? A dialogue between an economist and a jurist. *Study & Exploration*, 248: 60–63. [In Chinese].

NORDHAUS, William. (1996). Do Real-Output and Real-Wage Measures Capture Reality? The History of Lighting Suggests Not. *The Economics of New Goods* (ed, BRESNAHAN, Timothy F. & GORDON, Robert J.). Chicago: University of Chicago Press. 29–70.

NORTON, David L. (1976). *Personal Destinies: A Philosophy of Ethical Individualism*. Princeton, NJ: Princeton University Press.

NOZICK, Robert. (1974). *Anarchy, State, and Utopia*. New York: Basic Books.

OATEN, Megan, STEVENSON, Richard, & CASE, Trevor. (2009). Disgust as a disease avoidance mechanism: A review and model. *Psychological Bulletin*, 135: 303–321.

OI, Walter. (1967). The economic cost of the draft. *American Economic Review* 57(2): 39–62.

OKUN, Arthur M. (1975 [2015]). *Equality and Efficiency: The Big Tradeoff*. Washington: Brookings Institution.

OLSON, Mancur. (1965). *The Logic of Collective Action: Public Goods and the Theory of Groups*. Cambridge, MA: Harvard University Press.

OMAN, Nathan B. (2016). The Dignity of Commerce: *Markets and the Moral Foundations of Contract Law*. Chicago: University of Chicago Press.

PARRY, J. & Bloch, M., eds. (1989). *Money and the Morality of Exchange*. Cambridge: Cambridge University Press.

PETERSEN, Jennifer & HYDE, Janet Shibley. (2011). Gender differences in sexual attitudes and behaviors: A review of meta-analytic results and large datasets. *Journal of Sex Research*, 48(2–3): 149–165.

PIGOU, A. C. (1922). Empty economic boxes: A reply. *The Economic Journal*, 32(128): 458–465.

PIKETTY, Thomas. (2014). *Capital in the Twenty-First Century*. Cambridge, MA; London: The Belknap Press of Harvard University Press.

PIKETTY, Thomas & SAEZ, Emmanuel. (2007). How progressive is the US federal tax system? A historical and international perspective. *Journal of Economic Perspectives*, 21(1): 3–24.

PINKER, Steven. (2008). The Stupidity of Dignity. *New Republic*, 238(9): 28–31.

POLANYI, Karl. (1944). *The Great Transformation*. Boston: Beacon Press.

POLINSKY, A. Mitchell & SHAVELL, Steven. (1984). The optimal use of fines and imprisonment. *Journal of Public Economics*, 24(1): 89–99.

POTRAFKE, Niklas. (2014). The evidence on globalisation. *The World Economy*, 38(3): 509–552.

POTTERAT, J. J., BREWER, D. D., MUTH, S. Q., et al. (2004). Mortality in a long-term open cohort of prostitute women. *American Journal of Epidemiology*, 159(8): 778–785.

PRADOS DE LA ESCOSURA, L. (2016). Economic freedom in the long run: Evidence from OECD countries (1850–2007). *Economic History Review*, 69(2): 435–468.

PRASAD, Kislaya. (2012). Economic liberalization and violent crime. *Journal of Law and Economics*, 55(4): 925–948.

QUAH, Euston & NG, Yew-Kwang (2018). Ezra J. Mishan (1917–2014), in The Palgrave Companion to LSE Economics (ed, CORD, Robert A.). Houndsmill: Palgrave/Macmillan.

RADCLIFFE-RICHARDS, J., DAAR, A. S., GUTTMANN, R. D., et al. (1998). For the International Forum for Transplant Ethics. The case for allowing kidney sales. *Lancet*, 351: 1950–1952.

RANA, A., GRUESSNER, A., AGOPIAN, V. G., et al. (2015). Survival benefit of solid-organ transplant in the United States. *JAMA Surgery*, 150(3): 252–259.

RAWLS, John. (1971). *A Theory of Justice*. Cambridge, MA: Harvard University Press.

REISENWITZ, Cathy. (2014). Why it's time to legalize prostitution. *The Daily Beast*, 15 October. Retrieved from: www.thedailybeast.com/why-its-time-to-legalize-prostitution.

REITMAN, David. (1998). Punished by misunderstanding: A critical evaluation of Kohn's *Punished by Rewards* and its implications for behavioral interventions with children. *The Behavior Analyst*, 21(1): 143–157.

RICARD, Matthieu. (2017). Chapter 8: Altruism and Happiness. *Happiness: Transforming the Development Landscape*. Thimphu, Bhutan: The Centre for Bhutan Studies and GNH. 156–168.

RIPPON, Simon. (2014). Imposing options on people in poverty: The harm of a live donor organ market. *Journal of Medical Ethics*, 40(3): 145–150.

ROBERTSON, Christopher T., YOKUM, David V., & WRIGHT, Megan S. (2014). Perceptions of efficacy, morality, and politics of potential cadaveric organ-transplantation reforms. *Law and Contemporary Problems*, 77: 101–129.

ROBERTSON, Dennis H. (1954). What does the economist economize? Speech delivered at Columbia University, May. (Reprinted in 1956 in Dennis H. Robertson, *Economic Commentaries*, Staples Press, London, 147–154).

RODE, Martin. (2013). Do good institutions make citizens happy, or do happy citizens build better institutions? *Journal of Happiness Studies*, 14(5): 1479–1505.

ROSS, Thomas W. (1994). Raising an army: A positive theory of military recruitment. *Journal of Law and Economics*, 37(1): 101–131.

RÖSSLER, W., KOCH U., LAUBER C., et al. (2010). The mental health of female sex workers. *Acta Psychiatrica Scandinavica*, 122: 143–152.

ROTH, Alvin E. (2007). Repugnance as a constraint on markets. *Journal of Economic Perspectives*, 21: 37–58.

ROTH, Alvin E. (2015). *Who Gets What – and Why: The Hidden World of Matchmaking and Market Design*. London: Harper Collins.

ROTHMAN, S. M. & ROTHMAN, D. J. (2006). The hidden cost of organ sale. *American Journal of Transplantation*, 6(7): 1524–1528.

RUBOLINO, Enrico & WALDENSTRÖM, Daniel. (2017). Tax progressivity and top incomes: Evidence from tax reforms. Working Paper no. 10666, IZA Institute of Labor Economics. Retrieved from: http://ftp.iza.org/dp10666.pdf.

RYAN, Richard M. & DECI, Edward L. (2001). On happiness and human potentials: A review of research on hedonic and eudaimonic well-being. Annual Review of Psychology, 52(1): 141–166.

RYFF, Carol D. (1989). Happiness is everything, or is it? Explorations on the meaning of psychological wellbeing. *Journal of Personality and Social Psychology*, 57: 1069–1081.

RYFF, Carol D. & SINGER, Burton H. (2008). Know thyself and become what you are: A eudaimonic approach to psychological well-being. *Journal of Happiness Studies*, 9: 13–39.

SAHN, David. E. & YOUNGER, Stephen D. (2006). Changes in inequality and poverty in Latin America: Looking beyond income to health and education. Journal of Applied Economics, 9(2): 215–233.

SALONEN, Jukka T., TUOMAINEN, Tomi-Pekka, SALONEN, Riitta, LAKKA, Timo A., & NYYSSONEN, Kristiina. (1998). Donation of blood is associated with reduced risk of myocardial infarction: The kuopio ischaemic heart disease risk factor study. *American Journal of Epidemiology*, 148: 445–451.

SANDEL, Michael. (2012a). *What Money Can't Buy: The Moral Limits of Markets*. New York: Farrar, Straus and Giroux.

SANDEL, Michael. (2012b). If I ruled the world. *Prospect Magazine*, October.

SANDEL, Michael. (2013). Market reasoning as moral reasoning: Why economists should re-engage with political philosophy. *Journal of Economic Perspectives*, 27: 121–140.

SANDEL, Michael. (2018). Populism, liberalism, and democracy. *Philosophy & Social Criticism*, 44(4): 353–359.

SATEL, Sally, ed. (2008). *When Altruism Isn't Enough*. Washington, DC: The American Enterprise Institute Press.

SATZ, Debra. (2008). The moral limits of markets: The case of human kidneys. Proceedings of the Aristotelian Society, 108(3): 269–288.

SATZ, Debra. (2009). Voluntary slavery and the limits of the market. *Law & Ethics of Human Rights*, 3(1): 87–109.

SATZ, Debra. (2010). *Why Some Things Should Not Be for Sale: The Moral Limits of Markets*. Oxford: Oxford University Press.

SCHEIDEL, Walter. (2017). *The Great Leveler: Violence and the History of Inequality from the Stone Age to the Twenty-First Century*. Princeton: Princeton University Press.

SCHIEDERMAYER, David & McCARTY, Daniel J. (1995). Altruism, professional decorum, and greed: Perspectives on physician compensation. *Perspectives in Biological Medicine*, 38: 238–253.

SCHNEDLER, Wendelin & VANBERG, Christoph. (2014). Playing 'hard to get': An economic rationale for crowding out of intrinsically motivated behavior. *European Economic Review*, 68: 106–115.

SCHOLD, J. D., GOLDFARB, D. A., BUCCINI, L. D., et al. (2013). Comorbidity burden and perioperative complications for living kidney donors in the United States. *Clinical Journal of the American Society of Nephrology*, 8(10): 1773–1782.

SCITOVSKY, Tibor. (1976/1992). *The Joyless Economy*. New York: Oxford University Press.

SEIB, C., DEBATTISTA, J., FISCHER, J., DUNNE, M., & NAJMAN, J. M. (2009). Sexually transmissible infections among sex workers and their clients: Variation in prevalence between sectors of the industry. *Sexual Health*, 6(1): 45–50.

SELIGMAN, Martin E. P. (2002). *Authentic Happiness: Using the New Positive Psychology to Realize Your Potential for Lasting Fulfilment*. New York: Free Press.

SEN, Amartya K. (1973). Behaviour and the concept of preference. *Economica*, 40: 241–59.

SEN, Amartya K. (1987). On Ethics and Economics. Oxford: Basil Blackwell.

SGROI, Daniel, PROTO, Eugenio, OSWALD, Andrew J., & DOBSON, Alexander. (2016). Laboratory evidence for emotional externalities: An essay in honor of EJ Mishan. *Singapore Economic Review*, 61(03): 1640015.

SHANNON, K., STRATHDEE, S. A., GOLDENBERG, S. M., et al. (2015). Global epidemiology of HIV among Female Sex Workers: Influence of Structural Determinants. *Lancet*, 385(9962): 55–71.

SHIH, J. (2016). Taiwan's catch-22: An analysis of the Republic of China's conscription. Sigma Iota Rho Journal of International Relations, 26 February. Retrieved from: www.sirjournal.org/research/2016/2/26/taiwans-catch-22.

SILVERSTEIN, Matthew. (2000). In defense of happiness: A response to the experience machine. *Social Theory and Practice*, 26: 279–300.

SINGER, Peter. (2016). The case for legalizing sex work. Project Syndicate. Retrieved from: www.project-syndicate.org/commentary/case-for-legalizing-sex-work-by-peter-singer-2016-11?barrier=accesspaylog.

SKINNER, M. W., HEDLUND HOPPE, P. A., GRABOWSKI, H. G., et al. (2016). Risk-based decision making and ethical considerations in donor compensation for plasma-derived medicinal products. Transfusion, 56(11): 2889–2894.

SKOBLE, Aeon J. (2003). Neither slavery nor involuntary servitude. *Ideas on Library*, 1 September: 12–14. Retrieved from: https://fee.org/media/4393/skoble0903.pdf.

SLONIM, Robert, WANG, Carmen, & GARBARINO, Ellen. (2014). The market for blood. *Journal of Economic Perspectives*, 28(2): 177–196.

SMITH, Adam. (1776 [1982]). *The Wealth of Nations*. London: Penguin.

SOBER, Elliott & WILSON, David S. (1998). *Unto Others: The Evolution and Psychology of Unselfish Behavior*. Cambridge, MA: Harvard University Press.

SOLAR, Peter. (1995). Poor relief and English economic development before the industrial revolution. *Economic History Review*, 48(1): 1–22.

SOLIS, Alex. (2017). Credit access and college enrollment. *Journal of Political Economy*, 125(2): 562–622.

SPARKS, Jacob. (2017). Can't buy me love: A reply to Brennan and Jaworski. Journal of Philosophical Research, published online on 26 April.

STANFORD, P. Kyle. (2018). The difference between ice cream and Nazis: Moral externalization and the evolution of human cooperation. *Behavioral and Brain Sciences*, 41: e95.

STANOVICH, Keith E. & WEST, Richard F. (2000). Individual differences in reasoning: Implications for the rationality debate? *Behavioral and Brain Sciences*, 23: 645–726.

STARR, Douglas. (1998). *Blood: An Epic History of Medicine and Commerce*. New York: Alfred A. Knopf.

STEIN, Edward. (1996). *Without Good Reason: The Rationality Debate in Philosophy and Cognitive Science*. Oxford: Oxford University Press.

STEVENSON, B. & WOLFERS, J. (2008). Economic growth and subjective well-being: Reassessing the Easterlin paradox. Brookings Papers on Economic Activity. Spring, 1–87.

STIGLER, George. (1984). Economics – The imperial science? *Scandinavian Journal of Economics*, 86: 301–313.

STIGLITZ, Joseph, SEN, Amartya, & FITOUSI, Jean-Paul. (2010). *Mismeasuring Our Lives: Why GDP Doesn't Add Up*. New York: The New Press.

StrategyPage (2015). Morale: Israel considers cancelling conscription. *StrategyPage*. Retrieved from: www.strategypage.com/htmw/htmoral/20150115.aspx.

SUMNER, L. W. (1996). *Welfare, Happiness and Ethics*. New York: Clarendon Press.

TABELLINI, Guido. (2008). Institutions and culture. *Journal of the European Economic Association*, 6(2–3): 255–294.

TABELLINI, Guido. (2010). Culture and institutions: Economic development in the regions of Europe. *Journal of the European Economic Association*, 8(4): 677–716.

TÄNNSJÖ, Torbjörn. (2007). Narrow hedonism. *Journal of Happiness Studies*, 8: 79–98.

TAYLOR, James S. (2017). *Stakes and Kidneys: Why Markets in Human Body Parts Are Morally Imperative*. New York: Taylor & Francis.

TAYLOR, Timothy. (2014). Economics and morality. *Finance & Development*, 51(2): 34–88.

TEMKIN, Larry S. (1986). Inequality. *Philosophy and Public Affairs*, 15: 99–121.

TETLOCK, Philip E., MELLERS, Barbara A., & SCOBLIC, J. Peter. (2017). Sacred versus pseudo-sacred values: How people cope with taboo trade-offs. *American Economic Review*, 107(5): 96–99.

THALER, Richard H. & SUNSTEIN, Cass R. (2008). *Nudge: Improving Decisions about Health, Wealth, and Happiness.* Chicago: University of Chicago Press.

THIN, Neil, HAYBRON, Daniel, BISWAS-DIENER, Robert, AHUVIA, Aaron, & TIMSIT, Jean (2017). Chapter 3: Desirability of Sustainable Happiness as a Guide for Public Policy. *Happiness: Transforming the Development Landscape.* Thimphu, Bhutan: The Centre for Bhutan Studies and GNH. 39–59.

TISON, Geoffrey H, LIU, Changli, REN, Furong, NELSON, Kenrad, & SHAN, Hua. (2007). Influences of general and traditional Chinese beliefs on the decision to donate blood among employer-organized and volunteer donors in Beijing, China. *Transfusion,* 47: 1871–1879.

TITMUSS, Richard M. (1970). *The Gift Relationship.* London: Allen and Unwin.

TYLER, Tracey. (2010). Legalized brothels 'fantastic' for New Zealand, prostitutes say. thestar.com, 29 September. Retrieved from: www.thestar.com/news/gta/2010/09/29/legalized_brothels_fantastic_for_new_zealand_prostitutes_say.html.

TYRAN, Jean-Robert. (2004). Voting when money and morals conflict: An experimental test of expressive voting. *Journal of Public Economics* 88(7–8): 1645–1664.

TYRAN, Jean-Robert & WAGNER, Alexander K. (forthcoming). Experimental evidence on expressive voting. *The Oxford Handbook of Public Choice* (eds, CONGLETON, Roger, GROFMAN, Bernie, & VOIGT, Stefan). Oxford: Oxford University Press.

UGLYMUGS.IE (2013). Crime and Abuse Experienced by Sex Workers in Ireland Victimization Survey. Retrieved from: https://maggiemcneill.files.wordpress.com/2013/09/ugly-mugs-ireland-survey-september-2013.pdf.

UNAIDS (2013). Global Report: UNAIDS Report on the Global AIDS Epidemic. Retrieved from: www.unaids.org/en/resources/campaigns/globalreport2013/globalreport.

UNANUE, Wenceslao. (2017). Chapter 4: Subjective Wellbeing Measures to Inform Public Policies. *Happiness:* Transforming the Development Landscape. Thimphu, Bhutan: The Centre for Bhutan Studies and GNH, 60.

United Nations (2000). *Convention against Transnational Organized Crime and Its Protocol to Prevent, Suppress and Punish Trafficking in Persons, Especially Women and Children.* New York: United Nations.

US Department of State (2013). Trafficking in Persons Report. Retrieved from US Department of State website: www.state.gov/j/tip/rls/tiprpt/2013/.

VAHIDNIA, F., HIRSCHLER, N. V., AGAPOVA, M., CHINN, A., BUSCH, M. P., & CUSTER, B. (2013). Cancer incidence and mortality in a cohort of US blood donors: a 20-year study. *Journal of Cancer Epidemiology,* 2013: 814842.

VÄSTFJÄLL, Daniel & GÄRLING, Tommy. (2006). Preferences for negative emotions. *Emotion,* 6: 326–329.

VEENHOVEN, Ruut. (1984). *Conditions of Happiness.* Dordrecht: Kluwer Academic.

VEENHOVEN, Ruut. (2000). Freedom and happiness: A comparative study in 44 nations in the early 1990's. *Culture and Subjective Wellbeing* (eds, DIENER, E. & SUH, E. M). Cambridge, MA: MIT press. 257–288.

VEENHOVEN, Ruut. (2003). Hedonism and happiness. *Journal of Happiness Studies,* 4(4): 437–457.

VICENTE, Agustin. (2016). Prostitution and the ideal state. A defense of a policy of vigilance. *Ethical Theory and Moral Practice,* 19(2): 475–487.

VISCUSI, W. Kip & ALDY, Joseph E. (2003). The value of a statistical life: A critical review of market estimates throughout the world. *Journal of Risk and Uncertainty*, 27: 5–76.

VULKAN, Nir, ROTH, Alvin E. & NEEMAN, Zvika. (2013). *The Handbook of Market Design*. Oxford: Oxford University Press.

WAGENAAR, Hendrik. (2017). Why prostitution policy (usually) fails and what to do about it? *Social Sciences*, 6(2): 43.

WAGENAAR, Hendrik, AMESBERGER, Helga, & ALTINK, Sietske. (2017). *Designing Prostitution Policy: Intention and Reality in the Sex Trade*. Bristol: Policy Press.

WALLACE, David F. (2005). *Consider the Lobster and Other Essays*. New York: Little, Brown & Co.

WALSH, A. (2015). Compensation for blood plasma donation as a distinctive ethical hazard: Reformulating the commodification objection. *HEC Forum*, 27(4): 401–416.

WARNER, John & ASCH, Beth. (1996). The economic theory of the military draft reconsidered. *Defense and Peace Economics*, 7: 297–312.

WARNER, John T. & NEGRUSA, Sebastian. (2005). Evasion costs and the theory of conscription. *Defence and Peace Economics*, 16(2): 83–100.

WATERMAN, Alan S. (1993). Two conceptions of happiness: Contrasts of personal expressiveness (eudaimonia) and hedonic enjoyment. *Journal of Personality and Social Psychology*, 64: 678–691.

WATERMAN, Alan S., SCHWARTZ, Seth J., & CONTI, Regina. (2008). The implications of two conceptions of happiness (hedonic enjoyment and eudaimonia) for the understanding of intrinsic motivation. *Journal of Happiness Studies*, 9: 41–79.

WEI, Shang-Jin & ZHANG, Xiaobo. (2015). Immiserizing Growth: Some Evidence (from China with Hope for Love). Working paper.

WERTHEIMER, Alan. (1996) *Exploitation*. Princeton, NJ: Princeton University Press.

WHERRY, F. F. (2015). Markets, Moral Aspects of. The Wiley Blackwell Encyclopedia of Consumption and Consumer Studies. Hoboken, NJ: Wiley.

World Bank (2017). GDP per capita (constant 2010 US$). Retrieved from: https://data .worldbank.org/indicator/NY.GDP.PCAP.KD?locations=CN.

XU, Bing & Pak, Maxwell. (2015). Gender ratio under China's two-child policy. *Journal of Economic Behavior & Organization*, 119: 289–307.

YAN, L., XU, J., & ZHOU, Y. (2018). Residents' attitudes toward prostitution in Macau. *Journal of Sustainable Tourism*, 26(2): 205–220.

ZACHARSKI, L. R., CHOW, B. K., HOWES, P. S., et al. (2008). Decreased cancer risk after iron reduction in patients with peripheral arterial disease: Results from a randomized trial. *Journal of the National Cancer Institute*, 100(14): 996–1002.

ZAK, Paul J. (2011). Moral markets. *Journal of Economic Behavior & Organization*, 77(2): 212–233.

ZALLER, Nickolas, NELSON, Konrad E., NESS, Paul, WEN, Guoxing, BAI, X., & SHAN, H. (2005). Knowledge, attitude and practice survey regarding blood donation in a northwestern Chinese city. *Transfusion Medicine*, 15: 277–286.

ZELIZER, Viviana. (1978). *Morals and Markets: The Development of Life Insurance in the United States*. New York: Columbia University Press.

ZHU, Wei Xing, LI, Lu, & HESKETH, Therese. (2009). China's excess males, sex selective abortion, and one child policy: Analysis of data from 2005 national intercensus survey. *British Medical Journal*, 338: 1211.

ZWEIFEL, Peter. (2014). Book review of: T. Randolph Beard, David L. Kaserman, and Rigmar. Osterkamp, The global organ shortage: Economic causes, human consequences, policy responses. *Public Choice*, 161: 257–259.

Index

Abel, Gillian, 79
Academic journals, 96–97
Adler, Mortimer J., 131, 132, 133–134
'A dollar is a dollar' principle, 31
Affective altruism, 54–55
Alcohol, prohibition of, 66–67
Alesina, Alberto, 38
Allais, Maurice, 151
All-volunteer force (AVF), 86–87, 91–92
Altruism
    affective altruism, 54–55
    non-affective altruism, 54–55, 127–128
    preferences and, 126–127
    profiteering versus, 95
American Journal of Epidemiology,
        85
Amnesty International, 85
Anti-commoditization
    overview, 2, 3–5
    communitarianism on, 34
    'crowding out' argument (*See Crowding out*)
    exploitation argument (*See Exploitation*)
    repugnance argument (*See Repugnance*)
    welfarism and, 4
Anti-market sentiment
    anti-money sentiment compared, 17
    crime and, 16
    economic versus financial markets, 17–20
    historical background, 15–16
    inequality and, 15–16
    lack of rationality in, 16
    moral values, effect of market on, 14–15
    positive versus negative effects, 16
    procedural preferences and, 20–21
    2008 financial crisis and, 16
Anti-money sentiment, 17

Argentina, public opinion regarding free
        enterprise in, 2
Aristotle, 15, 131–132, 133
Arrow, Kenneth J., 9
Arts
    crafts compared, 56
    market expansion, effect of, 49, 56
Australia
    dollar, fluctuations in, 18–19
    progressivity of taxes in, 33
    prostitution in, 81, 82–83
    voluntary military service in, 92
Awards, sale of, 114–115

Baltic Dry Index, 20
Barrotta, Pierluigi, 152
Basu, Kaushik, 39–40
Beard, T. Randolph, 65–66, 124
Becker, Gary, 157, 160
von Beethoven, Ludwig, 49
Benjamin, Daniel J., 152
Berggren, Niclas, 49, 57–58
'Big society, small government', 88–89,
        124–125
Blood donation
    advantages of, 73–74
    blood sales compared, 73–74
    in China, 74
    crowding out and, 48, 73
    cultural attitudes regarding, 74
    excessive donation, 74
    kidney sales compared, 67
    in Singapore, 73
Blood sales
    blood donation compared, 73–74
    kidney sales compared, 61–62

Brennan, Jason, 3–5, 30, 110, 116
Breyer, Friedrich, 14, 15
Brülde, Bengt, 145
Buchanan, James M., 157
Business Insider, 78

Cambodia
    fines in, 104
    prostitution in, 80
Cameron, Judy, 50
Categorical imperative, 145–148
Cemetery excavation
    preferences and, 69–70
    in Singapore, 69–70, 110
Cempedak, 42–43
Certificates of entitlement (COEs)
    liberalization of, 176–177
    pay-as-you-bid method, 176
    in Singapore, 71–72, 175–177
    Vickrey auctions, 175–177
Charitable donation
    market expansion and, 58
    profiteering and, 95–96
    in US, 58
Cherry, Mark J., 63
Child labour, 39–40
Child selling, 110
China
    blood donation in, 74
    Cultural Revolution, 26, 70, 79–80, 113
    economic growth in and decline of
        inequality, 15
    failure of communism in, 53
    Great Leap Forward, 26, 70, 113
    kidney sales in, 61
    market expansion in, 1–2
    marriage in, 147–148
    New Year 'red packets' in, 17
    prostitution in, 79–80, 82
    public opinion regarding free enterprise in, 2
    speculation in, 93
    two-child policy, 82
Cigarette taxes, preferences and, 71
Civil awards, fines compared, 105
Clarke, Harry, 173
Coercion, exploitation and, 24–25
COEs. *See Certificates of entitlement (COEs)*
Commoditization. *See Anti-commoditization*
*Common Mistakes in Economics: By the
    Public, Students, Economists, and Nobel
    Laureates* (Ng), 170

Communitarianism
    overview, 2–3
    on anti-commoditization, 34
    on crowding out, 51–52
    economists versus, 51–52
    on lateness fees, 9
    on market expansion, 53
Conscription
    decline in need for, 92
    patriotism and, 91
    selective conscription, 90–91
Consumption, inequality and, 28
Contagion effect, lateness fees and, 9
Coolidge, Calvin, 76
'Coolidge effect', 76
Corden, Max, 42
Corruption
    arguments for prohibiting, 113
    market expansion and, 52
    prostitution and, 81
Costa-Font, Joan, 73
Cowen, Tyler, 49
Crime
    anti-market sentiment and, 16
    inequality and, 28–29
    prostitution and, 81, 82–83
    punishment of criminals (*See Punishment of
        criminals*)
Croatia, tourist overcrowding in, 102
Crowding out
    overview, 46–47, 122–123
    backfiring and, 47
    blood donation and, 48, 73
    civilizing effect of market expansion and,
        48–50
    communitarianism on, 51–52
    of intrinsic motivation, 46–47, 48, 50–51
    kidney sales and, 61
    lateness fees and, 6–7, 47
    literature on, 47–48
    of morality, 46–48
    nuclear waste and, 51
    price, effect of, 48
    reading and, 47

Davis, John B., 158
Default option in organ donation
    non-agreement as, 68
    presumed consent as, 68–69
Deng Xiaoping, 30, 93
Disgust. *See Repugnance*

Disincentive effects, 31
Division of labour, 55–56
Doux-commerce, 48–50
Downs, Anthony, 157
Draft. *See Conscription*
Duke-NUS Medical School, 66
Durian, 42

Easterlin paradox, 154–155
Economic growth
    inequality and, 15, 30, 38
    market expansion and, 58–59
Economic imperialism, 156–157, 160
Economic liberty, market expansion and, 58
Economics imperialism, 157
Education, profiteering and, 95
Efficiency
    fines, efficiency versus equity, 103
    humanistic argument for rights over
        efficiency, 22–23
    inequality and, 26, 30–32,
        36–37
    libertarian argument for rights over
        efficiency, 21
    parking and, 31–32, 39
    pluralistic argument for rights over
        efficiency, 21–22
    regressive measures and, 36
Efficiency, Equality, and Public Policy: With
    a Case for Higher Public Spending
    (Ng), 26
Efficiency gain, lateness fees and, 9, 10
Efficiency supremacy, 31
Egalitarianism, 34
Eghtesad, B., 61
Eisenberger, Robert, 50
Elías, Julio J., 51, 164
Emission trading, 121–122
Encyclopedia Britannica, 22
Environmental economics, 18
Environmental protection
    emission trading, 121–122
    fines and, 121–122
    littering, 119–120, 121
    profiteering and, 94–95,
        96
Equality, 28. *See also* Inequality
Esoteric services, 2
Ethnographic Atlas (Murdock), 38
Etzioni, Amitai, 2–3
Evolutionary biology

happiness and, 140
    prostitution and, 75–76
Exchange, 53–54
Exploitation
    overview, 24
    ability to pay and, 26
    benefits of equality, 28
    causes of inequality, 26–28
    child labour, 39–40
    coercion and, 24–25
    consumption, inequality and, 28
    crime, inequality and, 28–29
    disincentive effects and, 31
    economic growth, inequality and, 30, 38
    efficiency, inequality and, 26, 30–32,
        36–37
    egalitarianism and, 34
    fair benefits exploitation, 36
    fairness objection, 24
    fair process exploitation, 36
    globalization, inequality and, 29–30
    hypotheticals regarding, 34–35
    kidney sales and, 38
    of labour, 39
    market restrictions and, 35–36
    physical capital versus human capital, 29
    progressivity of taxes and, 32–34
    regressive measures and, 36
    'skyboxification', 38–39
    trafficking in human beings (THB) as, 37–38
    unacceptable exploitation, 37–38
Extension of traditional economic analysis
    overview, 5, 11–13, 168–169
    axioms from, 160–164
    economic imperialism and, 156–157, 160
    economics imperialism and, 157
    long-term effects versus current effects, 167
    market expansion, objections to, 167
    morality and, 167–168
    multidisciplinarity and, 158
    propositions from, 12–13
    reverse imperialism and, 157–158
    social equilibria, Pareto inefficiency of,
        164–166
    social welfare function (SWF) and, 159–160,
        166–167
    utility versus welfare, 158–160
    welfarism and, 11, 12
External costs
    immigration and, 173
    welfarism and, 122–124

Fair benefits exploitation, 36
Fairness objection to exploitation argument, 24
Fair process exploitation, 36
Falk, Armin, 14–15
Fees
    fines versus, 119–122
    lateness fees (*See Lateness fees*)
Financial crisis, anti-market sentiment and, 16
Financial markets, 17–20
Fines
    in Cambodia, 104
    civil awards compared, 105
    economic argument for, 103
    efficiency versus equity, 103
    environmental protection and, 121–122
    fees versus, 119–122
    imprisonment compared, 103
    lateness fees versus, 122
    for littering, 119–120, 121
    for murder, 105–107
    for parking violations, 103–104, 120–121
    in Singapore, 104–105
    under-utilization of, 104–105, 107
First-come-first-served principle, 39, 115, 125
France, public opinion regarding free
    enterprise in, 2
Francis (Pope), 15
Freiman, Christopher, 116
Freud, Sigmund, 152
Frey, Beat M., 58, 112
Friedman, Daniel, 41, 51, 66–67
Friedman, Milton, 86–87, 91
Friendship, sale of, 113–114

Gagnon, Julien, 51
Gan Kim Yong, 73
Germany
    prostitution in, 81
    public opinion regarding free enterprise in, 2
Globalization, inequality and, 29–30
Gneezy, Uri, 6, 7
Goldman Sachs Inc., 18
Goyal, Sanjeev, 51
Griffin, James, 145
Gruber, Jonathan, 71

Hansmann, Henry, 63
Happiness as only intrinsic value
    argument for, 135–136
    authentic happiness, 144
    categorical imperative and, 145–148

cognitive component of happiness, 134–135
    defining happiness, 130–135
    desirability of happiness versus pain, 137
    Easterlin paradox and, 154–155
    eudaimonic concept of happiness, 130–135,
        153–154
    evolutionary biology and, 140
    hedonic concept of happiness, 130–135,
        153–154
    hedonic paradox and, 154
    humanity and, 146–147
    indirect effects, 139
    intrinsic value of other things and, 155
    Kant, rejection of arguments of, 145–148
    lack of normative significance, 136–137
    maximin principle of justice and, 148–151
    morality and happiness, 131–132
    normative significance arising from
        happiness, 137–139
    objections to, 141–145, 152–155
    objective component of happiness, 132–134
    outdated normative principles, 140
    positive and negative moods and, 152–153
    preferences and, 142–143
    promotion of happiness through normative
        principles, 139–140
    Rawls, rejection of arguments of, 148–151
    secondary virtues and, 144
    social welfare function (SWF) and, 146–147
    subjective component of happiness, 130–132
    universalizability and, 146
    utilitarianism and, 141
    value independent of happiness, 140–141
    welfare, happiness concept of, 135
    welfarism and, 141
Harsanyi, John C., 22–23, 126
Hausman, Daniel M., 145
Haybron, Daniel M., 134
Hayek, Friedrich A., 30
HBO, 49
Healey, Catherine, 81
Healthy food, preferences and, 70
Hedonic paradox, 154
Hippocratic Corpus, 56
Hirschman, Albert, 49
HIV/AIDS, prostitution and, 82
Honour killing, 41, 45
Hornbeck, Richard, 168
Hospital admissions, 116–118
Human capital, 29
Human dignity, kidney sales and, 62–63

Humanism, welfarism compared, 22
Humanity, happiness and, 146–147
Huta, Veronika, 154

Ignorance, 13, 22–23, 24–25, 37–38,
     44, 166–167
Immigration
     benefits of, 171
     congestion concerns, 170–171, 173
     external costs and, 173
     inequality and, 173
     international terms of trade and, 174
     pollution concerns, 170–171, 173
     population density, benefits of, 171
     returns to scale and, 171–173
     unemployment and, 173–174
Imperfect information, 13, 20, 24–25,
     166–167
Imprisonment
     fines compared, 103
     whipping compared, 107–108
India, economic growth in and decline of
     inequality, 15
Industrial Revolution, 55
Inequality
     anti-commoditization and (*See*
          Exploitation)
     anti-market sentiment and, 15–16
     benefits of equality, 28
     causes of, 26–28
     consumption and, 28
     crime and, 28–29
     economic growth and, 30, 38
     efficiency and, 26, 30–32, 36–37
     egalitarianism and, 34
     globalization and, 29–30
     immigration and, 173
     kidney sales and, 63–64
     market restrictions and, 35–36
     physical capital versus human capital, 29
     progressivity of taxes and, 32–34
     regressive measures and, 36
     in Singapore, 101
     'skyboxification', 38–39
     water and, 101–102
Interest, 57
International terms of trade, immigration
     and, 174
Intrinsic value, happiness as. *See Happiness as*
     only intrinsic value

Iran, kidney sales in, 60–61
Ireland, prostitution in, 81, 85
Irrationality, 13, 20, 37–38, 40, 44, 123–125,
     166–167
Irrational preferences, 128–129
Israel
     Israeli Defense Forces (IDF), 92
     lateness fees in, 6
     voluntary military service in, 92

Jakobsson, Niklas, 83
Jaworski, Peter M., 3–5, 30,
     110, 116
Johnson & Johnson, 105
John Templeton Foundation, 47
Jonsson, Sofia, 83
Jury service, 116–117, 118

Kant, Immanuel, 96, 97,
     145–148
Kaplow, Louis, 48, 88–89, 160
Keniston, Daniel, 168
Kessler, Judd B., 57
Kidney donation
     kidney sales compared, 64
     presumed consent as default option, 68–69
Kidney sales
     blood donation compared, 67
     blood sales compared, 61–62
     in China, 61
     counselling regarding, 25–26
     crowding out and, 61
     debt repayment problem, 63
     exploitation and, 38
     human dignity and, 62–63
     illegality of, 60, 124
     inequality problem, 63–64
     in Iran, 60–61
     kidney donation compared, 64
     medical need for, 60, 64–66
     presumed consent as default option, 68–69
     repugnance and, 25, 43–44,
          62, 124
     reward concept, 64
     risks from transplants, 61, 66
     robbery problem, 67
     slavery compared, 109–110
     sperm sales compared, 63
     terrorism compared, 41, 45
     underground market in, 66–67

vouchers, 26
Koplin, Julian, 36

Labour
  child labour, 39–40
  division of, 55–56
  exploitation of, 39
Lateness fees
  overview, 6
  communitarianism on, 9
  contagion effect and, 9
  costs of punctuality versus, 7
  crowding out and, 6–7, 47
  day care service versus, 6–7, 8
  effect on punctuality, 9–10
  efficiency gain and, 9, 10
  explanation for lateness, 6–7
  fines versus, 122
  internal versus external costs, 8–9
  in Israel, 6
  level of fees, 8
  rational choice regarding, 7
  in Singapore, 7–8
Layard, Richard, 152
Lee Kuan Yew, 69, 70, 110
Leider, Stephen, 44
Li, Jane, 78
Lianhe Zaobao, 94, 104–105
Liberalism, 58–59
Life insurance, 57
Lim Chong Yah, 101
Lin Dai, 76
Lindert, Peter H., 29
Line standing, 115–116, 125
Littering, 119–120, 121
Lobsters, 38–39
Lotteries, 101, 115, 116–117, 125

Magnanti, Brooke, 78–79
Mäki, Uskali, 156–157
Mao Zedong, 2, 79–80
Market expansion
  anti-market sentiment (*See Anti-market
    sentiment*)
  arts, effect on, 49, 56
  charitable donation, promotion of, 58
  in China, 1–2
  civilizing effect of, 48–50, 125
  communitarianism on, 53
  community versus market, 54

  corruption and, 52
  division of labour and, 55–56
  economic growth, promotion of, 58–59
  economic liberty, promotion of, 58
  esoteric services, 2
  exchange, centrality of, 53–54
  liberalism, promotion of, 58–59
  medical practice and, 56
  misconception and, 57
  moral values, effect on, 14–15
  objections to, 167
  productivity and, 1
  reciprocation, centrality of, 53–54
  repugnance and, 56–57
  into social spheres, 3
  standard of living and, 1
  tolerance, promotion of, 57–58
Market failures, 124–125
Marxism, 39
Maximin principle of justice, 148–151
McCloskey, Deirdre N., 49
McNeill, Daniel, 41, 51, 66–67
Medical practice, 56
Michelangelo, 49
Migotti, M., 120
Military service
  Australia, voluntary service in, 92
  conscription (*See Conscription*)
  cost of voluntary service, 88–89, 92
  decline in need for conscription, 92
  E-F conflict and, 89–90
  increasing returns, importance of, 90–91
  patriotism and, 91
  preferences and, 87–88
  selective conscription, 90–91
  statistics, 86
  support for voluntary service, 91–92
  Taiwan, voluntary service in, 92
  taxation and, 88–89
  trend toward voluntary service, 86
  UK, voluntary service in, 92
  US, voluntary service in, 86–87, 91–92
Mill, John Stuart, 49–50, 141
Misconception, market expansion and, 57
Misinformation, 24–25, 40, 84, 110,
  123–125
Monetary payment, 53–54
Monogamy, prostitution and, 77–78
de Montesquieu, Charles-Louis, 49
Moral externalities, prostitution and, 83

Moral values
  consideration of others and, 14–15
  effect of market expansion on, 14–15
  responsibility-dilution effect, 14–15
Mozart, Wolfgang Amadeus, 49
Mueller, Dennis, 52, 159, 164
Mullainathan, Sendhil, 71
Multidisciplinarity, 158
Murder, fines for, 105–107
Murdock, George P., 38

Nanyang Technological University, 95
National Kidney Foundation, 60
National service. *See Conscription*
Netherlands, Tulipmania in, 20
Networks, 51
New Zealand
  progressivity of taxes in, 33
  prostitution in, 81
Ng, Yew-Kwang, 16, 26, 29–30, 35, 88–89, 90,
    127, 129, 147, 151, 173
Nilsson, Therese, 49, 57–58
Nixon, Richard, 86–87
Nobel Prizes, sale of, 114
Non-affective altruism, 54–55, 127–128
Norman, Neville, 173
Norway, progressivity of taxes in, 33
Nozick, Robert, 28

Okun, Arthur M., 21–22
Olson, Mancur, 157
Organ donation
  kidney donation (*See Kidney donation*)
  next-of-kin, objections by, 68–69
  non-agreement as default option, 68
  preferences and, 68–69
  presumed consent as default option, 68–69
Othman, Hasmiza, 104
Oxford English Dictionary, 22
Oxford University, 114–115

Paine, Thomas, 49
Pak, Maxwell, 82
Pareto inefficiency, 164–166
Parish, Ross, 31
Parking
  efficiency and, 31–32, 39
  fines for violations, 103–104, 120–121
Patriotism, conscription and, 91
Physical capital, 29

Pigou, A.C., 158
Prasad, Kislaya, 49
Preferences
  altruism and, 126–127
  cemetery excavation and, 69–70
  in China, 70
  cigarette taxes, 71
  conscription and, 87–88
  ex ante versus *ex post* concepts, 126
  happiness as, 142–143
  healthy food and, 70
  irrational preferences, 128–129
  organ donation and, 68–69
  procedural preferences, 20–21
  in Singapore, 69–70
  welfarism versus, 126–129
Presumed consent to organ donation as default
    option, 68–69
Price
  crowding out, effect on, 48
  disconnect between supply and, 99–100
  efficient pricing of water, 100, 102
Productivity, market expansion and, 1
Profiteering
  altruism versus, 95
  'being used', 96–97
  charitable donation and, 95–96
  education and, 95
  environmental protection and, 94–95, 96
  indirectly benefiting from doing good,
    94–96
  objections to, 98
  speculation, 93–94
  types of, 93
Progressivity of taxation, 32–34
Prohibition, 66–67
Prostitution
  in Australia, 81, 82–83
  benefits of legalization, 78–79, 82–84, 85
  bias regarding, 79
  in Cambodia, 80
  children of prostitutes, 84–85
  in China, 79–80, 82
  corruption and, 81
  crime and, 81, 82–83
  evolutionary biology and, 75–76
  female versus male attitudes toward, 76, 78
  in Germany, 81
  health effects of legalization, 82
  HIV/AIDS and, 82

ineffectiveness of policy regarding, 80
in Ireland, 81, 85
legal resources, effect of legalization on, 84
monogamy and, 77–78
moral externalities and, 83
in New Zealand, 81
ratios of prostitutes to adult males, 77
repugnance and, 45
sexually transmitted diseases and, 80
stigmatization of, 79
taxation of, 84
in Thailand, 80
in UK, 81
underground market, dangers of, 80–81
in United States, 82–83
in US, 81
Punishment of criminals
fines (*See Fines*)
imprisonment, 103,
107–108
methods of, 103
whipping, 107–108

Quotas, 121–122

Radcliffe-Richards, J., 25
Rape, 149
Rawls, John, 22–23,
148–151
Reciprocation, 53–54
Repugnance
causes of, 42–43
economic analysis, 42
historical background, 42
honour killing compared, 41, 45
kidney sales and, 25, 43–44,
62, 124
market expansion and, 56–57
overcoming, 44
prostitution and, 45
welfarism and, 41
whipping and, 107–108
Responsibility-dilution effect, 14–15
Returns to scale, immigration and, 171–173
Reverse imperialism, 157–158
Rhinoceros hunting permits, 116
Rights versus efficiency
humanistic argument, 22–23
libertarian argument, 21
pluralistic argument, 21–22

Robertson, Dennis H., 9
Rode, Martin, 58
Rössler, W., 79
Roth, Alvin E., 42,
44, 57
Rothman, D.J., 6
Rothman, S.M., 6
Royal Bank of Canada (RBC), 18
'Rule of 10%', 19–20
Russia, public opinion regarding free
enterprise in, 2
Rustichini, Aldo, 6, 7
Ryan, Richard M., 154

Sahn, David E., 117
Sandel, Michael, 2, 4, 24, 25, 38, 44–45, 112, 116,
119–120, 121, 168
Satel, Sally, 62–63
Satz, Debra, 63–64
Schnedler, Wendelin, 50–51
Science, 14
'Secret Diary of a Call Girl' (television
program), 78–79
Sentencing. *See Punishment of criminals*
Sexually transmitted diseases, prostitution
and, 80
Shakespeare, William, 49
Shavell, Steven, 48, 160
Showtime, 49
Simon, Julian, 173
Singapore
Automobile Importer & Exporter
Association of Singapore, 94–95, 97
blood donation in, 73
cemetery excavation in, 69–70, 110
certificates of entitlement (COEs) in, 71–72,
175–177
fines in, 104–105
Health Sciences Authority (HSA), 73
inequality in, 101
lateness fees in, 7–8
Ministry of Defence, 73
Ministry of Education, 73
National Blood Programme, 73
Singapore General Hospital, 66
Singapore Red Cross, 73
water in, 99–100
Singer, Peter, 76
'Skyboxification', 38–39, 168
Slavery, 109–110

Slonim, Robert, 73
Smith, Adam, 49, 55, 56, 167
Social equilibria, Pareto inefficiency of, 164–166
Social spheres, market expansion into, 3
Social welfare function (SWF), 146–147, 159–160, 166–167
Socrates, 56
South China Morning Post, 78
Soviet Union, failure of communism in, 26, 53
Speculation, 93–94
Sperm sales, kidney sales compared, 63
Standard of living, market expansion and, 1
Stigler, George, 157
Stutzer, Alois, 58, 112
Surrogate pregnancy, 110
Szech, Nora, 14–15

Taiwan, voluntary military service in, 92
Taxation
    in Australia, 33
    cigarette taxes, preferences and, 71
    in New Zealand, 33
    in Norway, 33
    progressivity of, 32–34
    of prostitution, 84
    in UK, 33
    in US, 33
    voluntary military service and, 88–89
Temkin, Larry S., 149
Terrorism, 41, 45
Thailand, prostitution in, 80
The Times, 114–115
Titmuss, Richard M., 48, 73
Tolerance, 57–58
Traditional economic analysis, extension of.
    See *Extension of traditional economic analysis*
Trafficking in human beings (THB), 37–38
Trump, Donald, 4, 34
Tulipmania, 20
Tullock, Gordon, 157
20th International AIDS Conference, 82
2008 financial crisis, anti-market sentiment and, 16

Unacceptable exploitation, 37–38
Unemployment, immigration and, 173–174
United Kingdom

Brexit referendum, 4, 34, 112–113
Poor Law, 29
progressivity of taxes in, 33
prostitution in, 81
voluntary military service in, 92
United States
    charitable donation in, 58
    progressivity of taxes in, 33
    prostitution in, 81, 82–83
    public opinion regarding free enterprise in, 2
    Supreme Court, line standing at, 115–116
    voluntary military service in, 86–87, 91–92
Universalizability, happiness and, 146
University admissions, 116–117
Usury, 57
Utilitarianism, happiness and, 141

Vanberg, Christoph, 50–51
Vicente, Agustin, 79
Vickrey auctions, 175–177
Vote buying, 111–113
Vote trading, 111
Vouchers, 26

Wagenaar, Hendrik, 80
Wang, Yan, 7–8
Washington Post, 104
Water
    disconnect between supply and price, 99–100
    efficient pricing of, 100, 102
    inequality and, 101–102
    restrictions, problems with, 100–101
    in Singapore, 99–100
    wastage, 100
Waterman, Alan S., 154
Webster's Dictionary, 22
Weimann, Joachim, 14, 15
Welfarism
    anti-commoditization and, 4
    categorical imperative versus, 145–148
    child selling and, 110
    extension of traditional economic analysis and, 11, 12
    external costs and, 122–124
    happiness and, 141

humanism compared, 22
littering and, 121
preferences versus, 126–129
repugnance and, 41
social welfare function (SWF) and, 159–160
Westmoreland, William, 86–87, 91
Whipping, 107–108
Wholemeal bread, 70–71
Willingness to accept, 70
Willingness to pay, 70
World Blood Donor Day, 73

World Public Opinion Survey, 2
World Value Survey, 83–84

Xiaokai Yang, 96
Xu, Bing, 82

Younger, Stephen D., 117
Yu Shyi-kun, 92

Zak, Paul J., 49
Zaobao Weekly, 77